Five Journeys through the Arctic
and a new Russia in search
of Willem Barents

JaapJan Zeeberg

With contributions by
Pieter Floore, Frans Heeres, Maurits Groen,
Dmitri Kravchenko, Robert LeCannu,
and Joost van den Vondel

JaapJan Zeeberg

Five Journeys

through the Arctic
and a new Russia in search
of Willem Barents

Aspekt Publishers

Five Journeys through the Arctic and a new Russia in search of Willem Barents

Aspekt Publishers | Amersfoortsestraat 27
3769 AD Soesterberg | The Netherlands
info@uitgeverijaspekt.nl | www.uitgeverijaspekt.nl

Cover: Gerrit de Veer, Willem Barents' writer, from a 1599 painting by Aert Pietersz, against terrain of Russkaya Gavan' (the former Cape Nassau). Back: Inostrantsev Bay, the former Ice Cape (photo's 1998).

Coverdesign: Maureen Vermeulen
Lay-out: Paul Timmerman

ISBN: 978-94-6462-914-9
NUR: 680

Contents

View across Matochkin Shar (photograph by H. Lund, from Grønlie 1924). *Anyone who has sailed through Matochkin Shar will probably never forget the remarkable beauty of the wild and magnificent panorama which constantly unfolds. What charm and variety in the combination of green sea waves with the bare, multi-colored rock, with the snow and the glaciers!* (Rusanov, 1907).

Crew of R/V Willem Barents, going ashore in Matochkin Shar with sloop *Lucie*. (Photo William Grant 1884).

Preface

Life is a journey and we move through its stages like a traveler through a landscape. This is all a book about the amazement of Westerners who traveled the world behind the former Iron Curtain, looking for traces of a small historical event against the backdrop of the ending of the Soviet Union. This is a book about the 'nineties.' Over one decade, we watched modern Russia take shape. We had exclusive access to an area that is tightly regulated, because of a common interest. The Russian Arctic has been the scene of some of the most inspiring explorations. One of these, the nine-month wintering of Willem Barents and his men on the Arctic island Novaya Zemlya, although a historical footnote, takes on new meaning in the 21st century.

For anyone growing up during the Cold War, Novaya Zemlya might as well have been on another planet. Trapped in the pack ice of the Arctic and then hidden in a hostile (or so imagined) nation the island has been inaccessible for generations. But the world changed, and Russians and Dutchmen searched together for the ship and grave of Willem Barents. Today, hostilities are back as if they were never gone.

A war is dividing our continent again. The attack on Ukraine came a week after the presentation of the Russian edition of this book, organized by the Moscow Library for Foreign Literature, to an online audience of 125,000 Russian viewers. The invasion, carefully prepared in plain view, for everyone to see, was the culmination of a series of events set in motion with the ending of the Soviet Union. Many of these events were witnessed by those who visited the Russian Federation in the 1990s: the August 1991 Coup, economic anarchy, wars in Bosnia and Chechnya, the crash of the ruble in 1998 and sinking of submarine *Kursk*. Also, the fatalism, the occultism and the obsession with Nazis, a scorn for 'foreigners': Russian sentiments over the past thirty years were clear and unmistakable.

Editor Denis Khotimsky wrote in his introduction: "Well-known events, famous places, names that have long been heard are viewed by the author from an unusual angle. He visited our country several times: Novaya Zemlya, Vorkuta, Labytnangi, Dikson, Khatanga and October Revolution Island – are for most of our compatriots more remote than the furthest foreign countries. The action unfolds in two historical parallels: on the one hand, these are events from the recent past: the Novaya Zemlya expeditions of 1991, 1993, 1995, 1998, and 2000, whose participants and witnesses are still our contemporaries, living in Russia and the Netherlands. On the other hand, events that took place more than four centuries ago and mark the beginning of the facts, stories, documents and persons that closely link our two nations."

With the melting of snow and ice, much of the mystery that has shrouded the Arctic for centuries disappears forever. We've captured a vanishing landscape, traveling past the remains of polar stations, so bravely maintained by their crews for much of the 20th century, and quickly repossessed by the elements. Willem Barents appears here and there in the background, reflected between ice floes and in the rotten beams of the wintering hut.

Between 1594 and 1598, navigator and cartographer Willem Barents, and his crew, showed that there is an open ocean at the top of the world. These early explorers entered a world unseen – long before the Arctic quest turned into a confrontation with nature. They were not unprepared: their story is that of the first successful wintering of Europeans in the high Arctic. The Arctic through their eyes is as alien as the 'Lost World' fantasies that they inspired much later. The original journals, excerpts of which are included here, have lost little of their imaginative power. This book reconstructs that Willem Barents ran into a lively network of fishermen, trappers and nomads around the White Sea, an important connection with the open ocean for what was then Muscovy. Novaya Zemlya, the 'New Land' wasn't exactly *New*, it was always there and known to the however few inhabitants, but it was new in the emerging context to chart, understand and control the planet we inhabit.

In our century, the effects of accelerated climate change and an ice-free polar ocean are felt across the globe. Mother Nature has been conquered and subdued – Joost van den Vondel in his poem from 1613, reproduced here, observed with remarkable foresight that this would be the ultimate price of the Dutch 'invasion' of the Arctic. Valerian Albanov's life or-death struggle in 1914 over ice floes and treacherous straits, with Fridtjof Nansen's book in hand, would qualify as extreme sports today. This is also a book about the Arctic and what it was like up there. We didn't just follow Barents' steps, but wanted to relive these classic journeys, and fill in all the mighty details that everyone has wondered about for centuries.

Nijmegen, January 2023

Team Kravchenko after raising their monument at the site of the wintering (1979); and their camp site just north of the 'Saved House' wintering location. Photo's by Yuozas Kaziauskas.

Chapter One

Into the Ice Sea

Winter was sweeping its last wet strokes across the saturated Dutch land when Dmitri Kravchenko arrived in Amsterdam on the morning of 3 March 1991. For more than a decade, Kravchenko – 55 years old, pallid beard and sunken face – had been obsessed by the glimpse into the past allowed him on a remote, snow-dusted Arctic Island. He was a man with a mission. Now his goal was the Rijksmuseum, the imposing two-towered 1885 brick building in the center of town. In a small suitcase he carried plans to complete Willem Barents' voyage around the continent. Kravchenko expected that in the Netherlands his reputation as Russia's investigator of Barents' wintering would open wide many doors, through which money would flow prodigiously. Confident of this success, he presented himself at the main entrance of the museum, queuing with tourists before the box office and nervously searching for words.

"One?" the woman behind the thick glass window asked when Kravchenko had stepped up to the counter.

"I must see Barents expert, Dr. Braat," Kravchenko began.

"Would you like to buy a ticket? Sir, you're holding up the line. This is the entrance to the museum," the woman replied. Kravchenko asked for an interview with Joost Braat, the Museum's curator and archivist. During the past twelve years, they had met occasionally in Moscow, and now Kravchenko was back – with a new plan.

"You're holding up the line," the woman repeated. "Please step back." Kravchenko hesitated and then, uttering Russian phrases, made his way outside. "Problem – but small problem," he muttered, backing away from the building to try and spot another entry. It soon transpired that he was not at the right address after all: the offices and archives were across the street from the museum. Next to a copper plate labeled 'Rijksmuseum' he rang the bell. Minutes later – at last – a familiar face! Much to Kravchenko's relief, he had found Joost Braat.

"Willem Barents' grave discovered on Novaya Zemlya," wrote Dutch national newspapers *Telegraaf* and *NRC Handelsblad* in bold headlines in 1979 [25-8-1979; 10-9-1979]. On the northern cape of Novaya Zemlya, the Russians claimed to have discovered several graves, one with a bear skull on it, evidently shot with a musket. Another one, had a pole on which the letters 'Bar' could be deciphered. Dmitri Kravchenko reported that the site of Willem Barents' wintering place elsewehere on the island was still littered with original objects. Many traces of the camp had been preserved under a 20 cm-thick layer of moss that had covered the site, as snow had done in the centuries before. "You know, my friend, that I have twenty years' experience in the Arctic territory," Kravchenko said to Joost Braat, a small, round-headed and smiling man. "At the site of the Saved House, we erected a cross six meters tall and a cairn in honor of Willem Barents and his men. Our monument is also a warning: this is an historic spot, which must be preserved!" Joost nodded approvingly. If it were up to him, he'd turn the Rijksmuseum into a big Novaya Zemlya shrine, with a reconstruction of the vessel and Barents' tomb and all!

Months after Barents' wintering on Novaya Zemlya, the wintering cabin had been covered by snow which eventually turned into an icy cover. In the spring of 1597, the castaways

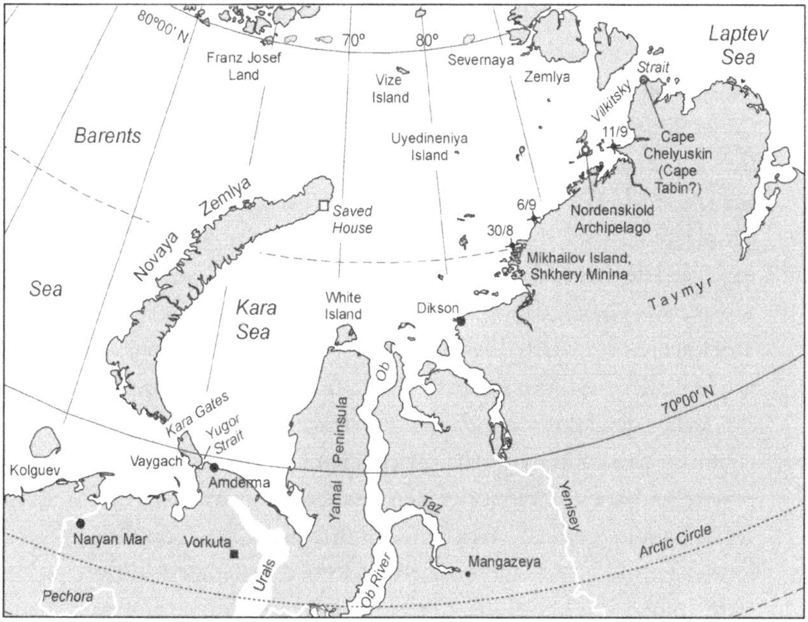

80°00' N
70°
80°
Franz Josef Land
Severnaya Zemlya
Laptev Sea
Strait
Vilkitsky
Vize Island
Barents Sea
Uyedineniya Island
11/9
Cape Chelyuskin (Cape Tabin?)
Novaya Zemlya
Saved House
6/9
Nordenskiold Archipelago
30/8
Mikhailov Island, Shkhery Minina
Kara Sea
White Island
Dikson
Taymyr
Ob
Yamal Peninsula
70°00' N
Kara Gates
Yugor Strait
Kolguev
Vaygach
Amderma
Taz
Yenisey
Naryan Mar
Vorkuta
Arctic Circle
Urals
Ob River
Mangazeya
Pechora

The Kara Sea and North Siberian Coast with locations mentioned in the text.

First photo of the Saved House remains, taken by the Milarodovich-expedition in 1933, some 60 years after discovery of the camp by Elling Carlsen (1871).

had used parts of the roof and side to make their two boats seaworthy, to escape from the island rowing and sailing. Snow encapsulated the camp and its interior. The snow in and around the building would become perennial, hardening to ice during the 'Little Ice Age'-centuries that ensued. When sea ice in the second half of the nineteenth century at last receded and people re-entered these barren parts, they stumbled upon a time capsule that had thawed and opened to deliver its treasure. The recovery of the cabin, in combination with Gerrit de Veer's 1598 account of daily life in those very quarters, enabled an unparalleled view into the past. Inside the tumbled remains of the 'Behouden Huys' or 'Saved House' was a sample of materials taken on this journey to the other side of the world. Linens, pewter tableware, a variety of Renaissance prints by Hendrick Goltzius and Jacob de Gheyn, a Gothic clock, wax candles, leather-bound books, and ornately decorated Venetian chalices were among the first finds. On Novaya Zemlya the explorers left carpenter tools, household goods, clothing, instruments, prints, merchandise, and armament they couldn't bring on their journey to safety. After the return of these objects and artwork to Amsterdam, they soon became the center piece in the Rijksmuseum's collection. "The hands of our seamen touched those objects," wrote maritime historian Jarig Mollema after viewing an exhibition in 1947, "and one leaves feeling as though their hands have grabbed ours."

As part of the next generation of curators in that classic building filled with the finest national treasures, Joost Braat was a civil servant, administrator, and ideologist: active member of the Dutch Communist Party. Thus, he was allowed travelling across the Iron Curtain and in 1974 met Mikhail I. Belov, a military officer and director of the Soviet Union's great Arctic and Antarctic Research Institute (AARI). Braat had immediately inquired how much really was left of Willem

Barents' wintering site. "Nothing... There is nothing left," came the reply, but in 1977, Belov arranged for Dmitri Kravchenko to organize an expedition to northern Novaya Zemlya and come up with a better answer. Kravchenko had participated between 1973 and 1975 in a search promoted by newspaper *Pravda* of the coasts of the Kara Sea for traces of the famous 1912 *Gerkules* expedition.[1] In 1977, inclement weather forced Kravchenko's premature return to Archangelsk, but two years later, he had better luck. Between 2 and 6 August 1979, Kravchenko plotted the remaining structure of the Saved House, as well as about 130 objects visible on the surface: pieces of leather, pottery, iron nails, tools, weaponry, and clothing [Kravchenko 1983; Floore 1998]. He recovered a human lower jaw, possibly belonging to one of the explorers interred during the wintering. A large, 4 m piece of wreckage on the beach – previously reported in 1871 and in 1933 – appeared to contain the same forged-iron nails as the Saved House. "The finds followed one after the other, as from a cornucopia, as if Lady Fortune herself had decided to join the exploration," Kravchenko wrote about his first survey [1981]. Russian television broadcast his documentary *In search of treasures* on 18 October 1980.

Years passed – and Kravchenko began preparing his ultimate experiment, one that was sure to have all the classic drama of an Arctic journey: to accomplish the Northeast Passage in Barents' name, in two small vessels. "We want to depart from Amsterdam by the end of May, 1991," said Kravchenko excitedly, seated before Braat's desk. "The first half of the voyage covers the northern shores of Europe and the Soviet Union towards Japan, where we'll arrive in November. In 1992, we will return by way of Alaska, Canada, Greenland, and Iceland. If you so desire, we could arrange to stop at northern Novaya Zemlya, so you could study the wintering site." Braat, smiling, explained that the Dutch investigation was only a paper project: cleaning and

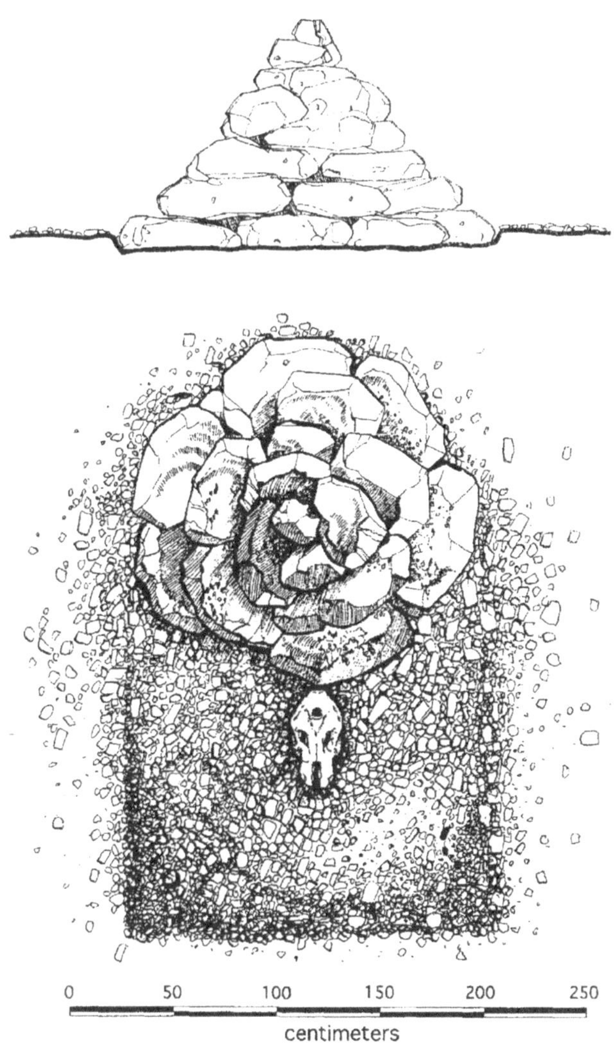

Drawing of the supposed double-grave on Cape Vilkitsy (north Novaya Zemlya) discovered by Dmitri Kravchenko, holding Willem Barents and Claes Adriaansz Goutijck (taken from Kravchenko's 1983 report).

sketching and preparing the winterers' objects found on the island almost a century earlier. For the adventure Kravchenko had in mind, he needed to get in touch with people who had dared to adventure before. At any rate, the Rijksmuseum was not the place where Kravchenko would find a crew for his vessels. Not knowing exactly what to do with the insistent Russian, Braat phoned the Amsterdam businessman Henk van Veen, who had made fortune as the inventor of the Kreidler racing motorcycle. He had been behind the archaeological expeditions to the whaling stations at Svalbard ten years earlier. Henk van Veen advised Kravchenko to visit the Maritime Academy in Enkhuizen, where a crew and possibly some equipment for his plan could surely be brought together, since Kravchenko contended that he personally was prepared to bear all expenses. His journey to the Netherlands, then, would be successful after all.

As a result of *perestroika,* the Soviet Union put its famous Arctic infrastructure of small ports, weather stations, and ice breakers to commercial use. Soviet leader Gorbachev in 1987 had announced in Murmansk, that the Northern Sea Route would be opened to foreign vessels of peaceful and commercial intent [Brigham 1991]. Ships and convoys would be assisted by the Russian ice-breaking fleet. Not a superfluous measure, because the 'Northeast Passage' traverses five different seas, each with its own ice season. The most unpredictable is the 1700-km-wide Kara Sea, an ice trap that appears open one moment but can slam shut the next. "This year, for the first time, we've been able to arrange permissions to take foreigners along the Northeast Passage," said Kravchenko to the director of Enkhuizen's Maritime Academy. "We definitely want Dutch crew, because, after all, Barents was Dutch." The school regarded Kravchenko's project as a fine opportunity for its students, albeit under the most daring conditions thinkable. If successful, the students would gather valuable information on one of the world's most elusive sea routes. With Kravchenko in attendance, the director phoned Frans Heeres, age 33, and Maurits Groen, age 28. Shortly thereafter, Kravchenko presented himself, along with two Russian crewmembers, on Frans Heeres' doorstep.

"What if we get stuck in the ice?" Heeres asked. "Then we'll walk," Kravchenko replied.

"Well, good, let's go then!" Heeres didn't need much time to think it over, and Kravchenko handed him an airplane ticket to Moscow. Next, Kravchenko visited Maurits Groen in Wijk aan Zee, alongside the wind-battered coastal dunes and billowing stacks of the steel factory. He sat down with the student's parents.

"I can imagine that you are concerned for your son," he started cautiously. "He will be sailing close to the Devil, on a strange ship with an unknown captain. It will be my task to return him safe and sound. I ask much of my crew, but even more of myself." A cup of coffee later, Maurits was also on board.

Three months later, by the end of June 1991, Frans and Maurits stood on the docks in Murmansk, somewhat incredulously inspecting the motor launches in which they were to brave the Arctic seas. They had been appointed first mates on *Aspol* and *Willem Barents*, which turned out to be free-fall lifeboats, just like those carried aboard larger vessels. These double-walled boats, ten meters long, each holding a crew of five, were to be their abodes for months. Within days, they equipped the vessels with radar, depth finder, and satellite navigation equipment brought from the Netherlands. Having each bunkered 700 liters of diesel fuel, enough for one week of continuous sailing, they cast off on the last day of June. Kravchenko had left instructions to collect him and the rest of the crew in Naryan Mar, a small port on northern Russia's Pechora River, some three days' sail towards the east. And so begun their adventure.

Through the Kara Gates

3 July 1991 – Aspol and *Willem Barents* maneuvered adroitly through the maze of sandbars and islands in the Pechora's estuary. "This is fun!" radioed Maurits from *Aspol's* helm to Frans, who was piloting the *Willem Barents*. "This is a lot of fun!" It was three o'clock in the morning, and the sun had risen a handbreadth above the horizon. The river reflected the spectacular colours of the Arctic dawn. They were sailing upstream to the *rendez vous* they had received in their instructions.

"At this rate, we'll be in Naryan Mar by tomorrow afternoon," replied Frans. The Dutchmen felt right at home between the sandy shallows and beaches that resembled their own North Sea coast. They had plugged all the cabin vents with gunnysacks to keep out the fierce Arctic mosquitoes. With the forward hatch closed, it was warm and humid below decks. The boats took wide turns around the tidal flats, their bow waves breaking up amid the reeds of a vast marshy area.

From the log of Frans Heeres [F.H.]:
"We'll continue until the ice stops us," Dmitri said to a journalist. Dmitri [Kravchenko] apparently is an authority because he is to take us into the closed Soviet Arctic. Between Murmansk and Naryan Mar, we tested our equipment. After four and a half days of sailing, we already experienced all kinds of troubles: oil suddenly spurted out of the engine, and we floated around adrift. *Aspol*, not noticing a thing, sailed on for about 5 km. Trying to make radio contact proved fruitless, and the bastards didn't even look back! The situation was not very serious, however, so we did not set off flares. We dropped anchor in waters about ten meters deep and managed to stem the oil leak. The Russians that

supplied us did not even understand the neccesity of outgassing diesel fuel. In Naryan Mar, I tinkered a bit with the engine. Luckily, I had brought all the manuals. I had read that Dmitri wants to approach the conditions under which Willem Barents lived and worked. Well, our steel saw was so rusty and worn out that it could have been Barents' very own. Before departing, I gave the decks a quick scrubbing to remove the last remnants of diesel fuel. Incredible! They just walk right over and through it. The decks are slippery as can be. It was not easy to stock up on provisions either, because everything is rationed. Money really has no value in Russia: packs of cigarettes are the coin of the realm. Six packs will get you one kilogram of salmon; twelve packs, a bottle of 95 proof cognac. Naryan Mar is the capital of the tundra. The town lies in a vast swampy area and lives off the trade in lumber, coal, fur, fish, meat, and oil. People stand on street corners vending their wares, usually tomatoes, sausages, used clothing, and shoes. There is not much entertainment here. I bought four pelts of reindeer or Arctic deer (they are soft and comfortable to sleep on), as well as coffee, honey, and ketchup. The vessels are pretty well stocked by now, but *Aspol* is listing.

The expedition left Naryan Mar on the Pechora River on 15 July. Shortly after midnight and a hundred kilometers from town, they reached the open sea. "We immediately find an orca playing with a tree trunk. Watch out for driftwood!" wrote Frans. On the following morning, the boats encountered their first sea ice: a floe ten meters long. "A splendid blue," wrote Maurits, feeling his heart in his throat at the sight of the massive floe. "Shake hands, slaps on the shoulder. Captain Valera who has already seen sea ice signifies through gestures that he's seen sea ice plenty, up to here by the neck," Frans wrote. "Later on, more fog and more ice. The weather is changing: a bit of rain's coming down. A high-pressure front is approaching, so the weather will improve. Over here, weather changes very fast." As the fog set in, Maurits went below for warmer clothes. By early evening, Vaygach Island loomed large and dark before the small vessels, with threatening outlines of sheer cliffs rising like behemoths from the ocean. Looking up, Groen shivered again.

"I've been here so often," boomed Captain Genadi Grishin from deep within his heavy beard. "No need to worry!" The expedition headed for the northern cape of the island to check in with the border guards that need to clear them for passage. 'KGB', Frans significantly noted in his log. Northern Vaygach was also scheduled to give Kravchenko the opportunity to inspect one of his enterprises. In spite of the ice floes drifting past, now and then, Kravchenko is not in a hurry. There, in Dolgaya Fjord, about 16 km long, the expedition spotted a dozen small boats, from which young men and women in yellow and orange oilskins were casting dredges to drag for kelp.

From the log of Maurits Groen [M.G.]:
There's a ship shrouded in fog surrounded by small icebergs. We sail slowly past, towards a small gravel beach where we can see a wooden cabin. Every morning, these people are towed to the kelp beds in big polyester barges to haul in kelp from the stone-cold waters. Thus, floating with the tides and winds, they traverse the bay.

[F.H.]: This seaweed is called *Laminaria*: it removes radioactivity from your body. They freeze it aboard the freighter. It is frustrating to be sailing up and down the bay without any plans. 'Awash', they say: That means 'no plan'. Dmitri is in no hurry. He says the Kara Gates is frozen over, so we can't enter the Kara Sea. It's about 50 km across the strait to Novaya Zemlya. The vessels could make the crossing in six hours, but it's too windy to go there today. I think we should be moving as soon as possible: it's no expedition in Willem Barents' footsteps without a visit to Novaya Zemlya."

The enthusiasm and skills of his young Dutch pilots, and their curiosity towards Novaya Zemlya appealed to Kravchenko – so much so, that suddenly he was determined to take them to the Saved House. It was an impulsive gesture. Technically, it could not be done, their schedule left no room for deviations; bureaucratically, it was as extremely difficult. The bottleneck of the northern sea route is Vilkitsky Strait and the rounding of Cape Chelyuskin. Frans knew from the *Arctic Pilot* [1990] that the Strait on average is navigable only from late August until late September. If they wouldn't cross before the end of September, they would be trapped. Maurits, thinking it already too late in the season, opposed visiting north Novaya Zemlya, but according to Frans, it could be done. Kravchenko was on fire: this was a onetime opportunity to bring Dutchmen back to the Saved House. The expedition turned into a race against time.

22 July 1991 – As the boats anchored near the military post at Cape Bolvansky, an oblong armored vessel came floating alongside. The amphibious vehicle was piloted by a young man in uniform, who took them to the compound for interrogation, rumbling with its tracks onto the beach. There were fifty soldiers on this base of prefabricated barracks surrounded by empty, barren cape. The visit lasted five hours, but Kravchenko could not persuade the commander to issue a permit for crossing the Kara Gates to Novaya Zemlya. "I first got to Novaya Zemlya as member of an expedition looking for German submarines from the Great Patriotic War," Kravchenko explained. "Later on, someone asked me, why didn't you go to Ice Harbor, where Barents wintered? I was just a sailor; I knew nothing about Barents' voyage, but then all members of our expedition began reading about it". His plea did not work. The guards had not forgotten that last year, *Greenpeace*, on their watch, had infiltrated the restricted waters of Novaya Zemlya to protest the dumping of radioactive waste. Measures have been sharpened to keep visitors away. Frans by request of Kravchenko wrote a letter to the commander to explain that his interests in the island were purely historical, but the officer would not budge. Now, more than ever, Dmitri wanted to go to the Saved House, and immediately he set course for Amderma, where he could take a plane to Moscow to obtain a permit from higher authorities.

29 July 1991 – [F.H.]: Dmitri and his wife Irina have flown to Moscow. In Amderma, we're killing time by drinking, gossiping, stocking supplies, and taking the boats for test rides. Visited a hydrographic research vessel. Got a complete tour of the ship. We were with the Captain when the entire ship, all 60 meters long, suddenly shook. We wondered what might have happened, but soon forgot the incident. We were sitting around drinking coffee when all of a sudden, our cameraman and another dead drunk idiot came stumbling inside. Maurits and I were annoyed. After mistreating a map, the dead drunk idiot spilled coffee on the carpet. That's when I grabbed his cup and we left. They had come to pick us up and banged into this nice ship, the first Russian vessel we've seen in good condition and well maintained. I sailed the boat away myself. The drunken bastard took off full-speed for the open sea, which was the last straw. Yelling and cursing, we steered him back towards the harbor.

Today, we took a walk to the airport on the beach to look over a four-engine propeller plane. It was just being loaded by a group of scientists conducting research into the earth's magnetic field at Novaya Zemlya. They wanted to fly along the island to the north. Our first question was whether they would also come near the Saved House. "Where's that?" the scientists asked. "Why don't you come and point it out to us?" I jumped in right away. For all the effort that everyone seems to be making to get to Novaya Zemlya, a top-secret island, this was an amazing chance. No limitations or nothing, I just took out my photocamera. One of the windows bulged like a dome, and there was an extra window in the floor. It was a plane without formalities: I could move all around. I even took a spell flying it, but we were yawing so much that the others came forward to see what was going on. Out and back in ten hours. We flew over the mysterious and little seen eastern coast. Saw a lot of long curving glaciers pouring out into the sea and sea ice everywhere. Also saw Ice Harbor, just as the map shows it. I hope Dmitri will get permission so that we can go there ourselves. In the evening, Maurits and I went fishing for an hour in the dinghy, just off the harbor's entrance.

North to Novaya Zemlya

Kravchenko returned on 5 August with permission to visit Novaya Zemlya. Now the schedule had become critical, and tension increased. Kravchenko grumbled about discipline and dismissed *Willem Barents*' skipper. Captain Valera is very sad but Kravchenko claims that two skippers on a boat is one too many. Next, a course was laid out for Ostrov Belyy (White Island) to refuel the boats. From there, the voyage would continue northward along the 70th meridian towards the Saved House. "The map we are now using probably will end up in a museum," wrote Heeres. "Plotting our course towards the Saved House is a historic moment." The skies were overcast, obliterating the distinction between the horizon and the sea. As the wind turned to the north, the waves came broadside. To steer to a more favorable angle and stop rocking left and right, Maurits turned a few points into the wind. Further on, scrawny *Aspol* fought the waves and watched the deviation of the other boat on its radar. The mariphone (a multichannel VHF-radio) crackled immediately and Maurits received a new GPS waypoint. This one about five nautical miles (9 km) off the coast of the island, to put him back on the old course. The weather deteriorated and soon all the men were seasick. The waves were so tall that at times *Aspol* would come to a complete halt, as if she had sailed into a wall.

7 August 1991 – [F.H.]: Arrived at White Island (which isn't white at all). Three people are off to see a fisherman 6 km away. They want to use his radio to call a polar station for a weather update. Both captains are ashore. The crew is asleep, except for Misha and me. Misha sleeps under his coat. When I asked him, "Why are you sleeping under your coat?" he replied, "I was never issued a sleeping bag." Entering the sea just east of the island is the Ob River, one of the largest rivers in Russia. It produces a fast current. Sometimes entire loads of lumber float past, felled trees or plain toppled trees. What am I going to do? Cast a net, or fish with a line? The polar station here is a disaster. In bygone days, this base launched meteorological rockets. But there was a huge explosion and an enormous fire. Storage tanks are still lying around. Talk about pollution! Never seen anything like this.

The journey continues past the Russian coast, against the currents and shrouded in blinding fog; our maps are old, and sandbars keep appearing where they are not supposed to be. At 2:00 p.m., a sudden clearing of the weather: no more fog, sun all around. Again, we encounter those huge white whales that we saw at our anchorage. It is an area of rugged beauty: an abundance of fish, birds, and seals. The weather forecast relayed to us yesterday afternoon by three tankers is good, but to us, a wind of 4-5 Beaufort and fog isn't all that good. The boats are very light and move up and down through the waves like a carousel horse. Replenished the water supply and showered while alongside a big, rusty freighter. Aboard I scrounged around for some forks, knives, and spoons, and some glasses, for we possessed only one mug and two spoons. Because the dinghy was taking on so much water, I hauled in the line, attaching it closer to the boat. When Dmitri found out, he was seriously angered. Well, what can you do? Tow a submarine, or tie the dinghy so that the water it takes on immediately runs back out? He didn't change its position, so he probably doesn't know of a better alternative either. It could be he's just grumpy or seasick. I hope the hole for the hawser doesn't wear out: if that happens, we'll be in trouble.

The expedition reached Novaya Zemlya on 10 August:
[F.H.]: 8:00 p.m. Seawater is freezing to a thin slice. A large floe blocks our way to open water. A dead end? After fifteen minutes of pushing and rearranging ice floes, we've found a passageway, which *Aspol* quickly traverses. Then, in reverse and turning around, we too are free. From 20 km offshore I can see Novaya Zemlya, black with white spots of snow against a sunlit background. It's still some 120 km to Ice Harbor – about twelve hours' sailing time. But there is a new mood on board again.

[M.G.]: We can see Novaya Zemlya under a splendid blue sky: brilliant sunshine and some feathery clouds. The wind is completely absent and because we are in sea ice, there is nary a ripple on the water.

In the distance, they could see gigantic tips of toppled ice floes sticking up from the frozen sea. In the evening, Maurits heard the ice crunching against the plastic skin of the small vessel and called out: "Hard starboard, throttle down!" and then, "Full speed, starboard out!" Slivers of paint remained on the ice and spread in *Aspol's* wake.

[F.H.]: For several hours, we've been in the ice (1/10 to 3/10 cover). We sail around the thicker fields. Every hour one can see a seal, and I'm intently looking for the first polar bear. Today is bitterly cold: last night, ice was forming on the boat. The wind has just turned a few points from southwest to west and grown stronger. I jumped onto an ice floe to study the situation. At lunchtime, the ice began to close in again. Just found enough of a small opening to get out. Left the area like a bat out of hell and back to the south because the ice forecasts are *plogge* bad.

We reach the wintering site

11 August 1991 – [F.H.]: We went closer to shore and sailed passed a huge wide glacier with a steep ice blue front rising up from the sea. It flows straight down from the ice-covered center of the island. Icebergs are all over the place! Then the low brown terrain of Novaya Zemlya again. Soon afterward, we arrived at Ice Harbor, and saw the cape of Willem Barents' wintering. With all the quiet of this remote and deserted area, we felt like sailing into something big.

On the beach, we could see part of a vessel, probably of the hull, with a number of timbers and various loose pieces. A large cross, put there by Dmitri, stands on the escaprtment where the house must have been. We sailed around the cape so as not to disturb any traces. Dmitri told us that we could not just grab up objects: we must not displace a thing. He hasn't been here for more than ten years and is emotional. We shoved the boats next to each other, sterns on the beach, and lowered the gangways.

Higher on the beach, the tables of Dmitri's old camp are still standing. It is a ten-minute walk to the Saved House. The only things remaining of the House are the floor beams and the roof support. Iron hoops from old crates lie behind the house. At its longest, the inside of the house is 28 feet (my own feet) long. The hearth was in the center. I picked up a piece of burnt wood there. All around are potsherds, piles of nails, and pieces of rotted planks. One can still recognize the site of the latrine. Two openings between the beams must have been the entry hall and the door. Behind the House, Maurits discovered a bullet. I picked up leather, fabric, and shards there myself. This is Dmitri's fifth time here, and he tells us there's remarkably little snow: only some perennial banks. Besides, there is only one iceberg offshore. The ground is rocky, all small, flat pebbles – a few mosses and no other vegetation.

At the margin of the snowbank against the escarpment on the beach, we found a blue shirt with long sleeves and a sloop's bench. The latter was completely frozen stuck. We started a fire to boil water. With an ax, a spade, and small amounts of hot water, we managed to dislodge the bench. The Netherlands does not have any [recent] relics from Novaya Zemlya because the KGB invoked military secrecy for the entire region. Our radiation counter indicates 40 x 10^7 millicuries. The chap who's carrying that thing around won't divulge too much about it. He says it will all be OK (in Moscow it indicated 18 millicuries, I think). Let's hope it will all be OK. I'm not going to lose any sleep over it. Chernobyl frightened me much more. Filming was a disaster: they are never ready for it. First, they stand around to see what's happening: first step on the beach, on towards the Saved House, excavation, and then we have to do it all over for the camera. Maurits got pretty crotchety because of that – me too! We were on Novaya Zemlya for ten hours. The weather was good.

[M.G.]: Four beams indicate where the House stood. To the west of the House, there are a few rusty, steel hoops that kept the staves of a barrel together. There are also pieces of glass, china, shreds of fabric and the heel of a shoe. There are many nails with square heads. According to Dmitri, those are definitive proof that Barents wintered here. He also pointed out a path that was used 400 years ago, he claims, to carry stuff from the ship to the House. Frans found an old piece of lumber. It turns out to be a bench for a rower. We excavated it and put it in a plastic bag. Dmitri does not want to take along much more – only the bench, which he will have examined. He also tells us that somewhere around here the ship's bell and a cannon are supposed to lie buried. Frans is happy and can't stop talking.

12 August 1991 – [F.H.]: After visiting north Novaya Zemlya, we are trying to escape the sea ice. Just passed another load. Damn! Neither one of Dmitri's positions is accurate. Each time, he's two to three kilometers off. Later on, we see more ice and a walrus. Back to White Island. The fine weather is gone. Three hours ago, a squall; now we have a Force 4 wind, and when we emerge from the ice, waves are forming. The wind has been growing and growing, and the waves are taller. At 6:00 p.m., we decide to run with the wind. We can seek shelter and refuel at White Island. The wind is now at 6 Beaufort. In this vessel, even under power, it is already difficult going.

15 August 1991 – [F.H.]: One moment, a very large ice floe threatened to scoop up our small boat. A large, submerged part of that floe found its way under our boat. Using a hook, we pushed ourselves off. Scram! We sailed about 60 m behind *Aspol* down a corridor between very large floes. We were barely 20 m past it when the corridor was gone. This event may have been slow to the eye but was a quick lesson in ice navigation. Massive ice formations appeared towards the coast. During my watch, Dmitri emerged every hour to check. Towards the end of my watch, he suddenly condemned me for not steering ashore. That's when I also got hot under the collar for a moment. Always following *Aspol*, which does not even know where it is going! Later on, he came to apologize. The ice forecasts are bad. Dmitri says Dikson is feeding us false forecasts. This causes discord among the team members. In the evening, we deliberated. That was Dmitri's idea this time. Well, I did have a few points to make. They never ask for my opinion or dismiss it, which makes me wonder, do they understand me, or not? The passage of a low-pressure front was discussed as something that cannot be forecast, which is not true. The wind's sudden turning, bombarding us with ice, is quite normal in such a depression. Now, Dmitri suddenly wants to look for a lost expedition from 1912. He wants to try to go on for one more week. Some agree, some don't. Where can we hide when the situation grows worse? The conversation briefly got mired in survival techniques. Dmitri stalked off, after accusing me of a lack of feeling for the boat. I felt incredibly affronted. How could he say this? He's the one who damaged the propeller by sailing into the ice! I went after him, and after much bullshit, we found we have the same goal: to preserve the boat and to get everyone home safely. Thus, we are 'good friends' and each can go off to sleep.

Right now, at 2:00 p.m., the route back is cut off. Our course was east-northeast, and the ice closed behind us. I saw a passage to the northeast, but Dmitri shied away. We were turning in circles – waiting. Finally, he decided to go ahead and all hell broke loose. He kept pushing between ice floes and getting stuck – tried to have us shove the bow free with boathooks. My advice was to push off astern and reverse the engine, because a boat then turns its stern into the wind. His reply was a furious shout: "Go to the cabin!" With great effort, we did manage to get the boat unstuck, and Dmitri just about wrecked the dinghy. By pushing on a massive ice floe, we obtained some space. *Aspol* had already been called for assistance but did not have to get into the action. Dmitri might just sail us into damnation. Yesterday, he promised to be better, but today he is worse than ever. He took over my watch and refused to get any rest, so I told him that I would get some rest if he would not. At 3.30 a.m., I located our position on the chart and lay down on my bunk. We are currently in thick ice (6/10) and looking for a way out.

Dikson

On 19 August 1991, the expedition arrived at Dikson, in the estuary of the Yenisey River. It was cold and a caravan of icebergs was passing on the horizon. As the boats approached the pier of the port, they saw a policeman running towards them, followed by several border guard soldiers. "If the police are running in Dikson, then something serious happened," said Kravchenko. Then came news of the coup by hardliners of the Soviet Union's Communist Party against Gorbachev in Moscow.

[F.H.]: What's happening? A Putsch? Revolution? What is going on!? Michael wants to go to Moscow. We hear that there are tanks in the streets, tanks in Sverdlovsk, shootings, and skirmishes at the airport of Moscow, which was very busy. Everyone is glued to the radio. Dmitri says we are in trouble because we are sailing under the white-blue-and-red flag of the Russian Federation, and there are no such flags in Dikson yet. Irina made it from a Dutch flag that we brought by reshuffling the colors. The local prosecutor demanded that we lower that flag. They haven't seen many foreigners here in the past years and are very suspicious about our showing up. The authorities went over our documents for three full days and all this time a police guard posted with us.

Two men from *Willem Barents* then departed. Struck by the departure of their friends, the vessels took in drinking water in a somber mood. Frans and Maurits weighed their chances and considered abandoning their attempt for the Northeast Passage. On 23 August, late in the afternoon the expedition was released and hurriedly set sail again. At 8:00 p.m. they were back in the middle of sea ice. Maurits put a man on the bow and carefully piloted *Aspol* from one open spot to the other. Genadi was standing next to him, peering intently, fatigue etched on his face. The Arctic summer was coming to an end and darkness weighed more heavily each night. The navigation beacons swept across monstrous pieces of ice. The man on the bow gestured that *Aspol* had to back up. Maurits turned the wheel, and *Aspol* again found open water.

[F.H.]: Perhaps the sea ice will regress a bit and we will have a chance to traverse Vilkitsky Strait, but weather forecasts are such that it may freeze over within a week. We don't talk much; everybody has his mind on the ice. During the day, it is 13°C, but the sea is subcooled, and a wind change will cause a drop in temperature and freezing of enormous surfaces of water. Seawater turns to ice through a stage of slurry called 'shuga' or 'nilas', a thick, greyish mass slowly undulating with the water surface. Nilas can harden on a moment's notice. Ice crystals began to block the engine's water inlet. At 6:00 a.m. Maurits, awakened by Genadi, got up to find *Aspol* moored alongside *Willem Barents.* Peering through the window, he saw Genadi and Kravchenko in consultation. Frans, seeing Maurits' face behind the glass, pointed out an enormous wall of ice stretching in the distance. "Are we going back to Dikson?" Maurits asked. "I don't think so," replied Frans. "They are looking for another route." Frans would have preferred to turn back. Since Dikson, *Willem Barents* had been sailing undermanned. There was a dense fog, visibility 25-30 meters and they seemed to be surrounded by cotton. Ice enclosed the boat from all sides. They were about a mile north of the mainland coast and could hear stress release from the sea ice crumbling into the big barrier, as if cannons were firing. Ahead, two miles away – a group of small islands.

Re-entering the cabin, Genadi reported the decision: to sail along the ice barrier for the time being. Maurits started the engine and brought the vessel behind *Willem Barents*. Boats and sea ice sped along in the strong current. The wind increased toward evening, and at dusk, the expedition finally sought shelter in an inlet of the Mikhailov Peninsula [Shkery Minina Archipelago]. The ice raced past in a twilight. Kravchenko told them this was the same inlet where the famous Russian explorer Vladimir Rusanov on Hercules sheltered during his ill-fated voyage in 1912-1913. Rusanov was never seen again, and in the 1970s Kravchenko led one of the search parties looking for traces of his expedition.[1] The next morning, when Maurits and Genadi climbed the tallest spot of the island to get a better view, their spirits sagged. As far as the eye could see, they were surrounded by ice. "It is impossible to go on," Genadi stated firmly. But shortly after, back on the boats, Dmitri wouldn't hear of it. Leaving the boats safely anchored in the inlet, they found their way to a polar station on the island, 9 km farther, to ask about ice conditions in the surrounding seas.

Trapped in the Ice

After two days, Kravchenko decided not to wait any longer: they left the Mikhailov Peninsula on 30 August, a week after their departure from Dikson. Before they set out, Maurits noted their location as 75°4' N, 86°29' E, and their heading as 40° northeast. Around 12:30, Dmitri raised Maurits by mariphone and directed Aspol to take the lead. "The ice is growing thicker again, but can still be compared to ice cubes in a glass of Coke," Maurits wrote. The radar showed pack ice 22 nautical miles (40 km) away. Maurits changed course towards the east to avoid the ice mass, but soon they saw ice shimmering in that direction too. Slowly, the small flotilla entered a rapidly thickening fogbank. Relieved by Genadi at 6:00 p.m., Maurits crawled into his bunk, but sleep was slow in coming. Eyes wide open, he lay listening to the engine stop and start again. They're trying to escape from the ice, he thought. Then, just as he decided he had better get up again, the small vessel heeled frightfully and came to a full stop, with an enormous blast.

[F.H.]: In the afternoon, the ice closed in behind us. After hours of sailing through a corridor toward the northeast, everybody was dead tired. Sometime later, the corridor ended and we entered a narrow, angular passageway. I was standing astern watching to see how Aspol would make it through. Genadi, at the tiller, took the turn too wide, and when he turned the wheel completely over, I saw how the stern exploded against the pack ice. Stupid, now you've done it! I thought to myself. Thick black smoke poured from the exhaust pipe. The engine was blown. And sure enough, *Aspol* came to a full stop, and people came out to inspect the propeller. The rudder was mangled and the propeller bent. Dmitri yelled for me to get a towline ready. I already had. Bow into the wind, we sailed back to *Aspol* down the ever-narrowing corridor. When the line was fastened, we still had to turn around. There was a strong wind and the ice was moving. An ice floe came between *Aspol* and *Willem*

Barents. Dmitri gave the order to push off at the bow. We got free, using our boathooks. Then, with *Aspol* on the towline behind us, Dmitri tried to force a passage. The moving pack ice by now was almost crushing our vessels. The corner of an ice floe worked its way in between the vessels. Clearly we would soon be separated, even if we played out more towline. Suddenly we listed radically, as the entire stern of *Willem Barents* was lifted out of the water. Dmitri threw Aspol's line overboard, saying something like, "Figure it out yourself."

[M.G.]: *Aspol* kept on rising, listing forty degrees to starboard. Everyone was screaming. We were suspended on the ice for a few seconds. Nobody moved. Then the ice started making crackling sounds, and *Aspol* sank back into the water. We righted ourselves and looked for *Willem Barents*, but she was in trouble too. Genadi had no idea what to do next. "For God's sake, send out a Mayday," I told him. After hesitating a moment in disbelief, he grabbed the radio and called out three times: "Mayday, Mayday, Mayday!"

[F.H.]: Slowly, we drifted apart with the ice floes. I yelled out to Maurits, "To each his own!" We were watching *Aspol* slip away in the fog. I told Dmitri that for me, this was the moment to send out an SOS. I scrambled below decks to gather up flares, the flare gun, and our logs and maps. Dmitri was totally lost to the world and kept repeating Mayday calls. I jotted down our position and drift and began collecting the most necessary items in case *Willem Barents* was destroyed. The radio, batteries, signal mirror, mittens and warm clothing, my fur boots, the Primus and a container of gasoline. I filled a satchel with navigation instruments, compass, clothes, maps, and chocolate. All around us, ice floes were being crushed, pushed up and under each other. Visibility was perhaps 100 meters. While I was out with Fedor to keep our boat away from the ice with hooks, Fedor, Dmitri's 12-year-old son slipped and went overboard. He disappeared straight into the narrow gap between the ice and the boat. But I managed to grab him by the hair and lift him straight out. The ice floe was pressed to the side and we heard it scratch like metal on glass. The five-ton boat squeezed out onto the ice. We lay on an ice floe with a slight roll to starboard.

[M.G.]: We prepared to leave the ship. Murat closed all *Aspol's* outlets. Daniel was topside trying to spot a route across the pack ice, thinking: "If polar bears can, so can we." However, the ice was drifting towards the open sea at three knots. Hopeless. So it seemed. I stowed the navigation instruments and maps. German distributed flares, and Alex, the orange survival suits. Then we all collected some personal items and gathered on deck. We kept trying to make contact with other ships. On the 2182 frequency band, we heard nothing but static. Genadi stood on deck in the darkness, a broken man. "Nothing but misery!" he said. Then he asked us if we were ready to abandon ship. I told him that all was ready. "We are staying aboard as long as possible," Genadi said. Just then, we felt the ice again shoving its way underneath the boat. *Aspol* listed and again fell through the ice, just like before. Everybody hunched down on deck and held on to the railing, except Daniel, who stayed with the radio, monotonously repeating the emergency call. Still no contact: possibly the transmitter is defective. Genadi went below decks and called Dmitri via VHF to ask if they, too, were sending a Mayday, but they didn't answer. Finally, the mariphone came alive. Dmitri has made contact with an icebreaker and she may be here within the hour. We were heaving an enormous sigh of relief.

[F.H.]: Via radio we've heard that the icebreaker *Vaygach* is in the vicinity. We only learned of her precise location when we heard that *Aspol* had been hoisted aboard. Meanwhile, we're still drifting at two knots on a course of 40° northeast, and on the map we see a rocky shoal approaching. The situation is so critical that the GPS, with a resolution of 160 meters in all directions, cannot determine whether we will hit it or not. Peering into the dusk, we suddenly see a pressure ridge of sea ice, apparently piling up on the shoals, approaching fast. Jumping off made no sense; the ice moves so much that when you think you've found a good floe, it is subdued by others. Besides, the ice itself will accumulate against the pressure ridge. *Vaygach*, observing the situation, contemplates sending in a helicopter. But they will have to act fast or else it won't be necessary.

"*Vaygach* to Expedition. Where are you, our radar cannot see you."

"Expedition to *Vaygach*. We are under the shore of a small unnamed island, which is probably why you can't see us. We see you well, from you the course angle of 170 degrees. Distance 9.3 miles."

"*Vaygach* to Expedition. What water depths do you show? Can you move the boat?"

"Expedition to *Vaygach*. The depth is not more than ten to fifteen meters. With a short tug, we will probably be released."

"*Vaygach* to Expedition. Start moving towards deeper water. We need a depth of 45-50 meters. We wait for you. Remain contact. Get ready to board. Report boat weight. We need to prepare slings for lifting."

[M.G.] At first, the icebreaker shows as a speck on the radar screen. *Vaygach* has us in sight as well, for she's coming straight at us. Then, a large searchlight swings across us through the fog. In answer, we turn on our floodlight. Only at a distance of 100 meters or so, can we see *Vaygach's* navigational beacons looming in the fog. Murat activates two manually adjustable searchlights. Daniel and I lower the small mast that has the antennas and prepare *Aspol* for hoisting. A high-rise building approaches us, so many windows and so tall! Like an extraterrestrial spaceship, the icebreaker's gigantic bow hovers over *Aspol*. High above us, hanging over the railings, are all smiling faces.

[F.H.]: When I climb towards the lookout to see if we had better get off or not, I see a small light in the fog. It belongs to an enormous structure. Right away, I fear being crushed by the ice that is stirred by this immense vessel. The sound of the cracking ice is deafening, like machine-gun fire. Slowly, they approach, until I see small figures along the railing and shout to direct their searchlight. The beam lights tangled masses of blue-grey ice, then swings away. *Praba, praba*! [to the right, to the right]. Suddenly, the light catches us. As large as the icebreaker is, she comes to a stop right before us. Everybody reaches out at the same time to touch the steel wall. I hold a line ready on the bow. The large deck crane lowers a hook of 500 kg. They attempt to lift the small boat with everyone on it, but *Willem Barents* won't give, because she is beset in the ice. The ice is still moving, and the stern line stretches to almost twice its original length. Ice accumulates around the icebreaker's bow. Suddenly, our line snaps. The order is given: women and children off the ship first, then Dmitri and I. A rope ladder unfurls alongside *Vaygach* to get us off the vessel. Fedor is hoisted hanging below the ladder. You only have a few seconds to climb aboard. When everyone is safe, *Willem Barents* is pulled from the ice and swings a good 25 m away from the ship. She comes up whirling. A short time later she lies on her side next to *Aspol* on deck. From all pouches of my survival gear, I haul flares I don't even remember having put there. By midnight everything was done. That night, I sat in the sauna and the swimming pool until 4:30.

That Distant Goal

Aboard the 150-meter-long, nuclear-powered icebreaker, the expedition traveled further east by the frozen Siberian coast. After two days, the icebreaker dropped them off, on Dmitri' s request, at 75°38'N, 88°47'E. The adventure ended here for Maurits: he had lost confidence and decided not to risk his life anymore. He stayed aboard the *Vaygach*, awaiting passage on a freighter heading for Murmansk. Kravchenko fired the rest of *Aspol's* crew. Frans agreed to stay to sail the boats back to Dikson and to quit there. However, Kravchenko could not resist temptation. Once free of the icebreaker, he rescinded his decision to sail for Dikson. Frans wrote: "Dmitri thinks the condition of the ice will be better in two weeks. Only Irina and his young son would follow him." For twenty years already, Dmitri had attempted to reach ancient Cape Tabin, the present Cape Chelyuskin, and now they were a within a few days' reach of it. It was still a bit more than 500 km to Vilkitsky Strait. Conditions were bad: *Willem Barents* again was suffering engine troubles and had to be towed by *Aspol.* "Wonder of wonders, by a stroke of good luck, we get the currents going our way for two days," Heeres resumed writing on 8 September. "The small vessels tied together by a line, we sailed right past some small islands at a speed of 13 km per hour, on toward Vilkitsky Strait." This late in the season, dusk falls around 5:00 p.m., and it is cold. Every fifteen minutes the water inlet became plugged with ice, causing the engine to overheat. Water splashed on the bow would freeze, and thick icicles adorned the water exhaust. A thick, greyish layer of ice crystals bobbed lazily on the sea surface. "I don't know what will happen," Heeres wrote soberly in his log. "Water that is now ice will not melt through the entire winter. We progress ever more slowly. Vilkitsky is freezing up. The route is closed."

11 September 1991 – [F.H.]: Suddenly, the final decision was made. When we stopped and dropped anchor, Dmitri came alongside as if shot from a cannon. Like lightning, I threw the line back. He grazed our vessel at a speed of at least 8 km/hr. When he came alongside again, a few moments later, he had tears in his eyes. "You are all going back to Dikson and I'm taking a vessel east," he said. He does not wish to see the expedition requiring one more bail-out from the pack ice. I rubbed his back and told him, "It takes time. Don't take unnecessary risks." We will turn around and head for Dikson, although Vilkitsky Strait lies before us. We've reached our northeasternmost position: 76°27' N, 97°23' E, the center of the Nordenskiöld Archipelago. Dmitri talked to Genadi. Neither came to the dinner table. Just after we made the decision to turn back, the wind began to change direction. The sea was completely frozen over with a layer of ice some 1-2 cm thick, sometimes thicker. The small 5-ton vessels climbed out of the water and slid over the crystal-clear ice until they sank through it. *Aspol* slid into open water and had to pull *Willem Barents* free. We took turns towing each other.

For two days, we waited in resignation for whatever might happen. With the pack ice, we drifted past a small island. From a distance, we inspected the place to see if we could winter there. But there was nothing onshore, not even grass. The ice around us was continuous (9/10 to 10/10 cover). It was all pretty well frozen. Ice formed all over our boats. It was nearly impossible to look around because everything glittered with reflected sunlight. On the third day, I was standing in the lookout when, at exactly 4:00 p.m., we spotted a ship. We succeeded in making radio contact at 5:00. It was the icebreaker *Rossiya*, leading two freighters, about 6 km distant. There was much discussion over the radio, but I don't know what they decided to do.

20 September 1991 – These days have been full of emotion and many changes. Dmitri is writing a letter to save his skin. Perhaps he'll have to defend himself before a commission. The entire project is bad for his reputation. Dmitri did not want to be relieved, and the icebreaker and its convoy sailed on in peace. They were already 9 km farther when the icebreaker began a wide turn to get us, together with its convoy. After we got aboard, the icebreaker sent a telegram to the Staff of Maritime Operations in Dikson. The answer to that telegram brought many problems. We were transferred from the ice-breaker to a research vessel. Once we were back in Dikson, the Staff of Maritime Operations came aboard. Our boats have been confiscated. We sat in the Captain's cabin, where a heated discussion about the expedition took place. A telegram was received asking us to prepare payment for our passage on this ship. I understood that payment was to be made to the Staff of Maritime Operations or to the Murmansk Shipping Company.

The most important thing the Staff wanted to know was, what's driving Dmitri? Some consider the expedition a romantic adventure, while others think he is out of his mind. The Captain of this vessel doesn't want payment for our transportation. But now and then, Dmitri is drawn into such a heated conversation that others must calm him down with gestures. This is clearly a situation where we find ourselves dependent on others. The vessels have been confiscated, and Dmitri has to explain two rescue operations. The discussion bogged down in a quarrel about racism when I remarked that people here had never seen a Negro. The Captain said he has seen only bad blacks in South Africa and Surinam. That's when I got up and turned in. Tonight we wanted to fly back to Moscow aboard a cargo plane. No 'No Smoking' signs or seatbelts: just sit or lie down. Unfortunately, the airport closed at 6:00 p.m. local time. Everybody was waiting. Even the pilots were ready for takeoff. But closing time is closing time, and we'll have to wait until tomorrow.

Chapter Two

Outpost at the World's End

1993 Journal of Pieter Floore

Suddenly they were there, in the Spring of 1992. Two Russian men with dark suits and thick-rimmed glasses walked into the corridor of the university's canal-sided institute in Amsterdam. Before them, Joost Braat of the Rijksmuseum strode into the room. For three years Braat had been issuing page-long letters and faxes about his excellent contacts in Moscow, his wish to begin research on Novaya Zemlya, and whether the university would be interested to move forward with this. But despite the ever-expanding research proposal, with protocols and declarations of intent, nothing ever moved. Until this day, when they knocked on the door. The men introduced themselves as Rauf Munchaev, Director, and Vadim Starkov, the Russian Academy's Chief Archaeologist. They sat down and were ready for business. The Amsterdam archaeologists: diver and maritime expert Jerzy Gawronski, and Pieter Floore sat on the other side of the desk, astonished.

That same afternoon, the collaboration between the Moscow and Amsterdam researchers was galvanized. They spoke ever more excited, about going to Willem Barents' wintering site on Novaya Zemlya, locate Barents' shipwreck, and search for his grave. It was unreal. The Dutch were uneasy and looked at each other expecting this would unfold as an office prank. But indeed, years of patient work had paid off. Here people had been brought together with the same dream: to travel to Novaya Zemlya and complete a historic adventure. They had come to invite them over and join.

There were a few problems. There was no money. Neither side had any funds to carry out such a great and dangerous expedition. The papers were full with a media scare over the 'vast' radioactive contamination of the island, which had served as testing ground to the strongest thermonuclear explosions on the planet. The Russian archaeologists were rather laconic about it. They had never heard anything of any radiation hazard. Moreover, radiation becomes increasingly weak as time passes. If anything, it would be almost completely gone by now. The Dutch really didn't have to worry. Novaya Zemlya wasn't like Hiroshima, now was it? Let us rather talk about money.

How would you manage to finance such a business in a year? Braat had thought of it all. He was in contact with Henk van Veen, who had organized the expeditions to the 17th century whaling station Smeerenburg on Svalbard, more than ten years ago. Van Veen's enthusiasm had been easily sparked. 'Nova Zembla,' Barents, het Behouden Huys – words from faded childhood books that suddenly got colour again. Van Veen contacted the board of directors of the Wegener newspaper group. The great nineteenth century endeavours to find an open polar ocean were sponsored by the New York Herald, so would this newspaper group not be interested to dispatch a journalist, at least? They did. And with little means they had, they agreed to sponsor this fantastic journey to Novaya Zemlya and even dispatch a journalist. Middle East correspondent Taco Slagter and the Rijksmuseum photographer René Gerritsen would report daily from the island – or at least whenever radio contact could be established. Transport would be arranged by the famed polar institute of St. Petersburg, which needed hard Western money to keep a small fleet of cannibalized helicopters in the air. By sacrificing one helicopter, a few others would remain airworthy and serve the remote polar stations that had been all but abandoned after the disintegration of the Soviet Union.

With the expedition only a few months away, the 'radiation problem' had not diminished at all. In yet another unexpected move of glasnost, 'openness,' Russia released the Jablokov Report, the environmental inventory produced by engineer Alexei Jablokov, advisor to President Boris Jeltsin. It was published in March 1993 and described in detail all the nuclear waste dumping sites on Novaya Zemlya. The report further advised to keep using the island for this purpose, with the expected flow of decommissioned Soviet nuclear submarines and icebreakers, and all radioactive materials from them. Novaya Zemlya's beaches and fjords provided a safe and isolated space to cool down in the Russian Arctic. Greenpeace during the autumn of the previous year had tried to reach Novaya Zemlya but their ship was intercepted and brought in by the Russian coast guard. As a result, even stricter rules to even approach the island were put in place.

This did not discourage the team. The complicated diving for a shipwreck was scrapped. Experts from the nuclear power institute advised that every expedition member would be outfitted with a dosimeter like the ones worn in power plants. Everyone would have to keep a sharp eye on the Geiger counters. Henk would personally lead the expedition. The group had no experience in the High Arctic and would have to rely entirely on the Russian hosts. An old Mauser rifle and some ammunition for protection against polar bears was smuggled through customs on the St. Petersburg airport. Henk and Vadim Starkov were entering forms here and receiving stamps there, while Taco distributed the sponsored gold-framed sunglasses. The smuggling was helped by the tumult caused by 52-year-old Svetlana Gusarova, oceanographer and the representative of the Arctic and Antarctic Research Institute (AARI), who was presenting herself as expedition leader to everyone within earshot. With little trouble they made it onto the domestic flight to Dikson, the 'capital of the Arctic,' on the shore of the Yenissei River. By helicopter they would then make the 460 km-jump across the frozen Kara Sea.

Thursday, 19 August 1993 – When Novaya Zemlya came into view below the low clouds, we all shrieked with excitement. We had been flying blind and suddenly were racing barely 20 meters over the sea surface towards our destination. This no one will ever believe. Arrived by helicopter on northern Novaya Zemlya yesterday evening. A biting northwest wind confronted us as we debarked. Stretching before us under the mists was a vast expanse of ice floes. For centuries on end, expeditions have wrestled to round the island's North Cape and arrive here, on the hidden east side where our countrymen erected their wintering cabin from ship wreckage. Henk begins measuring radiation with the Geiger Counter. There isn't a barrage of beeps or something, so I decide to quickly inspected the remnants of the Saved House. When all is clear, we set up our tents, about 100 meters away from it. I felt thoroughly tired and when all was done, I crawled into my tent with a fever attack. Lying in my sleeping bag in a deep sleep I didn't even hear the helicopter leaving. Henk van Veen and others flew with the helicopter to Mys Zhelaniya refuel for the flight back to Dikson. They are hoping to spot Willem Barents' alleged grave on the northern coast.

Emerging from a confused dream, the helicopter had not returned yet. Also, the weather had not yet cleared: the wind was blowing hard, but despite the wind, fog and dampness remained.

We found out that the Russians had not brought proper tents. They have only one miserable small tent for themselves, holding barely two people. Dirk asked Svetlana but she told him to mind his own business. After all, she's accumulated some twenty years of Arctic experience. In the same angry mood, she issued commands to her compatriots to prepare the tent. She decides she will not be staying herself. She manages a small scientific travel agency under the auspices of the AARI in St. Petersburg. When our helicopter returned from refueling, Henk and photographer René Gerritsen step out enthusiastically from their trip to the one of the most remote polar stations in the world and a flight past the ice cap and its glaciers. No grave, not yet.

Friday, 20 August 1993 - In the morning, I didn't quite feel 100 percent, but I decided to get up because I felt I had missed enough action. The air was clear as a bell and the temperature a few degrees above zero, with a breeze coming from the north. This fine weather is excellent for our archaeological work. For the first time ever, I could now see where exactly we had landed. With our small dome tents, we are situated in a vast, barren expanse exposed to the full brunt of the northeasterly wind. The land is flat, smoothed by thousands of years of glacial erosion. The sun shines on the silvery snow that covers the faraway hilltops. The camp is approximately 100 meters south of the Saved House, which stands out against the environment as a green, flattened hump. To its east stands the wooden cross, six meters tall, that Dmitri Kravchenko erected in 1982, both to honor the winterers and to clearly mark the spot as seen from the sea. The ground consists of clay-like material and fine gravel. All around me, I can see a variety of coarse and fine rocks. Frost-heaving processes in the annually thawing soil have sorted the rocks on the ground surface. Large rocks form interlocking wreaths around the smaller rocks in their midst. Many rocks are clothed in lichens—yellow, grey, and bright orange.

The escarpment on which we stand descends about four meters towards a gravel beach about 150 meters wide. It is a band of undulating ridges sloping towards the sea, each ridge lower than the preceding one. Out at sea and parallel to the shoreline lies a belt of ice floes about 200 meters wide. The floes float in from the north and run aground on shallows offshore. At the point where the ice abuts the shore, yesterday's polar bear emerged from the sea and headed for our camp. The few small plants growing on the beach are largely unknown even to Dirk. Here and there, widely dispersed, one can see the tiny, yellow flowers of saxifrage. These plants look like red spiders, their roots sticking out of the soil in small curves. It appears that those small curves will grow out again to become other small plants. Although the fiery colors of the flowers suggest that they are meant to attract insects, we have not seen any insects here. If fertilization is brought about by the wind, then it would be better to speak of turbo fertilization. Close to the tents, a few plants with ligneous stalks, small branches, and small, oval green leaves grow over the rocky soil. These are dwarf birches, and it takes years for them to blossom and produce seeds. While the dwarf birch is actually a small tree, it grows so small and flattened that it is scarcely noticed. Reindeer apparently consume this species, but the few samples near the tent have been lucky so far. Most profuse, however, are the lichens. If a tiny spot features the least bit of cover from the wind and some moisture, or is nutritious because of bone or excrement, then it will grow a small pillow of moss. The site of the Saved House is a huge moss pillow 15 meters in diameter. It covers all the remaining floor and surroundings of the wintering cabin. Low heaps of refuse in and around the wintering spot has given rise, these past four hundred years, to abundant growths unknown in these regions. The mosses ensure that this spot remains moist, even muddy, during the summertime. Other flowers and plants are therefore also thriving in excellent fashion. Lumber lying in and on top of the mosses is moldering, in contrast with lumber lying farther from the House in a dry bottom. It disintegrates when you pick it up. The northernmost floor beam lay partly buried in the soil, partly covered up by mosses. During removal of the mosses, the beam partially disintegrated from the loss of cohesion.

The excavation of the Saved House started yesterday. Vadim Starkov and his assistant Victor Dershawin began by making a detailed drawing of the remnants. Hans Bonke, our 45-year-old engineer-historian, performed a quick survey of our surroundings. Hans and Vadim showed me what they have stumbled on so far. Down below, on the beach, are pieces of lumber and iron that slid down the slope over time as the snowbanks melted. Vadim retrieved a large, grey piece of textile from the gravel. Cameraman Henri Hoogewoud recorded the find. Might it be clothing belonging to the carpenter who supposedly was buried somewhere beneath the escarpment? That we'll have to determine in the next few days. Some pieces of lumber are recognizable as boards and planks from an oak wood vessel. At first glance, we see no timbers here that might have come from the ship. Carlsen, describing the discovery of the Saved House in 1871, noted that large parts of a ship were on the beach. These fragments were still there in 1933, according to Russian geologist B.V. Miloradovich[2]. But where are they now? Frans Heeres and Maurits Groen still reported the wreckage during their flash visit two years ago. Clearly other visitors have been here in the past years. Traces from a tracked vehicle can be seen around the Saved House, and not far away, a rusted Coca Cola can lies in a fissure in the rocks. Remnants of campfires and glass shards indicate that our campsite had been used several times before our visit. Worse yet, a few meters to the north of the

Helicopter arriving with a new power generator. The remains of the Saved House are visible up front (1993, René Gerritsen/Stichting Olivier van Noort).

Standing night watch (René Gerritsen/Stichting Olivier van Noort).

Saved House are two deep pits. Who dug them, and why?

The Saved House itself looks much better and, judging from the intact moss cover, has remained untouched for decades. This afternoon, René experimented with kite-aerial-photography, but a clumsy maneuver brought the kite crashing to the ground, breaking its fiberglass frame. That experiment, at least for today, has come to an end. Bad luck continues to affect the expedition. Not even an hour after the kite crash, the power supply for the satellite phone conked out, before we had even made contact with the Netherlands. Taco Slagter started grumbling that his article for the newspaper had to be at the editorial offices tonight. Henk van Veen, our expedition leader, said that Taco could always dictate his text via the radio transmitter. Then, however, a power surge from the gasoline-powered generator burned out the transmitter. This gave rise to hectic scenes inside Henk's tent, because now we are entirely cut off from the rest of the world.

Saturday, 21 August 1993 – Again I found myself in bed with a fever for most of the day. Troubles with the communications gear have kept Henk van Veen and Henri Hoogewoud busy the entire day. They turned the camp upside down searching for a bottle of battery acid, which I last saw when we were loading the helicopter in Dikson. Without the acid, we cannot charge the small battery, which leaves us with no power supply for the transmitter. After a few hours, Henri managed quite ingeniously to string up the batteries from his camera in such a way that they can serve as replacement. They established contact with Radio Scheveningen, a central receiver in the Netherlands that relays messages to and from seagoing vessels. When I stepped outside for a moment in the afternoon, the weather was clear with little wind. René managed to repair the broken frame of his kite using tubes from his camping chair and tent. He launched the kite and took some air photographs. Thank God, something still works!

Hans Bonke and Dirk Van Smeerdijk are still busy with wooden spikes, laying out the archaeological plot over the Saved House. I have measured the amount of radiation around our campsite with the Geiger counter. Every now and then the meter registers a tiny beep, but not any more than in Amsterdam, I think.

Sunday, 22 August 1993 – Polar bears have found us. In all, some six of them showed up around camp. The fire and smoke from the campfire did not repel the animals but attracted them instead. A mother with two cubs lay down a few hundred meters from the camp and started nursing her young. When she arose afterwards, we tried steering her into another direction by firing off two flares. Sometime later, about 400 meters out on the sea ice, another bear showed up. This animal was soon joined by two others. They remained on the ice facing our camp the entire day. Also, a lemming was loitering near Kravchenko's cross this afternoon. The last resident of the Saved House has been driven off by our excavating activities.

Around the Saved House, we are now gathering the last loose items, including large glass shards from bottles and soles and other parts of shoes, and we encounter nails and pottery shards all over the place. The finds are well preserved, especially when they come from dry spots. In the evening, we again made contact with Radio Scheveningen, and Taco's small article was relayed without any problems. Although that, of course, brought great joy, the mood was quickly shattered when the newpaper's editor Jos Goos told us that he had arranged for a relief helicopter with a new satellite phone to arrive on Tuesday. That helo will also bring back Svetlana. Henk vehemently protested this useless and very expensive endeavor and went to great lengths to explain that it is not needed, but all in vain. Everything and everybody appear to have been mobilized, and this operation cannot be halted! Now that it had come to this, Henk just asked for another generator, with clean, high-octane gasoline, extra drinking water, and charged batteries, items that are sorely needed here.

Monday, 23 August 1993 - Pale sun, and the temperature climbed to a pleasant 6.5°C. Today, I finally feel quite chipper and ready for action. Whiling cleaning loose items from the surroundings of the Saved House, we have concluded that the winterers' activities were mostly in the lee of the building. There is bare, unvegetated rock on the north side of House, indicating that refuse was not thrown out here. The situation is entirely different on the south side, where the thick carpet of mosses extends out 15 meters. René flew his kite again this afternoon, and it was soon attacked by two Arctic terns. Dirk has discovered a nest nearby, and somewhat farther inland, by a small lake, hundreds of terns are nesting. With a digital camera mounted underneath the kite, we took wide-angle photographs at altitudes of 20, 50, and 70 m above the excavation site. Vadim Starkov did not quite understand what we were trying to accomplish with this, but when René had downloaded the images to his Macintosh computer, Vadim almost fell back in amazement. René was immediately invited to photograph Russian excavations in the years to come.

After the imaging session, we finally began our digs. Vadim and Victor started off inside the House, while Dirk and I worked outside, on the west side. At first, I tried to dig the shovel into the ground, but the moss is very tough and I had to shred the tiny plants by hand to see if there was something in between there. Digging through the soil with a small trowel turned out to be the better method. Here and there, many large rocks, moss, and wooden slivers still have to be taken out. Historian and engineer Hans Bonke added the last details to his layout drawing of the four beams and, together with Vadim, measured the elevations of the surface.

Tuesday, 24 August 1993 - The temperature is 2°C, the sky is cloudy, and there is a breeze with some snow. After the usual breakfast of slippery oatmeal and pieces of windblown charcoal, Hans and I started to work. The grid across the House forms one-meter squares, which will be excavated square by square. Pottery fragments, bones, iron nails and other conventional findings we will collect in a large plastic bag inside each square. Rare finds will also be marked and annotated on the chart. Today, I take care of the find administration, also to demonstrate to the Russians how we would like things to be done. Starkov considers everything prima, and Victor does exactly as Starkov wants it done. As far as that is concerned, then, I don't have to expect any opposition. Right inside the first square where he started, Vadim discovered a splendid find. Exclaiming "Barents seurkel! Barents seurkel!," he showed us a pair of iron dividers [drawing compasses], still intact. Henri Hoogewoud immediately ran to get his video camera. When he returned, Starkov had to put the instrument back into the soil and rediscover it before the camera's eye. But the emotion was gone, and no matter how hard Henri tried, he couldn't repeat the spontaneous drama of the earlier moment. Vadim was asked to reenact his scene a few more times until Henri eventually accepted a half hearted, dull imitation of this discovery.

Hans and Dirk are working on the western side and outside the projected limits of the House. They hope to find remnants of the fox traps. All the wood they find in the ground is left there. Perhaps they will eventually come up with some framing. After lunch—soup this time, with some canned mackerel—a number of us made a reconnaissance trip to Kravchenko's camp. Situated on the coast of Ice Harbor, the camp is about 15 minutes from the excavations. Tables and other structures still stand on the beach. You could set up your tent there, and all the benches and the stove would be in their usual places. A small blue inkwell is on the table. It was left there eleven years ago, but it could be used anew today. Surrounding the camp is quite a lot of refuse, among which we found several batteries destroyed by frost. We returned and resumed our digging. I wrote out the small data cards for the finds of this morning. At night, I pulled "bear patrol" from ten until midnight.

Wednesday, 25 August 1993 - Today the weather was drizzly. On with the excavations! Against all expectations, we are finding few bones and little fabric, yet at day's end, the results were not disappointing. The House's floor yielded two knives and a pair of pewter and brass buttons, and outside we found many clothing remnants. Dirk is digging inside the squares along the southwestern corner. Here, there are thick lumps of textile, but also leather and bones just below the surface. It clearly is a pile of refuse that was thrown out. There are pieces of clothing, which probably already were worn during the wintering or were used as rags. The cold climate has ensured that much was preserved. There is finely woven material, felt, but also knitted goods. One cannot distinguish the original colors. A single piece is dark blue, but in general, the fabric has taken on the undefined, dark grey hue of the soil. Besides, the small roots of the lichens have grown into it, making these finds difficult to pry loose from the soil. If it turns out that on-site preparation is impossible, we place the entire clod in a plastic sample bag to be carefully dissolved in the lab. Vadim Starkov has started to uncover the hearth, a flat bulge (20 cm high and 1.5 m in diameter) in the center of the House. The gravel is uncommon in the immediate vicinity of the House and was collected on the beach. It puzzles me why the winterers put so much effort into creating a hearth. It is constructed the same way it would have been done at home in Holland, where one often had to deal with a combustible substratum of peat or wet mud. On Novaya Zemlya's rocky soil, however, that is not necessary. Did they wish to place the fire somewhat higher, so that it would radiate more heat? Or were they troubled by the thawing soil? The fire eventually burned neatly on this hearth for almost ten months. Around this very spot the men huddled to keep warm.

The fire was their salvation, but at the same time, it almost caused them to perish. Today, Vadim also discovered small, shiny pieces of charcoal along the edge of the stove. These undoubtedly are the remnants of the charcoal that was burnt on 7 December 1596, during a terrible cold spell. In order to profit as much as possible from the warmth, the men plugged up every crack in the House. The air around the unsuspecting men soon filled with choking carbon monoxide gas. The sick man was the first to be bothered by it. Soon after, everybody became dizzy, and it would not have taken much for them all to lose consciousness. Through extreme effort, the strongest of the group succeeded in prying open the doors and chimney. The biting Arctic wind, which they had viewed as their greatest enemy for so long, rushed in and saved them from certain death. Roald Amundsen almost died of carbon monoxide poisoning on one of his last voyages in Northern Siberia, and Richard E. Byrd, wintering on Antarctica in 1934, almost succumbed to a faulty kerosene stove. Byrd was aware of the carbon monoxide danger, so at night he left the door to his shelter open. However, after a few weeks of continual exposure to the gas, he began to suffer terrible headaches. For weeks he lay on his bed. His body had incurred considerable damage. The men in the Saved House did not possess Byrd's knowledge but experienced this danger firsthand. Only after a severe shortage of wood did the winterers dare, very carefully, to burn a little bit of coal again. They understood that they had to keep the chimney clear.

Hans Bonke was pulling a smoking battery cell from our GPS-tripod that we meant to use to chart the excavation site. We split the battery charger open, but the molten plastic parts spoke volumes. The instrument that uses a large number of measurements, which it averages to get a one centimeter-accuracy. Occupied as administrator of the excavation's data, Hans does not find much time to engage in lengthy satellite measurements. Every measurement takes at least ten minutes. The optimistic plan that we had entertained at home, to record the position of each archaeological find piece by piece, was quickly abandoned. For our daily tasks, we just make do with a tape measure. Actually, we find an unexpectedly large number of items in the Saved House. Almost the entire day I am busy filling out small data cards for the excavated finds. I note which square each find came from, what materials it consists of, and who dug it up. Subsequently, Hans gets all the small sample bags with finds delivered to his tent. He then separates the finds according to material (metals, ceramics, glass, leather, organics) and describes and sketches the more remarkable items. Thus, we create detailed distribution charts of the various items, and in this manner we have determined, among other things, where the refuse heaps were, where the winterers were mending their clothes and shoes, and how matching pieces of a pot got scattered all over the House. As we have learned from other archaeological digs, distribution patterns usually reflect the very last activities in a certain spot.

Before we began to excavate, our hypothesis was that the floor had been thoroughly worked over during the treasure hunts of the past 120 years. Vadim Starkov is still under the impression that the floor of the Saved House and its immediate surroundings were completely turned over by Kravchenko's competing expedition. I don't think that is the case: the substratum is undisturbed, and we regularly find items that are still clearly in situ. Starkov himself, for instance, found large fragments of a leather shoe: its threads have long since gone, but the loose components still lie together. I discovered the complete bottom of a ceramic frying pan, fractured, but nevertheless in the same spot where the cook had abandoned it in 1597. Most finds are covered up by a very compact layer of mossy remnants and soil. Treasure hunting apparently was restricted to large items on the surface. However, there is evidence of Kravchenko's haphazard digging. On the west side of the House, immediately outside the western beam, there is a half rotted layer of moss turfs on top of which new mosses are growing. Although authorities forbade him to do so, Kravchenko stuck his shovel into the ground here and there. In both his reports, he mentions dug in poles, which at one time were parts of the now-vanished supports of the House. Kravchenko could have determined this only by digging. Perhaps the two holes in the ground north of the Saved House are his handiwork as well, but we can only speculate about that. Taco established contact with his editor Jos Goos in Utrecht through Radio Scheveningen and relayed our adventures of the last days.

Thursday, 26 August 1993 – After a breakfast of crackers with cheese, chocolate, and gruel, I was off to work, with a stuffed feverish head again. Excavations inside the House are progressing nicely. I believe tomorrow we'll be done with the inside surface. Victor Dershawin, especially, digs fast and turns over quite a lot of soil. It is not easy to determine whether he is also precise in gathering data. Yet, he often comes over and asks us to make a note of special observations, and his productivity is no less than that of the others. Today again, they made some interesting finds: three small, leather clad, brass gunpowder containers for a bandoleer, a couple of round lead bullets, a pinecone petal, and an iron candlestick of the type we already have in the collection of the Rijksmuseum. Hans discovered the almost intact skull of a fox, probably one of those the winterers caught in their traps

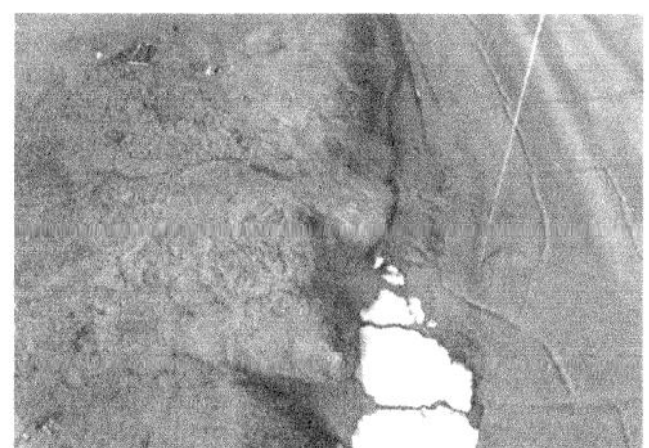

(A) Kite photograph of the remaining beams of the Saved House with a prominent hearth visible in the center (René Gerritsen). (B) The wintering locality on a frost-eroded cliff. The last of the eternal snow banks can still be seen. Beach polygons indicate shallow permafrost. (C) Hoops (ca. 70 cm) and remains of barrels for water, beer, and wine used by the winterers (photo Yuozas Kaziauskas).

and then consumed with relish. Outside the House Dirk is still "gritting," as he puts it. Fabric, leather, and pottery. And we already have hundreds of iron nails now!

All morning, Henk van Veen and Taco Slagter had been scanning the horizon through binoculars to spot our helicopter, in vain. We were expecting the helo to come in from the sea, but suddenly it came swooping in from the west. Around noon, the helicopter arrived. We could already hear its clatter from a distance, but visibility was so poor we only spotted it when it got very close. All Now our problems with communications and electricity would be solved, provided a new generator and the satellite phone were on board.

When the helo had landed, Svetlana Gusarova was the first one to disembark. She was quite excited and, gesturing wildly, called out for our "doctor" to come over immediately. Taco quickly boarded and stumbled on a gravely injured young Russian, about twenty years old, whom Svetlana had taken along from the polar station on Cape Zhelaniya, where a big fire had broken out several days ago. The lad had suffered extensive steam and fire burns on both hands and face, but he could not be evacuated until our helicopter had refueled. All that time, they had kept the victim quiet with vodka, but done nothing at all about his burns. On his hands, I spotted gigantic blisters the size of chicken eggs, some of which had already broken and run dry. Taco and Dirk immediately started taking care of the most serious burns as best they could.

Fire erupted two days ago at the polar station, and the flames engulfed this young mechanic. He belongs to the crew of the northernmost polar station and one of the most desolate sites in the world, where the helicopter had stopped to deliver some goods and refuel. Pushed by Gusarova, the pilots agreed to bring him along. Even a First Aid kit is apparently lacking on that bizarre station. He was burnt over 20% of his body, notably on his hands, arms, and face, and part of his hair is singed away. Although he was being remarkably brave, pain was apparent on his pale face. Taco asked him for his name and he weakly answered, "Sascha." The polar station has a primitive sauna, and for unexplained reasons, boiling water exploded on his hands and arms. A flash fire followed. It took us two hours to bandage Sascha's wounds and drip half a liter of I.V. fluids into his circulatory system. The lad didn't bat an eye during that treatment and started protesting only when Taco decided to cut open the sleeves of his training jacket to clean the blisters. This is probably the only jacket he's got. At last, they managed to get his arm out of the sleeve. Then Taco started an intravenous drip to compensate for loss of fluids. Henri and Yuri kept busy warming the I.V. bags around the campfire. There isn't enough firewood and we're using lumber from the Saved House to keep the fire burning.

While Taco and Dirk were taking care of the young Russian, Svetlana marched straight to Henk to demand payment for the helo flight, and for her flights from St. Pete. She wanted cash right away. A cool $17,000 is involved, but Henk thinks that this should be charged to the newspaper; after all, they need that satellite phone more than we do. Besides, the only money we have here is to pay for our return trip. Henk sat with Svetlana on a tree trunk, an ax between them, and soon drove her to despair. Tempers flared. She threatened that we might as well pack our bags, because Aeroflot would abandon us on the island on 31 August (our planned departure date). Henk was not impressed. "Then we'll spend the winter here," he said dryly. Henk put his foot down and at last Svetlana gave in. "Henk, you sly polar fox!" she hissed at him. After lengthy bargaining, the helicopter crew agreed to $280. Those greenbacks she passed on to the pilot. We gave Sascha painkillers, antibiotics, and the special burn bandages to carry along. Saying goodbye, Sascha had thanked us profusely and, as token of his gratitude, gave us two packs of the unsmokable Russian cigarettes. I recall that it was this lad who, during our visit to Mys Zhelaniya, had sought to contact us with a few words spoken in German. As the helicopter slowly took off and disappeared rapidly into the cold haze, Taco felt overcome by sadness. We fervently hope that in the economic anarchy of Russia, he'll receive proper medical attention.

Friday, 27 August 1993 - A cold day! The hearth, in the centre of the House, has now been completely unearthed. Few objects are found in the hearth itself, but small items in its immediate surroundings betray its intensive use. We have found the small bones of Arctic foxes, a welcome supplement to the winterers' menu. The small skulls were cracked so they could consume everything, even the brains. It has been suggested that this helped to stem the outbreak of scurvy, the much-feared disease that results from Vitamin C deficiency. The human body cannot make Vitamin C (ascorbic acid) by itself: we derive it primarily from fresh fruit and vegetables. But Arctic foxes can produce ascorbic acid from glucose, so their meat contains a certain level of Vitamin C. The winterers were able to snare almost 30 foxes. Victor Dershawin excavated the lower part of a fox's paw, its knuckles still all in place. Perhaps it was tossed into the fire during a meal and remained there.

We have also found bones of larger animals, which turned out, after cleaning, to be cow and pig ribs hacked into pieces. There was salted meat on board, and De Veer described how the winterers pulled a barrel of meat from the ship to refill it with fresh water. During this operation, a couple of passing polar bears peeked around the corner. One of them paid dearly for that: he immediately received a bullet and dropped dead on the spot. This bear was stood up until it froze and probably remained in front of the Saved House all winter long. Possibly the pile of polar bear bones seen by Kravchenko in 1979 and by Frans Heeres in 1991, near the spot where the cross now stands, was the remains of that animal.

All victuals aboard were dragged into the House, which was soon filled with barrels, crates, and bags containing not only provisions, but also merchandise. The winterers lived off these provisions during their entire stay. They were not too concerned about their supplies' spoiling. After all, they were living inside a natural freezer. Although we have found a great deal of trash on the floor, it's likely that the House was reasonably well kept during the wintering. Skipper Jacob van Heemskerck would have maintained the rigid cleaning routines followed aboard ship even during the cold and dark months inside the House. The huge piles of trash on either side of the House are simple proof of that. Besides, flammable refuse would certainly have disappeared into the fire.

Most of our finds are concentrated on the northeast side of the hearth. Here, we discovered a space of three to four square meters full of leather cuttings, lead bullets, pottery, buttons, and smaller bits of fabric: a few hundred objects in total. This is in stark contrast with the near lack of data in a two-meter-wide strip on the eastern side of the interior, suggesting that the cots were alongside this wall. A seaman's locker, harboring expensive and personal items, stood in front of each cot. This locker was also used to step up into the cots. Crates and barrels would probably have been stacked up against the north and west walls. A door in the south wall opened onto a porch. There probably was also a cot in the southeastern corner of the House, right next to the door. The etching of the interior of the Saved House in the German edition of De Veer's account [Hulsius edition, 1598] would then represent a north south bisection. Although the House's dimensions in that picture are too generous, individual

(Above) Mast bench removed by the winterers to make place for people and goods on the return journey. Uncovered by Dmitri Kravchenko (r) in June 1991 (courtesy F. Heeres). (Below) Brass gunpowder shell (10 cm) in which Willem Barents rolled his declaration. The object and letter provide material connection to the historical record described by G. de Veer (June 1597 'hung in the chimney' before their leaving the island).

details correspond quite well with the archaeological data. If there were six cots, then each cot was meant for three men. Aboard ship it was also customary for several men to share one cot. In the Saved House, that would have allowed them to profit from each other's body warmth. A cot measured approximately 1.5 to 1.7 meters long. Even though the mariners were not very tall—Van Heemskerck's body armor in the Rijksmuseum is small—they would probably have slept in a half sitting position, as people were wont to do in those days.

Svetlana has been a complete no show at the digs. Together with Yuri, she keeps busy in the kitchen. The culinary level of the field kitchen has been considerably raised by her arrival. Today, we'll be getting Uga, a delicious soup with fish from the Yenisey River. This afternoon, the weather also took a turn for the better. The fog lifted and the sun broke through the clouds. Henk, Dirk, and I took a walk towards the ruins of the wooden lighthouse on the cape to gather firewood for our camp. After keeping a fire going for almost ten days, we have to walk farther and farther to gather firewood. Driftwood on the beach in front of the Saved House was already in very short supply, but now it has been depleted. Sometime during the 1950s a wooden lighthouse a good 15 meters tall was constructed on the southern tip of the promontory. There is a small shelter next to it. The glass prism of the lighthouse's lamp lies spread about the remains like a sort of eternal ice. From what's left of the wooden tower, one gets a grand view of the entire cape until far past Ice Harbor. It is so clear that objects on the horizon don't grow blurry, but rather become too small for the eye to see. Everything is flat, the sea as well as the land. In the nineteenth century, Charles Francis Hall of the United States spent two years with the Eskimos in Northern Canada. One day, Hall was with an Eskimo hunter and viewed his surroundings with a telescope. Although the hunter boasted sharp eyesight, with the telescope he could bring closer those things that were barely visible even for him. He told Hall that the telescope provided a view into tomorrow. Hall wondered at the remark, and when I read it I did not understand it either, but now it suddenly makes sense. Here, you can easily see 30 km, and if you are at a higher elevation, even farther. However far you can see, you will see as far across the landscape as you can cover by foot in a day. You will always be looking at today.

Saturday, 28 August 1993 - The wind gauge indicates a Force 8 wind. Large waves are crashing in a haze of ocean spray along the coast, and foam is gusting up almost to our camp. The coast had been almost free of ice for the last few days, but now many ice floes come floating by out of the north. Reluctantly, we started our work near the Saved House. It was so frigid that I could hardly look into the wind. A few minutes later, a polar bear alert sounded. Two young bears had headed out to sea not too far from camp, only to come plodding along the beach towards the lighthouse. We had barely started again when Vadim showed us something unbelievable. Yesterday he astonished everyone with a leaden compass case casually left behind near the hearth, in the center of the Saved House. This could be the compass De Veer wrote about on 29 January 1597. In the square that he has just started to dig, Vadim is working around the end of a glass drinking horn preserved in the soil. The object is made from crystal clear glass, decorated with gilded paint. Two of these extremely rare horns are kept in the Amsterdam Rijksmuseum. In the sixteenth century, it was nearly impossible for most glassblowers to produce such colorless glass. Only the masterful Venetian glassblowers proved capable of this tour de force. This is not to say, yet, that this horn originated in Italy. Attracted by financially strong buyers, Italians had long been working in countries bordering the North Sea. These types of objects, however, are unusual on a ship, and I believe this horn is part of the precious cargo taken aboard in Amsterdam.

Van Heemskerck and Barents carried a highly diverse sample of arts and crafts available in the Dutch Republic. Their cargo was not a specific trade cargo, because they did not know for sure yet what might interest the peoples of Cathay and Japan. Jan Huyghen van Linschoten, during his stay in Goa, learned from missionaries that the Chinese Emperor was particularly enamored of clocks. The Gothic clock that Carlsen discovered in 1871, also depicted on Hulsius' print of the Saved House's interior, certainly was not a ship's clock. This timepiece with weights was totally unsuited for shipboard use and was likely selected as a gift for the Emperor. It was probably already eighty years old when it was packed. The two very large maps of the United Netherlands recovered from the remains of the Saved House were also intended to impress the mightiest of Asian Rulers. Commercially and politically, the voyage of Barents and Van Heemskerck was very much experimental.

Today, work progressed slowly because everybody soon became cold and tired in the icy wind. It remained to be seen if we could finish our research, for toward the end of the afternoon it started snowing. Powdery snow has continued to fall all during the evening. I transferred the data from Kravchenko's field sketches to our charts to compare the results of the two investigations. This afternoon, Hans researched the spot outside the northeast corner, where Kravchenko had marked his largest concentration of discoveries. As expected, it delivered scant results: a few small shards and nails remained, but nothing else. This was probably a spot where debris and scrap had been deposited during the disassembly of the House by Carlsen and Gardiner in the 1870s. The refuse heap on the southwest side that we dug into this week is totally overgrown with a thick layer of moss and small plants, as can be expected after 400 years.

A big ivory gull (*Pagophila eburnea* – somewhat rare in these parts) was soaring about our camp all day long. Yuri tossed some food remnants at it. The bird is very tame and flies away only when you come close, so just about everybody has already taken its picture. Oh yes, the new satellite phone went dead tonight. Will the newspaper send us a new one again?

Sunday, 29 August 1993 - I unzipped my tent to a white Novaya Zemlya. It snowed all night, and the accumulation is 30 cm for sure. This year may see an early winter. Thus, the investigations have come to an end for Vadim. He is of the opinion that all work has to come to a stop. Two days ago, he suddenly announced that he has to go to Spitsbergen on 30 August, and could we just call for the helicopter? Everyone was surprised, and Henk van Veen was clearly dumbfounded. "Couldn't this man have announced his itinerary before our trip?" said the expression on his face. "We sat around the table for days, and besides, the schedule and all agreements were already documented months ago." Vadim probably already sensed that repeating his urgent request would arouse resistance from his Dutch colleagues, so he brought Svetlana along to buttress his arguments. She also wants to go home because her mother is ill. It seemed best to everyone to just continue working and avoid further discussions. After a few hours in his tent, Vadim rejoined the excavations, continuing his tasks as though nothing had happened.

The snow made it hard to locate the Saved House, but the wind was helping us already to clean things up. A few hours later, the entire scene was bereft of snow. I created very detailed drawings to scale of all the floor beams. The south beam is 6.20 meters long. Both ends have been notched halfway through so that this beam can be used log cabin style. This beam matches the north beam in both length and girth, so I can assume that the interior width of the House was about 6 meters. Both beams have two notches, 1.20 m apart, at their center, in which two standing beams would have been placed to support the roof structure. There probably was a door between those standing beams on the south side. The north beam is somewhat sunk into the ground and may still be in its original position. The east and west beams were probably placed on rocks embedded in the soil. Kravchenko moved these beams, as photographs from his investigations indicate; however, they have been put back in approximately their original positions. The refuse heaps on either side of the House also demark a width of a little more than 6 meters. The length of the House is more difficult to determine. The location of the hearth in the center of the House indicates a length of 8 to 8.5 meters.

You won't be seeing a trace of Taco all day. I walked past his small tent: "Hey, Taco babe, what are you doing?" "Get lost, man. I'm freezing!" "This is something different from your Holiday Inn, eh?"

Ten meters to the east of the Saved House is a pile of rusted hoops. Most are broken in half, but some are still intact. These hoops, at one time, were part of the barrels containing beer, bread, bacon, and sherry. Almost everything aboard a sixteenth century vessel was kept in barrels. Often a cooper was part of the crew especially for that purpose. Certainly there were loose staves and hoops aboard so they themselves could make barrels. Indeed, a few staves were still lying around near the House, but many others must have perished in campfires, along with the greater part of the Saved House, in the ensuing years. In De Veer's diary, we can read how during winter those staves would disappear into the fire and the hoops would be tossed onto the roof to hold down the sails. At winter's end, the roof was demolished, and those hoops may very well have been tossed onto this pile.

Henk and Henri showed up at the end of the day. In between their repairs of the last few days, they have assisted here and there for an hour or so, but now that the excavations are coming to an end, they would very much like to excavate "a part with many objects." I put them to work on the refuse heap on the east side of the House. Dirk took 10 liters of soil samples from the area around the hearth. He had expected more from this particular site and thinks that, by sifting the soil through a fine mesh, he may obtain less obvious objects, such as seeds, very small bones, and fish bones. Between 4:00 and 5:00 p.m., a polar bear suddenly appeared, not even 50 meters from the digs. These ursine visits had become less frequent in the last few days, and we had dropped our guard somewhat. Nobody had seen the animal coming, especially because it had the sun at its back. Victor first sounded the alarm and jumped up, and then everyone started hollering. Even before Victor could get to a gun, the startled beast turned around and ran in the direction of our camp. No one could see this coming. Victor ran after the animal, firing his gun like a cowboy, and managed to drive it away from the tents. The bear disappeared, trotting towards the south.

Monday, 30 August 1993 - The excavation isn't easily cleaned up. Many things still need to be done, but this last day, of course, is way too short to complete the entire wish list. Thirty meters to the south of the House is a large beam that I notice almost every day, but to which I have not yet paid much attention. Hans finds that it is a complete cross beam of the Saved House, 6.20 meters long. On either end, there are notches in which the narrowed end of a standing beam fitted. Where exactly this beam fits in the construction of the house is unclear. Why would just this piece of the House have been preserved? The quality of the lumber is outstanding, and it is of the same silvery color as the floor beams. Other parts of the building most likely were of similar quality. Dirk sifted the entire hearth, which was excavated yesterday by Vadim and Victor, through the four-millimeter and then the one millimeter sieves. He has saved the remaining fractions for

The memorial marker placed by research vessel *Willem Barents* on 23 August 1881 on top of the smallest of the Orange Islands, with Henri filming and Vadim Starkov explaining (1993, credit René Gerritsen); view from the larger Orange Island towards Cape Carlsen, Novaya Zemlya's North Cape (1998, JJ Zeeberg).

future investigations. Amid the gravel he still finds three musket rounds and a large number of small nails (from burnt wood?). I hardly saw Vadim and Victor today. Towards the end of the afternoon, they suddenly emerged from their tent and started to string up their bags of collected wood, to get ready for transport. This morning already, I had noticed Vadim sitting inside his tent, all packed and ready to go.

Tuesday, 31 August 1993 - The helicopter was supposed to come around noon to collect us, but it showed up early, at ten o'clock while we were still busy breaking camp. As on the outbound flight, it was full of cargo and personnel for polar station Mys Zhelaniya. Henri, Henk, Vadim, and I are going along to once more scan the area from the air for potential graves. One can never know! After last week's disaster, someone had the bright idea to equip the polar station with a fire extinguisher, which almost fills the plane. Boxes of provisions and tools are stacked on and around this module. If the people of Mys Zhelaniya depend on whoever happens to be flying to northern Novaya Zemlya for their provisioning, then I feel deeply for them.

The passengers on the helicopter hardly reacted to us at first and cared little to introduce themselves. They acted as if it were the most mundane thing for a group of people to hop aboard on north Novaya Zemlya and take a seat on top of a box of books or a crate full of eggs. Once we were aloft, the tension evaporated, and I started a conversation with a small Mongolian who had made himself comfortable in the tail end of the helicopter. We became pals, and thus I had to share a drink with him. He dug a half liter bottle of vodka from his bag and pulled off the steel cap with his teeth. After handing me a mug full, he drank what was left in the bottle. Drinking made us hungry, so that same bag produced a raw fish, from which the Mongolian proceeded to rip off large pieces with a dull knife. When he asked if it tasted all right, I nodded affirmatively, my mouth full of fish bones. He pushed a second fish into my inside pocket, for when I get home. Of course, this grand gesture could not go unanswered. Searching my coat pockets, I discovered a pair of rubber household gloves, a small eraser, and a refillable pencil. These gifts were gratefully accepted, and while I was in such a good mood, I generously passed out a few left-over find administration cards.

We crossed the Kara Sea, wedged in by our gear. Tipping forward, the helicopter skimmed barely ten to twenty meters above the surface, shaking and vibrating violently in the turbulent air. Seated right underneath the engines, we felt the cabin grow blazing hot. Smelling vodka, a blond Russian named Alex came crawling aft. In broken English, he managed to inform me that two of them were going to Franz Josef Land to work two months at a polar station. Alex is a veteran of the Afghan Wars. He was an officer during the war and now lives in Moscow. Forward in the helicopter, Henri and Henk were seated next to a man with a peculiar, large reddish head and an equally reddish moustache. I thought fleetingly that he might be the one who was burnt a week ago, but this man seems to be much older. Henri was babbling a bit with this person, using the few Russian words he knows. The man, heavily besotted, leaned against Henri and kept on talking. Eventually the helicopter descended to land near the fuel station at Cape Zhelaniya. From the air, I could already see thousands of empty oil barrels around the polar station, which will probably remain there for eternity. We noticed during our first visit what a terrible mess this place is, with big piles of refuse in between the buildings. Now that we have come back, however, I understand how the residents cope with the mess: a layer of snow half a meter thick has already covered all of Cape Zhelaniya.

While the helicopter was refueling, we found out that the pilot had no intention whatever of investigating Novaya Zemlya's northern shore. Actually, our survey does not make sense now that winter has started and the surface is hidden beneath a thick pack of snow. Meanwhile, the fire extinguisher was being unloaded. The man with the red moustache turned out to be in charge of this operation. Wearing only a jacket over his clothing, he strode around in the snow issuing orders to the workers, who paid little attention to his instructions. A large diesel pump was the last item remaining inside the helicopter. After unsuccessfully trying to dislodge this heavy piece manually, some men walked off to get an oil barrel, clearly intending to roll the pump out of the helicopter.

I decided to walk over to the polar station, to look over at the fire ravaged building where that Russian lad was injured. A small yacht with a big hole in its hull lies on the beach. On a small escarpment, we could see two gravestones: a sad and lonely burial place at the edge of the world. The engine room, where several generators were working again, is the building farthest away from the living quarters. Between the buildings stood countless demolished trucks and tracked vehicles, and shy Arctic dogs loitered amid the scrap heaps. When I came back to the helo, Henk told me a man had died. It was the man with the red moustache, who had collapsed while unloading the diesel pump. He was put in the cab of a truck, where he died shortly thereafter.

I walked over to the truck and saw the man seated, half slumped over, ashen grey in his face. Henri was upset. He had caught the man when he sank to his knees but did not know what to do, nor had he realized the seriousness of the situation. He blamed himself for not knowing precisely what to do. The helicopter crew did not make any attempt to help, and still they appeared unaffected. In fact, none of these men has shown any concern over the corpse. The base commander approached Henk van Veen with the request to take the body to Dikson. Regulations require that an autopsy be conducted. Henk grudgingly agreed.

It was a weird flight back to Cape Spory Navolok. We were touched, Henri most of all. The man with the red moustache lay aft in the tail end on a wooden board, covered by a small blanket. Back in camp, we encountered an entirely different mood, because the other expedition members had organized a going away mixer with champagne. Although our announcement of the man's death put quite a damper on the festivities, we nevertheless raised our glasses to toast the successful conclusion of our field work, or whatever will have to pass for such. We lowered the flag and fired the last rounds from our rifles in a salute.

Crammed together with the others in the helicopter, I tried, half standing, to sleep away the flight hours. At Dikson, a police van awaited us. Henk had already been dreading the bureaucratic troubles that we might have in Russia, and now that we were returning with a dead man, he feared the worst. To our amazement, the police were interested only in whether we had shot any polar bears. They asked if they could inspect the helicopter to see if we brought along any polar bear skins. To Henk's query about what to do with the deceased, they replied that someone else would come to address that issue. Indeed, ten minutes later a flatbed truck arrived, and two youths tossed a stretcher underneath the helicopter, and then walked away. Together with Victor, I rolled the man's body onto the stretcher and, aided by the two policemen, we placed him on the truck bed. His small fur hat flew off his head as the truck got underway. The sky was grey and snow was falling.

For all we've seen of it, Dikson is one big mudhole. The dreary weather has cast a pall over the cheerful colors of the wooden houses. Aboard a big bus, we traversed the muddy streets lined by useless machinery and empty containers. Sagged pipes run atop a bed of oil barrels clear of the frozen ground. The city lies somewhat elevated, and the sea can be seen from anywhere in town. Sidewalks consist of wooden walkways, where dapper, well groomed ladies in fur coats stepped along. They stopped and stared in amazement when our shabby and unshaven bunch disembarked from the bus. We were led to a large hotel. Inside, the heat was soothing, very comfortable to the cockroaches in the room, who ran for safety when I put my bags down. I have the feeling that I am not far away from Ice Harbor. But when dark falls towards evening, after twelve days of daylight, I can tell that I am homeward bound again.

Chapter Three

AMSTERDAM, TWO YEARS LATER

There had been a spectacular development. In May 1994, parts of Willem Barents' vessel were identified in Moscow by Rijksmuseum experts.[3] The wreckage was being kept in northeastern Moscow, in an inconspicuous building, incidentally a stone's throw from the city's 'Monument for the Conquerors of Space.' The largest fragment, apparently part of the vessel's hull, was almost four meters long and consisted of two layers of oaken planks, each 4 cm thick and held together by cast iron nails and 2.5 cm-thick wooden pegs. These were the ship parts on the beach near the Saved House documented by Norwegian walrus hunter Elling Carlsen in September 1871. Frans Heeres had seen them still 120 years after that, but in 1993 there wasn't a trace of them left. Only when Moscow's Heritage Institute established contact with the Rijksmuseum did it transpire that they had secured the wreckage in June 1992. And because it had been partly excavated from the beach, more was likely to be found under the gravel, buried by sea ice in the course of time. The Moscow-based institute claimed full authority, illustrating a quiet power transfer from the St. Petersburg academy to Moscow. The invitation for a joint Russian-Dutch expedition by the Heritage Institute, in October 1994, came with the promise of all permits and logistics taken care off. It provided opportunity to complete the archeological survey of the Saved House – and to inspect several burial mounts reported along the northern coasts of the island. In May 1995, at last there came green light for a seagoing

Poster advertising the panorama painted by Louis Apol after visiting Matochkin Shar with R/V *Willem Barents* (1897).

expedition and a dozen researchers, Russian and Dutch (one Russian for every Dutch).

A follow-up expedition to north Novaya Zemlya was outfitted in the summer of 1995 to search for ship wreckage and inspect the potential graves of Willem Barents and Claes Andriesz. The famous team that had made headlines two years earlier, was joined by ship experts and a pathologist. On Tuesday, 27 June 1995 I met some of my teammates for this summer. Six weeks we had to ready the expedition. We gathered in the morning sun at 7:00 a.m. by the canal in front of our Amsterdam office.

A vessel had been chartered from August 15 to carry the expedition to north Novaya Zemlya, where two parties would be landed about 80 kilometers apart. In a rush, we had to list sponsors, for everything, to collect all our gear and supplies. As a good start, the military offered to provide us with clothes and equipment, sleeping bags, to search for our national hero, Willem Barents, and his vessel. The military proposed to train us, particularly the Air Force 'bomb squad,' to work with their metal detectors. They also offered to train us city people to use our guns and protect against polar bears. As we drove out of Amsterdam and onto the highway, Jerzy Gawronski, the expedition leader, steering with one hand, turned around and leaned back to hand us a newspaper. We had barely met and were on our way to collect our first expedition materials on the airforce base.

"Well, that is interesting', said Bas Kist, the Rijksmuseum's historian and archaeologist, dryly. He began reading the article out loud. Ocean currents off the coast of Novaya Zemlya dragged Barents' vessel away; Barents was given a burial at sea, and the paper stated that there would be nothing left of the Saved House. The car filled with laughter. I was confused.

"Nothing to worry about," Jerzy, our research leader smiled in the rearview mirror. The men have known each other for fifteen years. "We worked on Spitsbergen together, excavating the whaling station of Smeerenburg," Bas started telling me. "The pathologist, George Maat was uncovering the whalers' bodies at Zeeuwse Uitkijk [Ytre Norksöya], an island nearby." This was all new to me. Even Amsterdam was new to me. I had met Pieter Floore six weeks ago and he had handed me a stack of Xeroxes of a manuscript in Gothic lettering that would probably take me 25 years to decipher.

Bas Kist since 1964 has been curator of the Rijksmuseum's Dutch history section, colleague and good friend of Joost Braat. In 1978, forty-four years old, he camped four weeks amongst the remains of the whaling settlement Smeerenburg, on Amsterdam Island, all by himself.

"Spitsbergen was a wild frontier then," Jerzy recalled. "It wasn't like a place for hiking or camping as it is today. There was nothing there. You would really be alone and at the mercy of the elements." Photographs from the turn of the twentieth century show tourists posing behind rows of human skulls. One hundred years later, Bas found there was nothing left on the surface. He witnessed the erosion of the site. Upon returning from a tour of the desolate island, he found tourists debarking:

> "I really can't believe my eyes. All over the low part of the island I see people strolling. There are easily one hundred of them. Through my binoculars I spot them, partially wrapped in fur coats and for the rest in cheery vacation dress. A number of inflatables are lying on the beach. In the bay lies the ship on which they have arrived; it's called *World Explorer*. Closer up, I discover they are German tourists. Several of them pinned business cards on my tent and are now approaching me, stumbling in their city shoes, to take my photograph and to pose all kinds of questions. I don't know whether to laugh or to blow up when I notice them walking

> through and trampling all over my exploratory plot, carefully laid out with stakes and rope. I accept their cigarette but am otherwise too dumbstruck to have any questions. After this event it does not surprise me that Amsterdam Island retained so little of earlier activities. This in contrast to the Danish Isle, where apparently less people come. All that the Norwegian authorities have done to protect Smeerenburg, except for establishing some regulations, is putting up a sign that says 'Historical Monument'" [Kist 1981, pp. 61-63].

At 9:00 a.m. we arrived at the airbase and were received by the 'Explosive Ordnance Disposal Group'. The men were getting ready to depart for Bosnia, to clear roads for the UN peacekeeping forces. The sergeant-major taught us a few tricks of his trade and instructed us in the use of mine detectors and 'bomb locators'. Any object will have a distinct signal for which the men have developed appropriate jargon: a *clinger*, a *sticker*, a *warhead*, and so on. For training purposes, the group has a collection of anti-personnel mines, cluster bombs, and heavy aircraft bombs, as well as homemade projectiles and roadside bombs from the former Yugoslavia. On our first day, we worked on a training field on the base while jets thundered overhead. A second exercise took place in the woods, where the retreating Germans in 1944 blew up one of their compounds. In a few hours, we recovered a pile of rusty munitions from underneath the forest litter. Back in the lounge the men showed us a corroded pair of navigational dividers, discovered inside the glove of a Junker-88 pilot crashed deep in the mud of a Dutch polder.

Being the geographer of the team, I was set to the task of aquiring an automated theodolite and laptop computer; sophisticated hardware that we could never afford. My job was to support the archeologists and get a little work done on the side while visiting this very exclusive region. I was, of course, dreaming up my own plan: reach the ice margin, some twenty kilometers inland from the wintering site. The ice cap rests on land, unlike most glaciers which terminate in a fjord or a valley. What could it possibly be like? Would everything be frozen stiff? The landscape we would traverse getting there, has never before been crossed and will tell tales of glacier's former size and dynamics.

Among the instruments that came at our disposal was a Garmin global positioning system (GPS). Pieter and I unpacked it with awe. The GPS is a compact, rod-shaped instrument, which easily fits in a hand. Despite its minimal size, the GPS carries the full potential of space-age technology. A satellite receiver calculates its position by triangulation of the signals of at least three satellites, not unlike the navigation of seafarers measuring the azimuth of the sun and stars. The push of a button enters the retrieved coordinates into a memory-chip, plus or minus 20 meters. Batteries, we need many batteries. All the equipment that was coming in we packaged watertight and stored in the basement of our institute. Also gathered here were meteorological instruments to record weather conditions at Cape Spory Navolok. I particularly was hoping to document the famous *Bora*, a katabatic wind generated by Novaya Zemlya's ice cap. These are conventional instruments – thermometers, a hair-hygrograph, a barometer, and an anemometer – some with rolls of recording paper and powered by springs. After we tested them and left them in the basement, they were producing a reliable ticking sound.

Wednesday, 19 July 1995 – Doctor Maat arrived this morning and I interrupted my inventory of packaging to meet him. He is a pathologist from the University of Leiden, who worked with the Amsterdammers for more than fifteen years. Maat (1948) and his assistant in 1980 examined a sample of fifty skeletons at a burial site of 183 whalers on 'Zeeuwse Uitkijk', a small island (1.5 km^2) near Amsterdam Island, in the northwestern corner of the Svalbard Archipelago. This study and earlier observations of this Arctic seventeenth-century cemetery demonstrate that the bodies and clothes of Willem Barents and Claes Andriesz Goutijck are potentially well preserved. Bastiaan Baljé, crewman on R/V *Willem Barents*' in 1878, wrote what he found in his diary: "[Thursday, 20 June] During the evening a visit was paid to Fuglesangen Island, which apparently had served as cemetery for the Zeelanders who temporarily resided here some two to three centuries ago. Denied a stay on Amsterdam Island by the then-powerful Chamber of Commerce of Amsterdam, those from Middelburg and Veere, as early as 1617, established their train-oil boilers on this island of Zeeuwse Uitkijk, so that the nearby Fuglesangen Island rightfully can be considered the Zeelanders' cemetery. We counted, give or take a few, several hundred burial mounds, all covered by rocks of various sizes. One of these graves was opened and the coffin raised, which was found to be in such excellent state that it had to be opened with an ax. The decayed corpse, now merely bones, was clothed in a still well-preserved sweater with long Icelandic stockings and a knitted woolen nightcap, in which the hair remained stuck when we removed it" [Bastiaan Baljé 1878, in: Mörzer-Bruyns 1985, p. 89].

Dr. Maat specializes in identifying human skeletal material dug up anywhere, but is also the expert in forensic investigations to identify murdered people, and even disaster victims. His special interest, however, extends to pathological research on skeletons. "In the past, diseases ran their natural course," he says. "Now medicine is always intervening. These days I study joint-erosion diseases, which in the Netherlands have enormous economic effects because of the aging of the population. When you are able to learn about a disease's complete course via archaeological investigations, you're able to find clues that may help to lessen or cure disease."

Barents and Claes Andriesz had been ill during the last months of the wintering and died probably from the effects of scurvy. "Barents and his fellow traveler Claes Andriesz Goutijck had at their death been weakened by scurvy. When you have scurvy, you're bleeding internally," George continued his lecture. "These hemorrhages show as black discolorations along the bones. Loss of teeth accompanies chronic scurvy, and from their complaints it appears that the winterers had reached this stage. Bleeding gums and loose teeth are symptoms that help diagnose the disease, but they are not of any vital importance. Covered by six layers of clothing, which naturally were never taken off, symptoms such as swollen knees remained hidden."

Scurvy was a well know threat aboard ships. Winters were long and lack of vegetables or a disappointing herring catch would make that even under good circumstances people were close to being undernourished. The Grim Reaper worked overtime aboard those vessels that set sail too early. Drinking water deteriorated rapidly once a ship took to sea, and water was drunk with the teeth closed to sieve out small creatures and algae. A never changing menu of salted flesh, ship's biscuit, and grits usually brought an outbreak of scurvy after a few weeks. During the second expedition to northern Russia, scurvy reared its head in September. "Many of our crew became sick and plaintive from scurvy, stiff, both in legs and loins, with rotting of the gums, terrifying to see and hear, for the most caused by the steady cold weather and other bad humidity, but also because we didn't have any clean clothes or sufficient cover or protection [Van Linschoten 1601, 28 September 1595]. On the admiral's vessel, seven people died and sixteen others were unable to leave their bunks, on a crew of 40. French navigator Jacques Cartier experimentally determined the devastation of the human body brought about by the disease. During a bitterly cold wintering near present day Montreal in 1536, a strange malady erupted. To the French it seemed as if the native populace was spreading the disease. The large number of victims astonished Cartier. Even pestilence would not strike with such vehemence. After ten months, only ten out of the 110 men were able to take care of the rest. Every day sailors would die – usually very suddenly, while they were still trying to talk. The torment dragged on for weeks until an Indian woman brought a simple extract of tree bark and leaves. To Cartier's utter amazement, the ill recovered within hours – as if a miracle had occurred. When they hesitate to cross the Kara Gates (called Weygats by De Veer), the Dutch in their boats were driven back by ice to an island at the southern tip of Novaya Zemlya. "We went back to the island, and to our great fortune. Because we found spoonwort or scurvy grass there which served us well, like God had sent us there, because many of us were ill from scurvy to the extent that we could hardly move. These plants helped us recover and remarkably quick, so much so that its amazed us and we thanked God. We ate it whole hands full. We heard of its power back home and discovered that this power is even greater than we could have thought [...] Some could eat biscuits again, which they could not before" [De Veer 31 July 1597].

Russian researcher Dmitri Kravchenko in 1979 sowed the seeds for our expeditions when he reported his discovery of a grave, ship parts, and much of the original plan of the wintering cabin. "Willem Barents' grave found on Novaya Zemlya," the

Dutch newspaper *NRC Handelsblad* wrote on 10 September 1979 (p. 2): "With the discovery of Willem Barents' grave on Novaya Zemlya's coast, a Russian expedition has located one of the most important remains of the voyage of Van Heemskerck and Barents, well known to every pupil. As proof, the Russians discovered a burial mound on this completely deserted and barren coast, with a pole on which the initials BAR can still be deciphered." Kravchenko was unambiguous about the burial site: "On the southwestern side of the cape [Vilkitsky] a beacon was discovered about 15 m inland from the escarpment so it can't be seen from the sea. The rocks for it were carried over a distance of 250-300 m and are covered on the south- and west sides with lichens. On the east side was the skull of a polar bear with a hole in the forehead of 18 mm. This resembles a musket shot. A rectangular part of the ground of 2 x 1,8 m had clearly sagged, probably as a result of disturbance of the permafrost. This and the size imply that it is a grave, possibly a double grave. If one assumes that the skull was put on top of it after completion, we can date the burial to the 16th, early 17th century" (Kravchenko 1979 [1983] p. 107-109). He was further quoted in a bulletin issued by the Soviet embassy in 1981:

> "A detailed analysis of the diary of Gerrit de Veer allowed us to conclude that in June 1597, when Barents died, the Dutch had approached Cape Carlsen: that is the northern tip of Novaya Zemlya, which is free of snow and ice. Our first search occurred in 1977 over a length of 15 km. [Barents and Goutijck] were buried on the coast. The grave on Cape Vilkitsky is probably theirs. Why would we assume that this is a foreign grave, not of Russian origin? Well, first of all, Pomors never buried their dead in permafrost, because that would be too much effort. They would cover bodies above ground with rocks".[4]

Pieter and George will go to Ivanov Bay, which is in the middle of the search ellipse reconstructed from Gerrit de Veer's journal. There are two hints that helped to narrow the area down: the winterers on their return journey had left the Orange Islands, and De Veer reports that they had arrived at the IJshoeck, and therefore could see the first glacier of 'Ice Cape' [16 June 1597]. "The skipper called to Willem Barents how he was doing and Willem Barents answered: 'Quite well, mate, I hope to walk before we get to Waardhuus' [Vardø, near Norway's north cape]. Then he spoke to me and said: 'Gerrit are we about the Ice Cape? Lift me up then, I have to see that cape once again.' [...] We had been sailing about five miles then from the Orange Islands to the Ice Cape." These five miles are a little bit confusing. Gerrit de Veer's map of the Arctic says: 'Duytsche mylen; 15. in een graedt' [German miles 15. in a degree]. One German mile measured 6.3 km (3725 Amsterdam fathoms of 1.698 m, Verhoeff 1983). So five miles would be about 30 km, meaning that they landed at or near the cape on the west side of Ivanov Bay. The path of the boats dotted on De Veer's map of the journey shows the same: the winterers landed on the island before crossing the large field of ice bergs discharged from Ice Cape.

The Dutch at the time of Barents' passing were on coastal ice close to land and would most likely have brought their dead ashore. On 17 June 1597, the drifting ice threatened to crush the sloops. De Veer wrote: "The situation cried for action and in this distress, with nothing to lose (it is easy to risk a drowned calf), I being the lightest of all managed to crawl from one floe to the other and bring with God's help a rope to the shore ice." Willem Barents and Claes Andriesz Goutijck were carried onto the belt of sea ice frozen to the shore, and the boats were hoisted out of the water; then the sick were put back into the boats.

The improvised camp was at or close to the beach, because the men collected driftwood for a fire to melt tar and repair the boats. Several men searched inland for birds and eggs. And in this situation, on the morning of 20 June, Barents and Claes Goutijck died.

"It is obvious that Willem Barents and Claesz Goutijck were interred together in one grave," says George. "Both passed away on 20 June 1597. But were they really buried? It almost must be, although Gerrit de Veer makes no mention of that. I think the description of the burial ceremony was omitted from the journal to prevent difficult questions. Perhaps they thought that they had not done as good a job of it as was customary in the Netherlands. And it would be quite difficult back home to explain that they could not do otherwise under the circumstances." Gerrit de Veer summarily reported the event of Barents' death and did not describe the burial. The fate of the bodies remains unknown. In the case of previous deaths, the corpses had been interred with some ceremony. During the wintering, the 'sicke' died on the evening of 26 January 1597 and was read Bible passages. The next day, psalms were sung before all went outside, despite the tremendous cold, to bury the deceased wrapped in linen 'in seven feet of snow'. Investigation of the burial rituals of Dutch seafarers in the seventeenth century on northwest Spitsbergen, where ground conditions are comparable to those on Novaya Zemlya, indicates that the dead were taken on land for burial according to Christian principles, i.e., facing east [Maat, 1981; Werner, 1990]. They were placed in improvised wooden coffins and buried on promontories in shallow graves (less than 0.6 m deep) marked with a cross. Boulders were collected from adjacent areas and piled on the coffins to protect the corpses from scavenging animals. Burial at sea was a hygienic measure during voyages in tropical waters where decomposition was rapid.

The three of us pass a black-and white photograph shot with a camera under a kite during the 1993 expedition. The film was developed on return and shows a clear mound on the edge of the eroded stream that runs by the Saved House. “I can’t believe we missed it in 1993”, says Pieter. “We must have overlooked it entirely.” Could this indeed be a grave? A man wás buried in this spot: “The 24th of September we buried him under the shingles in the cleft of a hill near a drainage of water,” wrote De Veer about the death of the carpenter. If not the carpenter, might this mound contain ‘the sicke’ who died on 25 January 1597 and was buried in seven feet of snow?

“The gun stays at home, George” says Pieter resolutely after the two of them have been going up and down about it for a while. “In case you are not aware, Russia is at war with Chechnya and very apprehensive about gun smuggling.” George replies in feigned indignation, “Why I need my revolver? It is a Magnum: two blasts... and he is down!”

Thursday, 20 July 1995 – This is one of the warmest Netherlands summers in living memory. In the morning, riding my bike to the institute, I already work up a sweat. It puts me in a rotten mood, and in our sunlit office I listen, unmoved, to Pieter’s jokes about his neighbors’ brawls. They scream and fight and Pieter puts on a good imitation. On the steel locker door in our office is a photo of the vessel that will carry our expedition to Novaya Zemlya this summer: R/V *Ivan Kiriev*. Next to it is a clipping from German magazine *‘Geoskop’*: “Sie gehört zu den gefahrlichsten Regionen der Erde” (This ranks with the most dangerous regions on earth), it reads. Just to be sure, I tried to collect information on the extent of radioactive contamination on Novaya Zemlya. Soviet experiments with nuclear propulsion were virtually unrestricted, and when things went wrong, vessels and equipment were simply beached on Novaya Zemlya

Seventeenth century whalers graves on the shore of Bellsund, Svalbard in August 1996 (JJ Zeeberg).

A 4-m long ship part in Moscow's Heritage Institute, with double, oakwood planks and beams held together with oakwood pegs and cast iron nails.

to 'chill out'. Novaya Zemlya became the *Island of Death*: in April 1993, just months before the departure of the Dutch archaeologists, the Russian government issued the Jablokov report, which listed sources of radioactivity in the Russian Arctic. The article was interpreted by experts from the National Institute for Public Health and the Environment (RIVM), who stated that background radiation in the Netherlands is six times as great as the levels reported for Novaya Zemlya (in terms of radionuclides 1800 Bq of ^{137}Cs in Netherlands as opposed to 300 on Novaya Zemlya). This is primarily because of the Chernobyl disaster in April 1986, when the radioactive cloud released by the burning power plant descended over much of northwest Europe. All vegetable crops had to be destroyed because they were contaminated. Fission products released during venting events at Novaya Zemlya were detected throughout Sweden in 1987 and 1990, and it is estimated that about 70% of the underground bomb tests at Matochkin Shar vented, some even forcing evacuation of the test area (Matzko 1993).

However, nuclear waste and fallout on Novaya Zemlya are reported to be limited to dumping spots and test grounds. The nuclear dumping ground closest to Cape Spory Navolok is Techeniye Inlet, 60 km to the southwest at 75°58' N, with two submarine reactors at 35 to 40 m depth [OTA 1995]. Water is the best isolator to block and confine radiation, but we have no information whatsoever on the ocean currents and the spread of radioactive sediments along the Novaya Zemlya coast. So, diving and sea floor searching for the wreckage of Barents' ship again was cancelled, as in 1993 – again much to everybody's disappointment.

2 August 1995 – These days it is blood-boiling hot, and one wonders where the otherwise cool, rainy Dutch summers have gone. We have the blinds down and the tilting windows open to promote ventilation. It has been most uplifting to see the expedition pull together these last months, especially at the increasing tempo of the last weeks, when the project has coalesced, gained momentum, and begun to roll. The many small tasks have kept us so intensely occupied that departure time has approached almost unexpectedly. Each morning Pieter and I make lists of what has to be accomplished that day. To support my mapping of the area, a Husky computer, specially designed for Arctic conditions, has arrived, but we have not succeeded in getting it to operate. There are telephone deliberations with its manufacturer in England: they will fax instructions. At 11:00 a.m., a representative of Japanese land-surveying concern Sokkia delivered the electronic theodolite that I will use. I spent last week training with land surveyors mapping out a large man-made flood hill (a 'terp'). A theodolite consists of a small but powerful telescope that can swivel about both horizontal and vertical axes. The inclination of this telescope indicates reciprocal and azimuthal angles, which, measured together with distances, can produce a map of surface forms. To measure distances, the electronic theodolite shoots an infrared signal to a reflector carried on a pole. It is very accurate and connected to a laptop computer, yields digital data that can be easily exported to the mapping software. The entire system, called a 'total station', is fast, accurate, and expensive. Fortunately, the company has courteously provided us with a specially fitted system. Sokkia's technical services insulated the instrument's casing with silicone rubber to make it water-resistant. Its hard disc was cleared, and older, more reliable software was installed. Under a tree on a grass field outside our office, we set up the theodolite before a curious cormorant swimming in the canal. The 'total station', with its digital beeps and heavy yellow tripod, contrasts sharply with the simple theodolite of the Arctic schooner *Willem Barents* showcased in Amsterdam's Maritime Museum.

Friday, 5 August 1995 – The entire team, thirteen people, gathered this afternoon for a briefing from 2:00 to 6:00 in Jerzy's basement office on the Plantage Muidergracht. To begin with, we decided not to work from the ship, but to erect a camp ashore because transport between ship and shore may be restricted by the weather. Henk van Veen says he will arrange a shortwave radio for us to maintain contact with the ship when it lies offshore. Funding has been allocated for a rescue helicopter from Dikson in case of emergency. After that, we were issued travel instructions and discussed which items will be brought as carry-on (hand) luggage, so that we can still start work should our cargo get lost in Russia. It is decided to send the cargo ahead next Tuesday. Unfortunately, we couldn't convince our national airline KLM to support the expedition, so we got the best tickets we can afford and will fly to Moscow via Switzerland. A bit messy, of course. Some people have new passports and will have to have their Russian visas amended. The adventure will be documented on film by director Anton van Munster, whose credits include filming in Antarctica and Africa, as well as the four-hour documentary about the excavations on Amsterdam Island (*Spitsbergen 79° N*, by Jan Bosdriesz & Anton van Munster 1981). There is no need for a script, he contended; he knows what to do and after all, he was permanent cameraman to the famous Dutch director Bert Haanstra (1916-1997) for almost thirty years. Anton talks as if he's delivering commentary on a Haanstra film, thoughtfully formulating his sentences full of archaic, 1950ish expressions. He is disturbed by the sloppiness he sees in film making these days. "Our power was in the time we expended on our films. We kept at them until they were good. Just shooting *Bij de Beesten Af* kept us occupied for two and a half years. Bert and I wanted marble statues and we struggled on until we had them. Young people cannot imagine that with limited means you can obtain fantastic results, eh? In my starting days, I had no more than three lenses. There was no zoom lens then, so if you wanted a close-up shot, you had to move your nose right in on the scene. We put all kinds of things together ourselves. Look, this is a picture of a sound-damping box, which I built around my camera."

George Maat last saw Van Munster on Spitsbergen fifteen years ago, and the men greeted each other as old friends. Before an attentive audience, George explained his plans for 'Mr. Barents' and how his 'legal-logistical decision making' works. He invited us to ask questions or make comments. He acknowledged the emotional impact of opening a grave but suggested that it is scientifically responsible to do so. Comparison of Barents and Claes Andriesz with the whalers of Spitsbergen will make a significant study. Maat's equipment comprises, in addition to instruments for measuring bone dimensions and bone diseases, a small saw for internal bone investigation to determine age, various brushes to expose the bones, and a magnetic compass to find the accurate orientation of the burial site. Furthermore, he has a set of forms with him to record a step-by-step analysis of each skeleton. Should there still be 'soft parts' of Barents' body left, preserved by the frozen ground, we cannot do much more than take note of this. The Russians prefer that upon opening of a grave, the remains not be disturbed at all. George has decided to restrict himself to superficial identification and to taking a small tissue sample for DNA research, because Barents' DNA may be contaminated after renewed human contact. The sample will be conserved until the rapidly developing techniques ensure optimal analysis. Salvaging the corpse is out of the question in this phase. Russian Orthodox religion would object, to say nothing of Russian cultural authorities. Human remains recovered at Svalbard were brought back to the Netherlands in paper boxes, but that is now unthinkable.

Further, George advised everyone to have a physical exam and to get gamma-globulin shots against hepatitis A.

Henk van Veen offered a moving final word. Henk, famous as inventor of the Kreidler OCR1000 motorcycle twenty years ago, has been protector of recent Dutch Arctic research. With calm face and the distancing cool of an accomplished man he recalled how Bas Kist sat alone on Amsterdam Island, then sketched the organization of the ensuing expeditions and the curbing of commercial interests during the 1980s. After pausing for a moment, he finished by saying that now, fifteen years later, the veterans are transferring their experiences to 'angry young men'. Much laughter followed. It is good that these things have been said, he concluded, a bit emotional. Then, Van Veen caught himself and spent another half hour urging that the group's decisions be harmonious and, above all, that we speak with one voice. He closed by summarizing the procedures and codes of conduct aboard a seagoing vessel and did not fail to state that in case of disaster, responsibility does not lie with the organization. We then went outside and René made a group photo alongside the canal, accompanied by the shrill calls of the gibbons in adjacent Artis Zoo and the screeching of the No. 7 tram. Afterwards, the expedition members rapidly scattered, because it was Friday evening, and everyone hurried home for this next-to-last weekend. Some left for a brief holiday. Next weekend we will be packing our bags and saying our goodbyes. There was this lady I planned to call and ask her for a drink. If she did not want anything to drink, perhaps we could just sit and talk. I did not call her right away, because such things require a well thought out approach. Doubt was killing me, and when at last I decided to call, she wasn't home. Only the third time I got through, and she agreed to a date in Utrecht.

Monday, 7 August 1995 – "Which way, Bas?"

"The sergeant-major is waiting for us at the gate with four spouts," Bas chuckled. Jerzy stepped towards the guard with four passports to get visitor's passes to the Gilze-Rijen airforce base. Gun practice, yes! Today we were invited for gun instruction and target practice. 'Bakkie' coffee first, and then a brief classroom introduction and safety instructions, before we proceeded to the target range. The structure of a semiautomatic rifle is a thing of splendor. The gasses released by each explosion are redirected to dampen the recoil and eject the shells. One by one, each of us took the FAL rifle and fired five bullets in rapid succession at a target 100 meters away, trembling after each salvo with adrenaline and concentration. A more primitive sensation is barely thinkable. To see and hear the devastating blow at the receiving end of your action makes you rather proud of your shot. I missed once, and that was not supposed to happen. Too eager! Again, kneel down, load, release the safety, aim, elbow high, exhale quietly, and there goes the bullet, without your realizing it. And once more. Our Remington hunting rifle with the magnum bullets thoroughly rattles you around. You feel your pulse race, your breathing grows steadier, hold your breath, everything merges in one murderous line, and then you unleash that certain thunder, which you feel travel through your brain as if hit by a glancing blow to the head.

The expedition is entering its final stage of preparation. During my physical examination, I had to touch my nose and tell the doctor how I was feeling (somewhat agitated but nothing serious). He had a pill for that. Today our cargo was to have been collected by the airline transporter, but the crates are still in the basement, untouched. It transpired that no cargo flight had room for them. Maybe next Friday. Yesterday Toshiba agreed to provide a computer, which is a godsend, because the special Arctic Husky computer remains unresponsive. I arranged its delivery to Sokkia in Almere for installation of the mapping program. Unfortunately, the computer did not arrive and must be traced; it will probably be delivered tomorrow, but we can hardly afford the extra day's delay. Other items have arrived, such as a chainsaw and its accessories made available by Andreas Stihl. Still lacking are a battery charger and a set of resistors. My list furthermore includes aspirins and other medicine; iodine, fungus-fighting ointments, active carbon, new bandages for the first aid kit; whistle, plastic spoon, fingerless gloves, belt-buckle, rope, duct tape, electrical tape, big thick plastic bags, sunglasses, field book, lithium batteries, mallets, underwear, soles and shoelaces, ice creepers/spikes, aluminum foil, thermal blankets, drafting pens, floppy discs, and extension cords with their receptacles. The laptop computer apparently needs a lot of 9V batteries, just what we don't have. I call Philips and they will express-mail us a box full. Haveco sent a supply of flares. By bike, I swayed through the city to an address where, behind closed doors, there is a gun store. I asked for OX-13 gun oil, specifically for cold conditions, "fustrol or ballistol, but no spray can," according to Dr Maat's instructions. No idea what I am talking about.

Friday, 11 August 1995 – The last few days have been anxious, with lists swirling incessantly through my mind. All snakes are in the bucket, and now I must keep them there. Broadcasting stations keep phoning to ask if the expedition to Novaya Zemlya has left already. "Gerrit de Veer, has he been there as well? Do you have his phone number?" Never knew there were so many news programs. The bigger stations are waiting for things to happen in a few more days. But we'll be gone then.

On Tuesday evening, I went to Utrecht for my date. While recruiting for Barents' famed voyage, men were selected "unmarried, as much as possible, to have a brave crew that would be less distracted by yearn for wife and children." It was 8 August, and during the twenty-minute train ride between Amsterdam and Utrecht, I recalled that exactly one year ago today, I was in Russia crossing the Polar Urals. On 8 August my two partners and I reached the mountain range's divide and could see into Siberia: a horizon as taut as the sea.

We had taken the long-distance train from Moscow, in old clothes and worn leather jackets to blend in, to the city of Vorkuta. Feared and respected as the gateway to the Gulag, a collective name for the thousands of prison camps that once dotted the Russian Arctic, Vorkuta is a long journey in a glowing hot train. The green wooden window frames were painted shut, because outside a bitter cold wind blows for most of the year. There was a lounger for every traveler, on which a mattress filled with straw, and a horse blanket. The last robber gangs got off the train two hundred kilometers past Moscow, in Yaroslavl. The train was on high alert until then and travellers would be looking after themselves. Then the pajamas and slippers appeared, and a homely buzz unfolded through the carriage as our fellow-passengers began to fetch boiling water, fired with brown coal and newspapers, to make tea or prepare vegetables. We were heartily invited. For two days the wagon shared dried fish, onions, and 'Ukrainian snickers:' salted cubes of pork skin. Railway workers spent their two weeks' leave traveling; to visit their home village in the south of Siberia or the Ukraine and return immediately. Pechora was the last stop for most on board. During goodbyes, a man warned us: "It is very dangerous what you do." One more day and one night to Vorkuta. The ancient Ural Mountains stretched across the horizon. A mountain range eroded and rounded by the forces of time. The city is in the middle of the tundra, an endless peat bog with frozen groundwater. Low, stubborn taiga pines stood widely distributed. A peat fire glowed next to the track, probably from a discarded cigarette. The plume of smoke like a comet protruded from the landscape thirty kilometers downwind, and the train passed through the tail only after another couple of hours had gone by. Russia's bottom said one. He demonstrated it and slapped the back of his trainers. Where Russia discharged its outcasts.

Coal was mined at Vorkuta from the 1930s and forced laborers paid with their blood for each ton of coal. When the mines transitioned from slave labor to hired labor, the city had grown to 60.000 inhabitants or so. It was a mixture of former prisoners and their former guards, now condemned to each other with nowhere to go. So they stayed, and worked those very mines. Worker camps lined both sides of the last stretch, the 450-km rail line from Pechora to Vorkuta, but have been razed to the ground in an effort to erase that bad memory. After 1991, the former coal mines and remaining exiling camps around Vorkuta were simply left to themselves. The entire region was abandoned without support from Moscow and fell in disarray. In Moscow, we were told that people would beat you to death for your boots. Our Russian colleague Michail agreed to come with us only after we gave him a hundred dollars. Then in our presence he bade his wife and child a strained farewell. Tears flowing.

After days on that hot train, and a transfer in Vorkuta, we debarked in the middle of the tundra with a group of Nenets, near a corral of these Arctic natives with tents that they call chum. Hours later, we found ourselves in the open at the foothills of the Urals, still far removed from the valleys into which we were to disappear. Every fifty paces, Michail would anxiously turn around and see if we were being followed. As night fell and we decided to make camp, we heard, far in the distance on gusts of wind, the hum of a tracked vehicle in the tundra. Michail, while wrapping himself in a clear plastic tarpaulin to compensate for the leaky tent, said that our killers were looking for us. The next day, we disappeared into the mountains, after cleaning all traces that could reveal our route. The Arctic swallowed us within a few hours. We climbed over endless, boulder strewn fields and up against steep reddish sandstone formations until we could see across the watershed. With binoculars I counted the oil rigs in the immense delta of the Ob River. Hundreds of thousands of insects billowed up from the marshy lowlands against the old and weathered mountain slopes. As we sat in front of our improvised tent toward the end of the day, eating berries and enjoying the low evening sun, Michail broke his silence and began to talk. He told us that two years ago, in 1992, he had been at the Dutch wintering camp on Novaya Zemlya. "Whose?" I had to repeat the question three times before I understood his mumbled "Willem Barents."

"The ship," he insisted, meeting with our ignorance: "we found the ship." Only now one year later do I realize that it was he who brought parts of the vessel to Moscow, identified by the Amsterdammers in May 1994. One other thing he tried to get across: there was an image, he said, six meters tall, a monument or a symbol. I never understood what he meant but saw it on a photograph: Kravchenko's seaman's cross, six meters tall in an otherwise flat expanse. Within weeks, I would see it with my own eyes...

"So how did it go?" Pieter asked the next day. I shrugged. "We talked about what she liked and what kind of work she was doing. And then she asked if I liked that, too. Talked too much about me knowing this and that... I guess it was all right." Pieter nodded, and we examined a flat wooden box with a tombstone-like object, weighing at least 100 kilograms, which had been delivered by mail that morning. This 'monument' was sent by a group of entrepreneurs from the island of Terschelling, twenty kilometers north of Holland's mainland coast. Willem Barents full name, according to his contemporary Jan Huyghen van Linschoten, was 'Willem Barentsz van der Schelling' and rightly or not, Barents figures actively in the public relations of the island Terschelling.[5] The tombstone consolidates the relation between Terschelling and Novaya Zemlya, and the engraving artist added a bit of himself to the creation: his name, and quite legibly, if you please. Whatever this monument memorializes, it is not Barents' wintering or the Saved House. There is no trace even of the five deaths that occurred during the voyage. Five small crosses, for example, would do. Yet, Pieter thinks it is marvelous that the memorial stands here before us. He envisions the stone one hundred years hence, corroded by salt air and covered with lichens, just like the marker that was left on the Orange Islands in 1881 by the Arctic schooner *Willem Barents*. That ship was unable to reach Ice Harbor. Now it is our turn. Pieter in 1993 saw the memorial on top of the Orange Island, a flattened rock with steep cliffs on all sides north of Novaya Zemlya. "The stretcher that they used to carry the heavy stone marker atop that rock is lying nearby, upside down, just as the gallant crew of the schooner abandoned it a good one hundred years ago," said Pieter. "It looks like no one has been there since." He smiled. "Our helicopter pilot said he knew exactly where our national hero lies buried..."

Riding my bike today, I was racing through hot Amsterdam, which was one big party this late Friday afternoon. Young people from all over Europe, who wanted to see the world, decided to come to Amsterdam; back-packers flock around the Central Station with no obvious place to go. Henk van Veen recommended that, in addition to the gasoline-fed Honda generator that we already have, we acquire a small wind-powered generator. He uses the same model on his Luxury Yacht in the Mediterranean. Carrying the 20 kg battery for this generator in my backpack, I returned to the office. Once there, I first pull a chilled can of drink from the machine to maintain my fluid balance. At day's end we concluded: we're ready. I am dead tired, and the city is restless. The last few nights I have to sleep well to restore reserves, and that's what this miracle doctor had pills for. I wondered whether the so-called 'placebo-effect' would lure me into sleep, but a half hour after swallowing that pill and chasing it with a shot, I am really reeling and groping around to find my bed. It's around midnight as I write this. The pill is making my eyelids feel heavier and heavier.

Saturday, 12 August 1995 – God, it's hot! So hot that perspiration is running down my face, chest, legs. The city is saturated, steaming hot, crowded, and smelly. Trams groan past; below on the street someone is singing an exotic song. Across the narrow canyon, people are reading the newspaper or watching TV, and a panty-clad girl is smoking a cigarette while vacuuming. The sun shines on my face through a small window; there is pigeon poop all over the windowsills. Someone whistles for his dog, someone else empties a bucket of water over a car. A little lady tends her begonias; somewhere on the block someone is playing the trumpet, nice and bluesy. Then, peering down the seams of a boot, just out of the oven and hot in my hand, while the molten waterproofing wax seeps down and I rub the leather until dull-black, I wonder if she'll be thinking of me, or if our date left her ice-cold. At night, the amber street lamps suspended in the middle of these tall and narrow streets swing gently in the wind.

Monday 14 August 1995 – At 8:00 a.m., I received my inoculations at the GG&GD (Municipal Health Service). "Where are you going?" she asked, waving the needle around my face. Stammering, I answered, "To R-R-Russia." My leg is stiff and I have been a little shaky all day. Jerzy went home for a while to "lie down for a bit." Last odds and ends at work turned out to be more than expected. I got home at 7:00, ate something, and made a few farewell calls.

Chapter Four

All aboard – White Sea to Barents sea

Wednesday, 16 August 1995 – The expeditionary vessel *Ivan Kiriev* is moored downstream of Archangelsk's city center in a quarter called Solombala. This is the old part of town, where Otto Sverdrup's *Eklipse* and the first icebreakers, *Yermak* and *Vaygach*, fastened eighty years ago, as did Otto Schmidt's icebreaker *Sibiryakov* in 1932. This is where Albanov, Konrad, and their rescuers of the Sedov expedition returned in August 1914, after their two-year ordeals up in the icy northern seas only to find themselves in World War I. And it was from here, in Mary Shelley's 1818 novel, that Robert Walton had departed when he found Victor Frankenstein, chasing the demon of his own creation across the ice. Not unlike our man Kravchenko. A tugboat passes, towing a huge float of lumber down the Dvina River. At 3:00 p.m. (Moscow time), preparations for departure are in full swing. The research vessel has been chartered for four weeks at 2000 dollars per day. Those twenty-eight days comprise our window of opportunity: no matter what, *Kiriev* will be back in port on 15 September.

Our vehicle for adventure in the coming month is a 1250-ton research vessel, not even twenty years old, built by Wärtsila in Finland. The vessel is 62 meters long, 12 wide, and boasts a fresh coat of paint. On its foredeck, under a canvas tarpaulin, lies our landing craft or *plashkot*, as the Russians say. High above the bridge stands the crow's nest: a one-man observation cabin, the only hint of the icy seas that *Kiriev* will be plying. One enters the ship through a heavy, watertight door that screws down securely with four steel dogs. Inside, a narrow corridor runs through the center, with steep companionways leading to the lower and higher decks. My cabin is below decks, near the waterline. I share it with Henri Hoogewoud, cameraman. He has the top bunk; I am below. Each cabin has one porthole, large enough to stick your head out, but too narrow for a man to crawl through. The bunks are comfortable, with small curtains that can be closed for a bit of privacy. We tried them out to catch a few hours' sleep. To welcome everybody on board, an 'icebreaker' meeting took place at 7:00 p.m. in the mess, the largest room aboard the vessel. The tables in the saloon are angled to the ship's steel hull and have a light-colored Formica wood veneer. We found them covered with bread, fish, cheese, pickled tomatoes, vodka, wine, and champagne cider. Above each table is a porthole. Prominent representatives of the Archangelsk Oblast (District) also attended our gathering. Pyotr Boyarsky of Moscow's Heritage Institute, the expedition's general manager, delivered a cheerful introductory speech and proposed a toast. We chatted until someone else rose for a speech, followed by another toast. Everyone had wishes for the best, and the mood rapidly grew mellow. We introduced ourselves. Our Russian colleagues have "years of experience with very interesting and complex problems." Some are; 'world-famous'. When, at last, Jerzy Gawronski was invited to speak, he began like a great orator: "Here we have a star... The famous and experienced...." He said he was taking along only the best possible manpower. "You have the honor... we have the honor to cooperate with..."

"I don't know how things are in your country," Boyarsky said through his colleague and interpreter, Yuri Mazurov, "but in our system it is unusual to personally lobby a minister or even the president for assistance. People in Moscow think we are troublemakers. We wrote them so often that they must have thought: "Let's just give them what they want, so we can get rid of them." Boyarsky stopped until the laughter died down. "When all those letters arrived from the Netherlands, we could show them: 'See, there are more of us! Even if we might not be normal, there are, after all, more people who are not normal.'" Also present, dressed in a smart, anthracite-colored suit, was the governor of the Archangelsk Oblast, who reminded us that it was his predecessor who commissioned Vladimir Rusanov's mapping of southern Novaya Zemlya's coasts in 1909. Then he rose once more to emphasize the fraternal bonds between the Russian and Dutch peoples, starting with Peter the Great. In rapid fashion, toast followed upon toast. Boyarsky ultimately closed by saying that the Russians, now that the Soviet Union has disintegrated, have become a people of the North.

"The Arctic is the backbone of our country," declared Boyarsky.

Next followed the tea, and at 10:00 p.m. the meeting was over. The guests disembarked and the expedition remained aboard.

As soon as the assembly had dissolved, the sailors emerged, and the television came on for tonight's football game of Russia against Suomi (Finland). Lenin's portrait was removed and replaced by the face of Ivan Kiriev. The ship is home to sailors, mates, boatswain, and engineers. Most of them are about the age of Herre Wynia and me, and they find us easier to talk to than our elderly, distinguished partners. They will invite you (with some light pushing) to their cabins for a 'small drink'. Here's your glass. "Chut, chut," I said: "a little bit!" "Nicht voll," the Russian smiled back at me. "There but for the grace of God go I," I thought, unable to think up another excuse not to drink. I noticed a terrible scar along his right arm, and the three remaining fingers of his mutilated hand clenched around the glass. An hour later, utterly wasted and drunk, I fell down in my berth and brushed away a cockroach.

Thursday 17 August 1995 – It appears that our equipment won't arrive before tomorrow night, possibly much later. The transport got stuck in St. Petersburg until the appropriate form, obtainable only on the spot, has been completed. Our contacts in St. Pete are being alerted, and we must decide: wait or sail? At 8.30 a.m., one hour after breakfast (white bread, tea, butter, sugar, and liverwurst), we had a lifevest demonstration and lifeboat drill: seven slow whoops and one long one over the intercom, repeated three times. After lunch, at 12:30, we climbed on a truck that took us to the Museum of Natural History and from there to a rather depressing Museum of Communism, exhibiting the brutal excesses of that regime. Leaving Solombala, we passed a narrow canal, which, according to our Russian friends, is the White Sea Canal that was constructed to Moscovia's primary harbor on the orders of the Czar. It was low tide, and sloops had settled on the muddy bottom. We passed through Archangelsk's historical districts, where Dutch, Flemish, Danish, and English merchants established themselves in the sixteenth and seventeenth centuries along the banks of the Dvina River. On the side of the road, Russian women with skirts and rubber boots and elderly men in worn suits offered potatoes, a bucket of berries, some dried fish, and one pumpkin.

Our first stop was the Museum of Natural History, to which Dmitri Kravchenko had delivered his catch, including a human jawbone, on return from Novaya Zemlya between 1978 and 1981. The museum was closed, but by appointment a lady showed up, and we followed her through the dark corridors of this sleepy institute to a dusty, paper-filled office. She turned on the light in the back of the corridor and there, pushed aside on the floor, we found a wooden object that we immediately recognized as a timber from Barents' ship. My inquisitive colleagues then questioned her about the jaw allegedly found near the Saved House. The question puzzled her and she began to search the office, but with no result. The curator was out of town, so she instructed us to come back later, much to the disappointment of Dr. Maat. Kravchenko had described the jaw as "small, that of a woman or a young boy." It possibly belonged to the sailor who was buried in 'seven feet' of snow on 27 January 1597. "We comforted him as best we could with a few biblical passages," Gerrit de Veer wrote. "Shortly after midnight, he passed away."

Two days in Archangelsk, then, our whole gang traipsing its deserted streets clad in red windbreakers provided by a sponsor, which makes us not exactly blend in. The city center is an empty plaza and one tall white Soviet-style (post-Stalin) office tower. Near the river are a silent boulevard and a wide, deserted beach with an empty playground and dead carousel. Where has everybody gone? Perhaps it was livelier here before the crash of Communism. I stared down the waterline as Jerzy paddled in the ice-cold water. I took the tram and walked through piles of fallen leaves under slowly thinning trees, past old wooden houses, back to the quays of Solombala. The air was filled with the full scent of decaying leaves. Our chances of reaching Ice Harbor are optimal at summer's end, when the Atlantic storms have blown the Barents Sea clear of ice. Autumn is settling in, and farther north winter is approaching again, day by day. On the docks, I spotted George Maat recording his impressions on a dictaphone given to him by Anton van Munster. Anton will trail Maat and Gawronski for his film.

"Dr. Maat, is there anyone you would like to operate on?", I asked him as he was standing there, posing, with two hands on the deck's railing. "Some look most interesting, but to know with certainty one would have to take them apart."

Friday 18 August 1995 – To our relief, the expedition equipment arrived at Archangelsk's airport, but clearing it was another story. "You have documents from the Ministry of Culture, the Dutch Embassy, and the FSB [Federal Security Service]. But not from me..." The customs officer leaned back in his chair and decided to ignore us. He waved to a colleague, who came running in and began to discuss an apparently unrelated matter.

"Please. That's why we have now come to see you in person," Jerzy pleaded. Our translator, Yuri Mazurov discretely turned towards Jerzy. "It takes a small sum...," Yuri said quietly, hands folded together behind his back.

"How much?" asked Jerzy impatiently.

"Six thousand exactly."

Jerzy retreated, talked to Bas Kist, and took the money from an envelope. The customs officer pulled the chair to his desk and, satisfied with our 'lubricant', blessed the expedition by completing our documents with his signature, adding three stamps in rapid succession. Then he got up and we followed him to the depot. I am not sure if this is the New Russia or a left-over from the Old Russia, but as it is we practiced our 'negotiating' skills.

Kiriev had come to life in our absence. Amid the hum of cranes and loading activity, I strode through the crowds to go aboard. The sailors and machinists after last night's drinks welcomed me with thumbs up. At last, departure had been set for 11:00 tonight. The Captain was in uniform and the bridge was brightly lit. Minutes before departure, friends, relatives, sweethearts, and officials poured out of the ship. They walked down the gangway and gathered on the quay. The bright lights of *Kiriev* turned the darkness away. The girls, tense, laughed loudly. Words flew back and forth, with much arm waving and a last kiss across the railing. The gangway was hauled aboard and stowed. Deckhands worked hard to pull in the thick cables that tied the vessel to the docks. Edging away from the concrete shore sides, *Kiriev* powered up, the hum of the engine vibrating through the steel deck. The waving crowd ashore was quickly absorbed by the night. I could feel the cold wind in my face grow stronger. The bow parted the dusk as we gained speed between the dark banks of the widening Dvina. Everyone hurried inside to celebrate, but I remained on deck a little longer. The dark vastness of the river's estuary was awesome. One could still discern the flat line dividing the overcast skies from the water. Victor, the bosun, apparently drew the first watch. His dark silhouette in a padded *Moreflot* overall was leaning on a short, steel post. I saw restless eyes in his sallow, unshaven face as we smoked cigarettes, their tips glowing in the draft. Sometimes, he would come forth with a few sentences in Russian, which he invariably started by politely and flawlessly pronouncing my name. I wanted to stay and continue to watch the horizon and that dark river but retreated to get some rest. This is the most impatient moment in every voyage.

In the fo'c'sle (forecastle), I knocked on the door of the next cabin to ask for quiet on behalf of my cabin mate Henri. However, when the door opened, the lads dragged me inside and pressed a water glass half full of vodka into my hands. They asked me how old I am and if I was married and showed me pictures of their wives. My Russian colleague, fellow geologist Dmitri Badyukov, 41-year-old, took me along to the chief's cabin two decks higher. It is more comfortable there, where the Dutch team has its quarters. Dr. Maat was curling his greying moustache as he added another line to his diary. Next door, Anton was sound asleep. The corridor ends in a spacious laboratory full of crates for the expedition. A bundle of lines is lashed over and about the cargo to prevent its slipping. The foremost end of the corridor terminates in two large corner cabins. The starboard cabin belongs to the Captain; the other, to Pyotr Boyarsky our general expedition leader. These cabins have several portholes that provide a forward view. Boyarsky's cabin was full of people; they were sitting on easy chairs and even at the desk. Boyarsky, a compact 52-year-old with a small, trim beard and a smile on his face, sat contentedly behind his desk. Cooperation with Russians means more than friendly collegial contacts: one has to be able to down a few glasses. The collective drinking is a 'bonding thing' and it opens minds normally shut tight. Participants are invited to take turns addressing the others, which – quite often – results in interminable and incomprehensible orations. This is where trust is built or lost. Few can afford not to participate, because these are moments of truth. Jerzy seems to handle the heavy drinking with ease and has the ability to come across as amiable and dignified in speech, thus forcing the basis for a friendly cooperation. This is significant because the Russians aren't too keen on our expertise and view especially our instrumentation with suspicion.

"Russians don't need computers: they rely on themselves." Boyarsky, who for reasons of (health) does not join in the drinks, got up to say this, and Yuri Mazurov translated it into English. Our Russian partners are surprisingly superstitious or, at least, serious believers. Many of them carry a small crucifix from the Orthodox Church. Now we listened to scientists, a drink or two under their belts, talk about flashing lights and unfathomable mysteries such as flying saucers. When, at last, I beat a retreat down the steep, narrow stairs into the ship's belly, I could hear singing and guitar-playing from below. Eugene and Konstantin, in the cabin across from Henri's and mine, had sailors Alexander and Andrei over. Alexander (Sascha) and Andrei enthusiastically signaled that I should come in, and they freed a spot between them on the cabin's small seat. Sascha, on a decrepit guitar with badly tuned, worn-out strings, was playing Russian folk songs that utterly fit my mood: passionate and sometimes melancholy sounds, raw and straight from the heart. He smoothly shifted his thumb to play the bass line. Andrei sung about black ravens circling a lovely valley and battlefield-to-be, still circling over bleached bones many years later. He passed out cigarettes and lit himself a fresh one. The Russian texts were incomprehensible to me, even when Sascha looked me straight in the eye to emphatically articulate some lines. Arm in arm, Eugene and Konstantin jumped around the small cabin, their hands waving in the air. Yevgeni – he calls himself Eugene or Jurgen, but everyone knows him as Zenja – is a slender 30-year-old sporting a Lenin goatee. Konstantin, his chubby young assistant, never leaves his side. From a drawer underneath his berth, Konstantin produced rolls of cheese and sausage. While cutting up a small *zakuska*, he ad-libbed a German translation of those songs. Sometimes, he missed a few lines, and then Sascha would interrupt his song and together they would clarify: "When your girl is ill," or "About Ivanovskoy Harbor." Ivanovskoy Harbor is a port where the women are so unattractive that your girl will feel sorry for you when she finds out you've been keeping someone there.

"So, was it somewhat quieter?" I asked Henri at our 8:00 a.m. breakfast. His wan expression told me that he'd had a bad night. "No," he answered miserably. "All night long, they kept calling and singing and slamming the doors." I promise I won't be drinking anything, from now on. I must get ready for the landings. I am seated in my cabin at a small desk illuminated by a desk lamp. Through the porthole the morning sun shines on my face. On the wall are a large sticker with the Czarist two-headed eagle, a crucifix, and several *Bombibom* chewing-gum pictures of cars. Except for the vibrations in the floor and the swinging wires, there is nothing to indicate we are under sail. Now that I sit so calmly, writing, it dawns on me that our preparations have been successful and that we are really on our way to Novaya Zemlya without too many problems. The vessel is a small world, propelled by a powerful diesel engine. I never been particularly fascinated by the ocean, so this is a new experience for me. In the distance, I can still see a narrow strip of land. Our traversing of the White Sea, the deep inlet between northern Scandinavia and Russia, will take a full day. Heavy weather is expected.

The public image of polar exploration over much of the 20th century was shaped by the race to the South Pole between Roald Amundsen and Robert Falcon Scott, in which Scott was given the role of a tragic hero. Scott entrusted his last words to paper: "I do not think I can write more." These polar records are about struggle, and survival on a planet that is hostile to humans. They are not tales of heroism, they're accusations. The other great story about that British Antarctic Expedition was given the tell-tale title *Worst Journey in the World* (Apsley Cherry-Garrard's 1922 memoir). The breathtaking photographs by Herbert Ponting have reached iconic stature, demonstrate the forceful beauty of the planet. The same is true for the photographs by Frank Hurley (1885-1962) of Shackleton's journey to the Antarctic, just four years after the Scott Expedition. The retreat of the men after the foundering of *Endurance* offer a spectacular pictorial analogue to the sojourn of the Dutch escaping from Novaya Zemlya [photographs in: Alexander 1998]. A less known but equally spectacular escape, resembling both the Dutch and Shackleton, is the 1881–1882 wintering of Benjamin Leigh Smith and the crew of *Eira* on the southernmost island of Franz Josef Land. A year before the intended wintering, Leigh Smith, one of the 'gentleman-explorers' of the era, surveyed the southern islands of the archipelago to select a suitable place for his wintering cabin. Following the construction of a prefabricated wooden house on Bell Island (*Eira Lodge*), Leigh Smith decided to look around and explore Nordbruk Island, 25 km to the east. (We sense where this is going). While *Eira* lay anchored off Cape Flora (79°05' N), sea ice 'brought in with the tide' accumulated around the vessel, nipping the hull, and to the horror of the seamen *Eira* started to sink [Credland 1980]. The British then spent sixteen days in driving rain to construct a 10-meter-long hut with turf and stone walls. Sails were stretched over the top to a center elevation of just over 2 meters. During the wintering, the twenty-four men spent most of the time in or on their beds. They had a routine of food preparation and three meals daily, as well as a service Sunday morning at 9.30 a.m. Christmas, New Year's Eve, and the Queen's Birthday (23 May) were properly celebrated. Simple routines are essential for maintaining good spirits and a sense of progression.

Poor ventilation produced an atmosphere so unhealthy that a pet canary soon died. Unlike the open chimney construction of the Saved House, the wintering hut on Cape Flora had an iron stove for heating, so steam from boiling stew permanently filled the cabin, condensing on the walls and ceiling. When coal ran out in January, the men began to cook with bear and walrus blubber, covering the entire interior with soot. In their bunks they looked like 'rows of blackbirds' [Leigh Smith, in: Credland 1980]. Soot also covered the faces of the winterers aboard *Saint Anna*, stuck in the ice northeast of Franz Josef Land (1914): "In winter, when the temperature in our quarters fluctuated between -2.5 and -5°C, and the air was damp and foggy, filled with particles of soot that continually floated around, [our oil lamps] were incapable of driving back the darkness which prevailed for months on end... The corners and outside walls were covered from top to bottom with thick layers of ice and rime frost. These were the cleanest areas: no soot stuck to them. Here one could watch the fantastic, glittering play of the ice crystals, which shone even in the light of our oil lamps" [Barr 1975; Albanov (1917) 2000]. Gerrit de Veer wrote: "A big storm covered the entire house with snow, and this produced so much smoke that we could hardly make a fire. All remained in their bunks except the cook, who had to maintain the fire... The cold and the smoke were both unbearable. We could hear the ice at sea crack although it was half a mile away" (1 December 1596).

Leigh Smith and his men escaped and journeyed home in open boats. *Eira* had four sloops for walrus hunting and whaling, which enabled the crew to sail and row the 800 km to Novaya Zemlya. Their crossing of the Barents Sea took forty-three days. They set out 'with a cheer' on Wednesday, 21 June 1882, after the evening meal. In the boats, hot tea was made during the journey and a hot meal cooked daily. On the evening of 2 August 1882, the boats reached the entrance to Matochkin Shar, which was already a familiar anchorage for trappers and explorers. The following morning, a vessel identified as the Dutch schooner *Willem Barents* came out of the strait. Allegedly, Leigh Smith stepped aboard *Willem Barents* carrying a mug of cognac to raise a toast to his rescuers. Decades later, this event was still giving rise to rumors that Willem Barents' 16th century bottles of rum had been found, still tasting splendid and ready for consumption! [*Algemeen Handelsblad*, 5 February 1924].

Our Russian colleagues find the wintering of Willem Barents on Novaya Zemlya an odd however interesting event, gently mocking our pride in it. There has been continued interest in this history since the Russians returned to the area, on the occasion of the Second International Polar year in 1933. To access the story, a translation of De Veer's account into Russian was prepared in 1936 by Vladimir Yu. Vize (1886-1954), then director of the Arctic and Antarctic Research Institute in St. Petersburg. Vize had participated in the Sedov Expedition of

1912. But before becoming a Russian scientist, Vladimir Yu. was in fact a German boy named Waldemar Kurt Wiese. Vize may have been inspired by artifacts retrieved from the Dutch winter camp by one of his scientists, geologist and paleontologist B.V. Miloradovich, in 1933. The Miloradovich expedition was one of nine sent to the archipelago that year, providing the first photograph of the pile of lumber that remained of the Saved House then. (Behind these cold facts is an interesting, perhaps, romantic and tragic story. Miloradovich had a 19-year-old female assistant, of which he writes very warmly in 1933 and whose name is, somewhat cryptically, given to the Eks Bay immediately north of Ice Harbor. Her future husband, 23 at the time, was there too as his deputy. They disappeared from view during the war years in St. Petersburg. And we don't even know Miloradovich's full name or death).

After an hour of reading, I got up to stretch my legs and enjoy the fine weather. The sea was calm and *Kiriev* was pitching lightly, causing objects to swing slowly to and fro. On deck I was quite comfortable in just a T-shirt. This quiet sailing provides opportunity to test our equipment and see how the instruments have endured transport. Judging from the steady drone it produced, the gasoline generator was working fine. Photographer René Gerritsen opened a large grey suitcase containing our satellite communication equipment and fitted the four quarters of the antenna dish together. This device will enable us to telephone the whole world from the Saved House. Our Russian colleagues were sorting their instruments, contentedly smoking *Belomore* cigarettes. Two men hauled a dripping CTD (Conductivity-Temperature-Depth) probe from the blue sea. The oceanographers, geographers, and archaeologists are making this journey on invitation of the Heritage Institute, in full the Russian Institute for Cultural

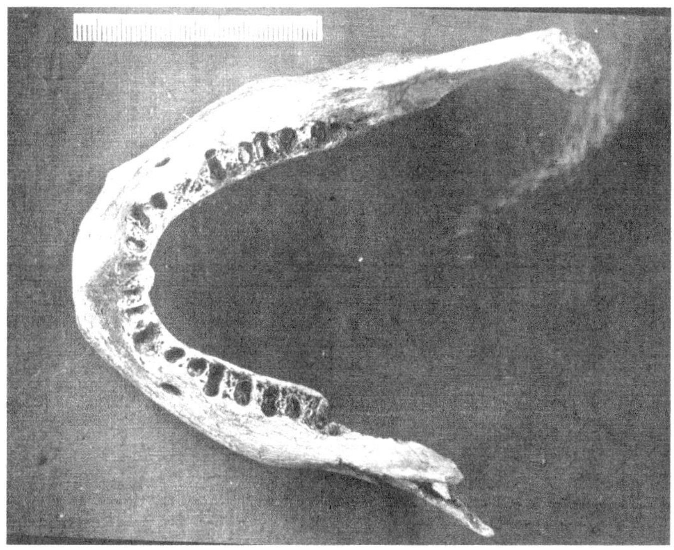

Human cheekbone found near the Saved House and delivered by Dmitri Kravchenko to the Archangelsk Historical museum, probably belonging to the 'sicke,' or the boy that died on 27 January 1597.

Crew of the R/V *Ivan Kiriev* in August 1995.

and Natural Heritage (RICNH). This institute is positioned between the Academy of Sciences and the Ministry of Culture of the Russian government. The government consults it on matters of Arctic interest, and it has much good will. Through Pyotr Boyarsky's relentless diplomacy, the institute has come to manage every historical artifact at Novaya Zemlya and Franz Josef Land, including shelters, encampments, shipwrecks, scientific stations, abandoned structures of atomic bomb testing, Pomor crosses, lighthouses, cairns, and graves – and thus, the Saved House. The Heritage Institute, across the street from Moscow's Kosmos Hotel, occupies several floors of a five-story building otherwise used as a boarding house. Many finds, including the remains of Barents ship, are on display on the second floor of this building. They will turn on the lights whenever there is a visitor.

Last night Pieter and George met with their teammates, and this morning they discussed a strategy for the survey. Among the four Russians, only Eugene holds a permit to dig. George will have to defer to Eugene, something that he had not counted on. Eugene appears to be highly orthodox in his religious beliefs and was likely given lead responsibility for exactly that reason. The Dutch will be able to determine the grave's contents, but without displacing any body parts, and tissue sampling is still a point of discussion. Eugene will supervise every step of George's investigation.

Pieter and George reported what they had learned to Jerzy. "As sober Dutchmen, we may think it's all poppycock, but we have to respect them," Jerzy opined. When I asked how he could be so sure that Barents and Andriesz had not been abandoned on the ice or dumped into the sea, George replied: "At Spitsbergen, we have established clearly that the living were continually dragging those stiffly frozen corpses around just so they could inter them properly. Many coffins were even filled with sawdust to absorb body fluids. The dead were buried in rows facing the coastline, like clothespins on a line. That was a very strong tradition and the best honor a shipmate could receive. Besides, burial at sea, where the deceased would vanish below weighed down with a cannonball, was very uncommon and considered disrespectful in those days. Also, the winterers on their way home did not have anything to make those bodies sink, and without weights, I can assure you, a corpse remains floating. How would that be, those two corpses bobbing between the floes, eh?"

We entered the Arctic around noon when we crossed the Arctic Circle. The GPS indicated that we were covering 17-20 km/hr, or about ten knots. *Kiriev* had traveled 189 km from Archangelsk, and I had progressed 2495 km from my first observation, in Amsterdam. Henk van Veen gave me the coordinates of the Saved House, which showed to be 1434 km distant ('as the crow flies'). On the undulating coast of the Kola Peninsula I could see big, dark radar antennae scanning the northern horizon for American bombers potentially intruding from across the polar ice. This is the throat of the White Sea, a sizeable inland sea and the heart of the Pomor culture, established by Russian settlers along its shores. The sea opens up to the north, widening there to more than 200 km, a body of water that our compatriots, returning from their wintering, crossed by rowing and sailing. This was the second major crossing in those two open boats, after the jump into the deep from Novaya Zemlya to the Russian coast. They hesitated to venture out into the White Sea, for the drinking water had leaked and they were low on reserves. The two boats had lost sight of each other. They looked back at the rocky coast along which they had crept forward with great effort after days of headwind. Now the wind had turned and they decided to take it. In the night they reached the other side of the sea. They heard the coast before they saw it, from the thunder of breaking waves. In the lee of a small island they found a settlement of fishermen. The return to civilization was celebrated exuberantly – and there is an exited reunion with the lost companions from the other boat, who had been out of sight for days at Cape Svyatoi Nos (De Veer gives an accurate map of it). Coincidentally, and without knowing it, the winterers had landed where the Willoughby Expedition froze to death forty-three years earlier, in the small bay of the Varzina River. It was the first English attempt to pass Novaya Zemlya, but all sixty-six crew members perished from the cold. Fishermen discovered them dead on board their ship the following spring.

Back inside the ship we noticed that in the mess the chairs had been tied down to the floor with rubber straps. This produced some guffaws, but in the afternoon, we began to appreciate those precautionary measures when the storm announced its proximity. First, a swell arrived and the ship's pitching motion increased; then the weather took a turn for the worse. At the first instability I already felt somewhat disoriented, and I took it for the first sign of seasickness. In my berth I succeeded in relaxing a bit, but an undeniable feeling of nausea remained. Soon, the waves were running three to four meters tall. *Kiriev* was built for ice navigation, with a shallow draft of 2.9 m and a rounded hull designed to rise above the crushing forces of the ice. Hence, in rough waters we roll like a pig, and this tall ship swings considerably. Now the water in the ballast tanks was sloshing beneath the deck of my cabin. I tried to stay on the open deck to breathe plenty of cold fresh air, but just like some of the others, I had to hang onto a steel beam and acknowledge, with growing nervousness, the signals from my intestines. Each time the water masses behind the vessel rose to an apex and crashed, the stern sunk into the swell but without disappearing.

The soup at 7:30 p.m. was sloshing out of the plates until one sudden, violent movement scattered all the tureens. Stacks of paper dispersed over the floor and, in the blink of an eye, the saloon turned into chaos. People were stumbling around and even the Russians now looked glum and ill at ease. The deck was rolling beneath my feet. Anton, who showed no signs of seasickness, thought it was marvelous. My head was abuzz. The sea thundered on, white capped and foaming, something primordial on which we float, infinitely insignificant; an omnipotent dark being capable of swallowing us without warning. Seaman Sascha, standing in an open doorway, peering into the tempestuous night, said this is his greatest love: fighting the storm. In the narrow passages, you're tossed around. I prayed that it would soon pass and tried to forget I exist, meekly swinging around in my tropically warm bunk. Boy, was I a mess! I could smell and taste myself, a most unpleasant experience. Bending forward, sitting up, or walking requires the greatest effort. I would have to hurry and lie down, with glowing cheeks, a cold sweat, and tears in my eyes. The toilet is a hot and hellish space. The biting smell of methane makes breathing impossible. All kinds of substances from the insides of human beings float in the rolling black water. People were groaning, gagging, and coughing in the companionways. I haven't prayed to the porcelain god yet and continue to resist doing so. This roller-coaster ride may last for days. The storm, centered over the Barents Sea, was moving northeast and at midnight, the Captain turned the bow into the wind to reduce heeling. At half speed, *Kiriev* moved farther into the Barents Sea. The loss of speed introduced a strong vertical motion. Sick and confused, I had to deliver myself to this steel vessel and the able hands of its crew.

Gerrit de Veer praised the great improvements in the vessels. Fifty or sixty people would work long days, for seven months to build a single vessel. Barents' journeys on behalf of Amsterdam and the Republic were carefully prepared. This confidence in the instruments of transport and solid preparation to venture into hostile surroundings is what the sixteenth-century explorers have in common with today's astronauts and kosmonauts. Space shuttle astronaut Joe Allen wrote in the preface to *Entering Space*: "These spaceships that now circle the earth and cross the solar system, incorporating aspects of every science and applying every technology of our age, are more than computer-guided craft of cold composites and metal. They are monuments to human innovation. Aboard such a ship, in every corner, in every nook and passageway, we sense the skills of those who built it, and their minds and spirit travel with us" [Allen and Martin 1984]. (This leads us to the curious design of the Soyuz-Apollo docking system, developed for the spectacular 1975 docking in orbit, an event that signalled the beginning of détente between the superpowers. Besides the ideological differences, many technical challenges had to be overcome. Neither side wanted to be in the receiving, or female position. Both the Russians and the Americans wanted to be equipped with a probe. Something had to be done, because two probes clearly ruled out any possibility of docking. A symmetric unit was invented, like a steel handshake.)

Sunday, 20 August 1995 – We have wet the tablecloths to offer increased friction to the plates and glassware, and thick steel deadlights are now secured over the portholes. I still feel reasonably uncomfortable, but tonight I discovered that even a half-hour's sleep relaxes my innards enough to allow a small trip. On the upper decks, the ship's motion is noticeably more violent. At noon I had a good meal, and with some firmness in my stomach, I feel a lot better. The swaying has become more natural and I can now succeed in moving around without getting sick. Yet it is not very pleasant. There is a woman working in the galley besides the chef and his quiet young assistant. She manages the kitchen, sets the tables, and brings us our plates. It takes your breath away to see her cross the mess in a straight line with her hands full and listing at an angle.

"What's the real name of the guy with those steel dentures?" asked George at the table.

"Starkov," Pieter answered. "Ringo Starkov." Vadim Starkov, 59 years old, is the representative of the Russian Academy of Sciences and, in that position, the official Russian research leader. The current Academy is but a ghost of the mighty empire it was for many years. Every Soviet State had its deputies, each heading a strict, pyramidal hierarchy. Connected scientists were required to become members of the Communist Party to be legible for community services, such as housing and family education. Only the top-level investigators would represent their science abroad, and just a few years ago, Starkov was one of them.

"Ringo Starkov, eh?" George repeats pensively. "What a strange name. Sounds more like something for an American. Ringo Starkov... Oh well."

"You don't hear that too often, for a Russian," I say.

"Ringo Starkov...," he says then. "Doesn't that sound like Ringo Starr?"

"It does, doesn't it?" we reply.

"Who was that again?!"

"The drummer of the Beatles!" We laugh out loud.

Cold War politics have created parallel worlds that meet and merge unexpectedly. I hear that 'The Island at the Top of the World' (1974), sadly dismissed by film history, has its like in

'Sannikov Land', the Movie (1973). This is probably private, but my image of the Arctic derives from a Disney movie. The Island at the Top of the World I saw in 1975. It started it all for me. Forget CGI, models were still dangling on suspension lines. But I saw a Zeppelin, orcas breaking through ice floes, an exploding volcano. Vikings. Its Russian equivalent is 'Sannikov Land' or Zemlya Sannikova. Most of our companions, I hear, may not remember the plot, but do remember the score, and especially its title song. The movie was based on a science fiction novel by Vladimir Obruchev from 1926. The book described Sannikov Land being an island high up in the Arctic, amidst eternal ice, but warmed by a volcano and therefore populated by 'troglodytes' and mammoth. (Here too the volcano explodes which ends it all).

Obruchev (1863-1956) was a pioneer researcher of loess, the windblown glacier dust that covers very large regions. He was also familiar with permafrost science and the woolly mammoth that emerged from the melting north Siberian soil. For his fiction work, 'Plutonia' in 1915 followed by 'Sannikov Land', he found further inspiration in Arthur Conan Doyle's 'The Lost World' from 1912. (Doyle himself likely went back over his memories of 1880, when he was serving as surgeon on board of the whaler *Hope*, meeting Leigh Smith and the crew of *Eira* on their way to Franz Josef Land). The 'Lost world'-genre that succesfully continues today reflects the activity of fossil hunters of every allure, from the American Wild West to the permafrost landscape of north Siberia. This inspired Conan Doyle, Obruchev, and American writer Edgar Rice Burroughs (1918), who produced *The Land That Time Forgot*, introducing another beast that had been unearthed and recently been put together in full majesty: *Tyrannosaurus Rex*.

Sannikov Land was not just a fruit of imagination of a science fiction writer. It was a geographic hypothesis that had roots in the sixteenth century concept of an Arctic continent. As such, it was outlined on Mercator's 1569 world map with four big rivers and a magnetic mountain at its centre. Willem Barents who, like Nansen three centuries later, had sounded the waters north of Novaya Zemlya and found great depths, and relatively warm water, did not hesitate to leave the continent out of his map. He instead drew Spitsbergen, whales, and some sea monsters. However, the idea of a continent in the North Pole persisted both as a myth and a dream. In 1809 Jakov Sannikov, a merchant and a hunter from Yakutsk, during Matvey Hedenstrom's expedition believed to have spotted land to the north of the New Siberian Islands. What he saw, a fog bank, an ice ridge, who knows. But it reinvigorated the idea of the Arctic Continent, now named Sannikov Land, an untrodden world. There was another sighting of this phantom landmass in the western part of the Russian Arctic, by Julius Payer in April 1874. Payer had pushed himself to reach and explore the northernmost island of the Franz Josef Land Archipelago. The unreachable land over at the horizon he christened Petermann Land, after the famed German publisher and advocate of the Open Polar Sea. The Arctic continent was taking shape once again. Fridtjof Nansen, while preparing for the *Fram* voyage, was forewarned he would be shipwrecked on its shores [Nansen 1897, p. 23].

Setting foot on and affirming the existence of Sannikov Land became Baron von Toll's Arctic quest. Baron Eduard von Toll (1858-1902) remains one of Russia's most inspiring explorers. That admiration is ambiguous. The Baron was a kind character who died chasing a mirage, which has tragic appeal for some. With this Baron-hood of the old-European elite he matched the European and American gentlemen explorers. But perhaps the greatest inspiration comes from his association with the grandeur of St. Petersburg and the last Czar, Nicolas II. The murder of the Romanov-family, the Czars (from 'Caesar' or 'Emperor') quietly resonates through the new Russian state. It ended a centuries-old bloodline and the aspiration to unite the Russians within this historically rooted entity. Von Toll is an agreeable hero of a period long gone. I 'met' him during a summer in Estonia. The Baltic state had been liberated from the communist yoke and was quick to claim the Baron as its native son. Just out of Tartu University, Von Toll was invited by Alexander von Middendorff and expedition leader Alexander Bunge of the Imperial Academy of Sciences to join the large expedition to the New Siberian Islands (glaciers in the Russian Arctic are named after Academy geographers, including these three). Von Toll who had studied Mediterranean fauna, flora and the geology, now was bitten by the Arctic bug and saw that elusive land himself. He wrote: "On 13 August [1886] I saw in absolutely clear weather, from the mouth of the Mogur River, below 76° N and ca. 139° E, the sharp outlines of four flat-coned mesas, to the east of which stretched a low plain." The Baron asked his companion 'Begleiter Jergely': "Would you like to reach that distant goal?"

"Once place my foot there, then die," Jergely replied.[6] Their fatal adventure started only fourteen years later. In the years between, Von Toll developed his specialism, returning to northern Siberia to study the permafrost landscape and search for mammoth remains released by the melting ground ice. His expedition in 1893 also established emergency depots for Fridtjof Nansen's visionary journey with *Fram*, which had been designed exactly to demonstrate that the Arctic is a deep, ice-covered ocean. Von Toll had befriended the famous Norwegian explorer, but even after the *Fram* journey and Nansen's proving of his hypothesis: North Atlantic 'Gulf Stream' water coming in at until great depths, Von Toll stubbornly persisted in his quest. In 1898 he presented his plan of an expedition to Sannikov Land to the Academy and got its approval. Nansen supported the plan as well.

At the beginning of summer, 1900, the expedition sailed with *Zarya* from St. Petersburg. *Zarya* had been fully adapted to resist the forces of ice by the builder of *Fram*. The Romanovs, the Imperial couple, were there to see them off. The Czar personally inspected the vessel, in presence of Grand Duke Konstantin, President of the Academy of Sciences who had liberally contributed to cover the expedition's costs. They would go through the Yugor Strait, then winter in the New Siberian Islands. Bennett Island, an elongated rock measuring 22 by 14 km discovered by George De Long in 1881 [see: Guttridge 1986, Sides 2014], was to become their stepping-stone to Sannikov Land. Von Toll with a party of three started from their wintering bay on Kotelny Island, taking dog sledges and kayaks to Bennett Island. While they were out, the western shores of the continent were brushed off the map once again. Hugo Wichmann, editor of *Petermanns Geographische Mitteilungen* (the National Geographic of the 19th century) wrote on 25 September of that year, drawing on the findings of Nansen and the Italian expedition of 1899: "There is no land to the north of Franz Josef Land. Petermann Land does indeed not exist" [PGM, Band 46, Heft IX, 25 Sept 1900, p. 219]. In the same monthly report: "According to a telegram from Arkhangelsk, on August 7 (20), Baron Toll reached the Yugor Strait on *Zarya* and on the same day wanted to enter the Kara Sea, which turned out to be free of ice. The Russian artist Borisov arrived in the Matochkin Shar, where he plans to spend the winter sketching and making scientific observations. As leader of the British Antarctica Expedition has been appointed Leutn. Z.S. Rob. F. Scott."

(Above) Eugène Lepoittevin (1839), Wintering of a Team of Dutch Sailors on the Eastern Coast of Novaya Zemlya. Oil on canvas, Beauvais, France. (Below) J.H. Isings (1951) Overwintering in het Behouden Huys, print for schools.

"A sad message from Siberia, unfortunately, leaves little hope that the indefatigable New Siberia explorer Baron Toll has succeeded in evading demise," wrote Hugo Wichmann on 28 January 1904. "Lieutenant Kolchak on 4/17 August 1903 on Bennett Island found a message from which it appears that Toll and Seeberg [plus two men from Yakutsk] were on Bennett Island between 21 July and 26 October 1902. It is highly probable that Baron Toll and his comrades met their death on the way to New Siberia. What happened – hunger or an accident in the water – will probably never be known" [PGM, Band 50, Heft I, 28 Jan 1904, p. 34]. Closing nearly two decades of covering Von Toll's quest for Sannikov Land, Wichmann concluded on 28 March 1905: "The exploration of Bennett Island has cost too dearly with the demise of this brave explorer and his companion, the astronomer Seeberg."

"From first to last the history of polar exploration is a single mighty manifestation of the power of the unknown over the mind of man," wrote Fridtjof Nansen [1911]. "Nowhere else have we won our way more slowly, nowhere else has every new step cost so much trouble, so many privations and sufferings, and certainly nowhere have the resulting discoveries promised fewer material advantages."

I got up from my small desk and looked through the water-splattered porthole across the southern Barents Sea. Now getting used to the vessel's moving and with a slightly calmer sea, I ventured back on deck. The ship moved forward with a steady, regular swing, together creating a spiraling motion. From the aft deck I watched our wake form and then dissipate in the distance. It was chilly out there, still +7°C with light rain and wind everywhere. We were leaving the summer behind us. On land, it would take us a day at least to get used to the thin winds: the same winds that drive us back to our warm bunks after a few minutes on deck. Through the fog we could glimpse the outline of Kolguev Island, ~30 m high and totally flat. In the gangway, I found Jerzy and Dima smoking cigarettes. We chatted until Anton told me to step aside so that Henri could film Jerzy as he leaned over the railing. Dmitri asked me to demonstrate our GPS system on the bridge. The Captain wants to compare GPS-based headings with those from the *Kiriev*'s instruments, which include a LORAN radio navigation system and the Russian *Glonass* satellite navigation. On a small outside section of the swaying bridge, shaking with nausea, I explained the workings of our small gadget. Drops of saltwater splashing from underneath the bow wetted my face and mixed with the rain. Endless wave trains were marching down the lead-black sea and passing unhindered below our vessel. I showed how to establish a 'way point' and how to enter the coordinates of a certain destination. I would have liked to stay around for a while, but suddenly I felt overwhelmed by seasickness. I did, however, find out that our course had changed. The continuing storminess of the Barents Sea has forced us to abandon the original route along the west coast of Novaya Zemlya. Now *Kiriev* is heading for the Kara Gates to arrive at the island's leeward side.

Chapter Five

Repulsed by the Storm

Monday, 21 August 1995 – By the end of the morning of the third day at sea, *Kiriev* is cruising off the south coast of Novaya Zemlya. The heading is northeast, waves come in from a westerly direction and the wind is straight out of the north. Last night, there was a gale, with wind speeds of 18 m/s (36 knots; 8 Beaufort). The sea is rolling with streaks and great white patches of foam. The ship's meteorologist confirms that a cyclone presently is passing over north Novaya Zemlya. Water flies all around as waves break over the bow. There isn't a single moment of stability. I bolster myself in my bunk by squeezing a pillow between the headboard and my head. I tumble backwards, drop a good distance, then tumble forward again, so that I eventually stand vertically and drop straight about one meter. The ship is going through a series of rapid vibrations. Rising, heeling, falling, vibrating, rolling, sliding. With every falling wave, *Kiriev* veers into the deep until buoyancy compensates. In the downward motion, you feel your stomach acid burn. In the upward motion, it becomes harder to breathe. Eyes closed, it is easy to imagine the ship's spiraling through the waves. One moment I can see the grey skies with sometimes a seagull or a fulmar, next the foaming sea, before the porthole goes underwater. After the White Sea, which was coffee-colored from humic acids transported by the Dvina River, the water in the Barents Sea is a deep, transparent blue. Alex the mate came by the cabin and told us not to go outside again. It is too dangerous on deck; going overboard would be a death sentence. Don't worry pal, I'm not going anywhere! Often the ship will remain heeling, only to return most unexpectedly to its old position. The resulting bedlam is unimaginable. Everything shakes and clatters, closets burst open, and kitchen utensils splatter all over the galley floor. I feel unstable and can't wait to set foot on firm ground.

This morning after breakfast, we were given our landing instructions. I'm assigned to the first group as Number Five. Jerzy is trying to maintain the morale now, because we must face that the Great Russian-Dutch Novaya Zemlya Expedition of 1995 will spend much less time on land than the three weeks originally planned. The Arctic weather remains a most unpredictable factor and now it forces us to readjust our schedule. "Get every bit of sleep you can," our commander told us. "When it's time for action, things will happen fast." Our way east is blocked by an exercise of the Russian Northern Fleet. At 9:00 our location was 46°15' E; still north of Kolguev Island. The landing craft remains tied down on the foredeck, covered up until we're ready to lower it.

Most of the time I have stayed in my bunk, reading or sleeping. The very moment the seasickness ceases, the body relaxes. I intended to do a lot of reading, but the wretched stay aboard this stuffy vessel has prevented me from ordering my thoughts. I can't read, think, or write. Lie down and sleep: that works. My brain returns time and again to the same question: how to escape from this situation? At mid-morning, instructions from the bridge echoed throughout the vessel: in five minutes we'll be changing course. The Captain was executing a series of tactical maneuvers off the Kara Gates to pass east through the Russian fleet, but, eventually, around noon, he decided to drop anchor in a relatively protected bay of southern Novaya Zemlya. The barren coast is close by: black capes and rock faces thirty meters

The Island at the Top of the World, movie poster from 1974.

Afbeeldinghe van drie Beyren die ontrent het ſchip quamen / daer van de eene achter een ſchots ys bleef legghen / ende d'ander twee naer ſchip quamen / d'eene nam een ſtuck vleijs uyt de robbe daert in te ververſchen ſtont / ende werdt midlertijdt gheſchoten dat hy neer ſtorte / d'ander niet wetende wat zijn macker overghecomen was / ſtont langhe ſtil ende roock hem aen / ende liep ten leſten wech. Daer nae quam hy weder teghen ons volck aen / ende rechte ſich op zijn achterſte pooten / om op ons aen te vallen / maer wert middelertijdt doode gheſchoten / ende wy rechten hem op zijn pooten / ende lieten hem alſoo bevrieſen.

This spectacular rendition of an encounter with a polar bear is illustrating events described by Gerrit de Veer on 15 September 1596: two men are keeping the bear at bay while the third reloads the gun. The wintering journal was a modern 'Lost World'-style pictorial.

tall, their undulating stratigraphy highlighted by a dusting of snow. The sky over the Barents Sea is slate-grey, almost black. On deck is the chief engineer, who resembles Czarist Russia's evil monk Rasputin more than a little. He growls as he points at the bay, ear defenders around his neck. This place is called Pigs' Bay. In its confines, the waves leap with sharp crests. Fulmars dart between those crests, and their short wings don't even touch the undulating sea surface. In the seventeenth century, these birds swarmed over whale carcasses, and Spitsbergen whalers called them *mallemokken* ('silly birds'), but the robust Arctic petrels are anything but foolish. Some of the crew are using the opportunity of our lying here to cast a line with bait. They haul the small fish aboard and cut them open with rapid motions. Their innards are a clear orange and teem with worms, some several decimeters long. The fruits of the sea don't look too healthy, and I also recall that the light of the 'Czar Bomba' (and several nuclear devices similar to it) once brightly lit this area.

In the mess room I drink tea with George with Novaya Zemlya's dark rocks outside our porthole window. One way to tell the age of the rock pilings that Pieter and George will search and study, is to look at its lichens: the greenish white or orange 'paint splashes.' Lichen growth is directly related to mean summer temperature and precipitation and may have been limited by snow cover during the 'Little Ice Age'. Diameters of 30-40 mm have been established for blubber ovens and whaling graves from the mid-seventeenth century on northwest Spitsbergen (Werner 1990, 1993), I tell George. Looking at mean summer temperatures, North Novaya Zemlya is colder than West Svalbard, with a mean summer temperature of 2°C at Cape Zhelaniya, compared to 5°C Svalbard. So they should be looking for fairly small lichen circles: probably just 20-25 mm in diameter.

Tuesday, 22 August 1995 – Second day at anchor! Storms are moving by on all sides. Again, we will lose a day. People sleep or stare idly at the deck head, dizzy with the continuous motion. This lying at anchor is getting on my nerves. Waiting for the weather to improve, we try to maintain our momentum by endlessly sorting materials. Those who lay frozen in the pack ice for months, years on end, trapped aboard their much smaller ships – how did they do it? How did they reconcile themselves to the long wait? Nansen describes their year in the ice vividly: totally in control of the situation, enjoying food and company he watches his comrades fatten up while ice ridges thunder outside and the aurora dances above their sturdy abode. One hundred years ago. We do some reading and faithfully write for about an hour every day: no wonder every Arctic journey produces a stream of diaries. Our expedition's doctor, Nicolai Labutin, is in his element, investigating the adaptation of the human body to the conditions that we are presently experiencing. Every day, he descends into the narrow passageways with tubes and measuring cups. George inspected *Kiriev's* small clinic and was very satisfied. He and Labutin are now the best of friends. The first experiment is aimed at determining the physical fitness of every participant. Already, there are some who wish to stay out of Labutin's way and are trying to remain hard to find. Today it finally was my turn. I considered the half hour in sickbay atop the bicycle a welcome distraction. Look at me: the gauges are really smoking!

Life is rather monotonous, but it never is dull aboard ship. Days are necessarily spent in close quarters, and you can hide behind your profession, but not for long. Truth will out. Life here is intense, and I find it fascinating to realize how on this trip I share long days with others, while at home I sometimes don't look another person in the face for weeks, in a manner of speaking. When we sit together in the mess, the most diverse

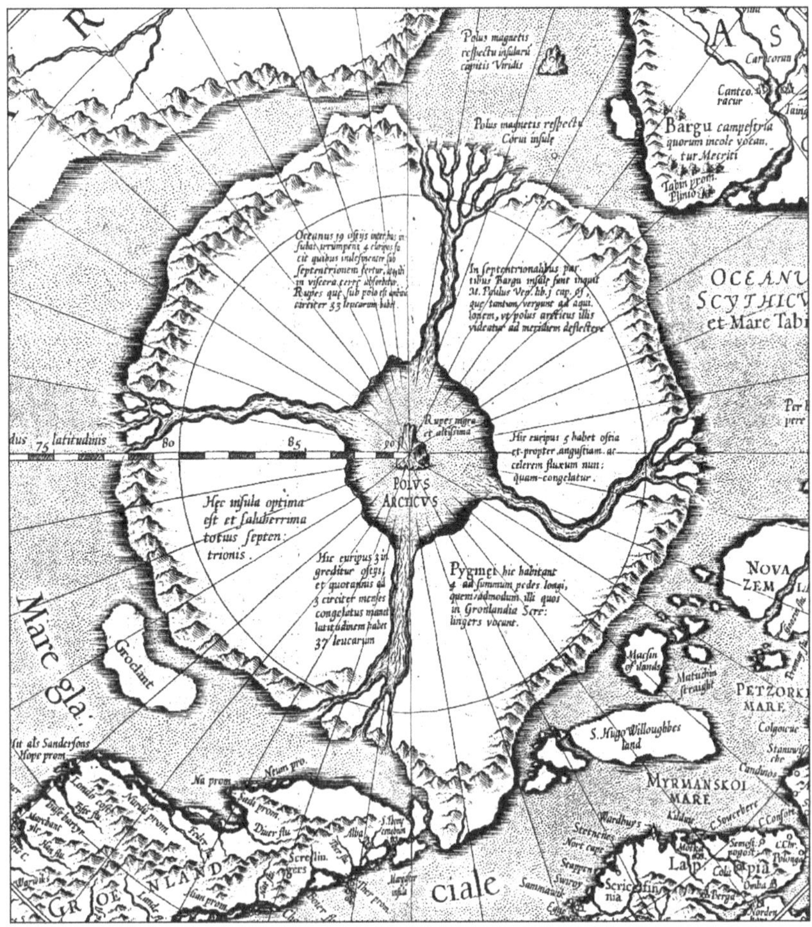

Gerard Mercator showed the (imagined) Arctic Continent on his world map of 1569, that he later reworked into a new folio plate for his famous 1595 atlas. (Gerard died in 1594 and the Atlas was published by his son Rumold, who died not much later.) Prominently featured is Matochkin Shar, the passage that divides Novaya Zemlya's northern and southern island. It shows the knowledge of the archipelago that had been collected in Amsterdam prior to the Arctic journeys.

topics of conversation cross the tables. We tell our stories in an atmosphere of confidentiality. Bas Kist, now 61 years old, with a grey and stubby shadow of a beard that grows up to cover his round head, is the senior authority of our group and Jerzy's been his apprentice for a while. Bas grew up in bomb-ravaged Arnhem and witnessed the failed crossing of the Rhine by the Allied armies in 1944. These events are at the bottom of his preoccupation with weapons, patriotism, and the colonies. He is a very knowledgeable man, always prepared to discuss any military conflict. The political machinations at the Rijksmuseum, long fought together with Joost Braat, are also readily discussed with much cynicism and apparent pleasure. He tells me that amongst the remaining mysteries are two notebooks recovered from the Saved House, the pages of which have never been unstuck. They have never been opened and may contain notes taken during the last or previous-to-last voyage.

George, on the other hand, has not been his imperturbable self these days. Seasickness has affected him more than he had expected. Also, he is coming to terms with a fifteen-year-old trauma, sustained after his last stay in the Arctic. In 1980, George Maat and his assistant Menno Hoogland worked for several weeks in isolation on Ytre Norksöya, northwest Spitsbergen. Towards the end of their stay, the researchers were caught in severe weather that flattened their camp. The blizzard that hit the island forced the expeditionary vessel, *Plancius*, to seek refuge.

"Every day I would climb to the tallest spot to transmit radio messages," George recalled. "Because I was unable to receive anything myself, I did not know if someone would actually hear me. Later on, it turned out that they were able to hear me very well at the base camp on Amsterdam Island. But these scientists were much too busy quarrelling... It never entered anyone's mind to come and help us." Ytre Norksöya provided little shelter. Now in critical danger, the men kept warm by moving around. "We were covered head to foot with ice," George told us. "I was completely white. I'd told Menno, thus, that we would be placing all our gear near the water, not because I'd been expecting us to depart but purely to keep moving. When everything was dragged there, we began carrying it back up." Maat determined that the limits of their endurance would be reached. Desparate, they now send out the international emergency message SOS. *Plancius* relayed the message to Amsterdam Island, but expedition leader Laurens Hakbord replied they should remain calm and wait until tomorrow. At that point, *Plancius*' captain sprang into action, George told us. *Plancius* left its shelter and came cruising by in a driving storm. "Two sailors had been ordered to get us off the island. Of course, we had no idea what was happening and were overjoyed when we saw the flaming orange survival gear approach. Anton had joined the two sailors and stood up to his chest in the icy waters to keep the Zodiac off the rocks." They felt abandoned and now is the first time since then that George has returned to the Arctic.

The Russians appear not to be overly concerned with the certain delay that accumulates with every hour that we lie still. There is much work to be done, and bad weather will likely claim several days once we are ashore. Each lost day is at the expense of my trip to the ice cap, and if we lose just a few more days, I can kiss that adventure goodbye. So close and yet so far: I don't think I will ever get another chance to move through this remote land. Even better it would be to cross the ice cap. This has been done once, I read, in 1913 by members of the Sedov Expedition to the North Pole. Georgy Sedov's original journal and observations were discovered in the archives of the Hydrographic Service of the Navy in 1956 and a great paper was written about it by William Barr in 1973.

The expedition that would cross Novaya Zemlya's ice cap sailed with *Sv. Foka* from Archangelsk on 24 September 1912. The ship's destination was Franz Josef Land, from where Sedov intended to sledge to the North Pole. The crew included geologist Mikhail Pavlov, Vladimir Vize, and photographer Nikolay Pinegin (all remembered in the glaciers and a cape – the expedition named the Inostrantsev Bay after their geology professor, Alexander Alexandrovich Inostrantsev). Vize would be the director of the polar institute and with a German background, in the 1930s translated De Veer's diary from German to Russian. Sea ice forced the expedition to winter on Novaya Zemlya's west coast and the unplanned stop-over was used to study the island. Sedov, a 37-year-old officer in the Imperial Russian Navy, wrote on 3 October 1912: "Our expedition apart from reaching the Pole, will pursue still wider scientific work, and since Novaya Zemlya, which belongs to our Motherland, requires exploration above all, we will in the meantime direct our fresh energies to a detailed and multi-facetted study of it". On 30 March 1913 Pavlov, Vize, and sailors Konopler and Linnik began a crossing of Novaya Zemlya's 1500 m high ice cap with a dog team, skimming its crest at an altitude of 913 m. They reached Vlas'yeva Bay on the Kara Sea coast and then returned the same way, climbing the ice cap again. The expedition never reached the Pole and Sedov died on the ice of Franz Josef Land, after another wintering in 1914. The expedition – these Arctic relays are plentiful of happy and unhappy coincidences – did pick up Albanov and Konrad, survivors of the Brusilov expedition that involuntarily repeated Nansen's journey.[7] Both expeditions had been isolated for over two years and upon returning from their match with Nature sailed straight into the First World War. On 10 August 1914 they encountered fishermen: "Haven't you heard that a terrible war has broken out, a war that started in Serbia?

Germans, Austrians, French, English, Serbs, almost everyone is now involved in this violent conflict. [...] German submarines could be patrolling the Murmansk coast. We were certainly in the danger zone" [V. Albanov 2000].

Between breakfast at 7.30 a.m. and dinner, twelve hours later, there is little to do but sit and nap. The sounds of the waves and the engine, the whistling of a turbine, the drone of a generator, the crackle of turning book pages – they put me to sleep. One more day gone. I feel restless and tinker around. The Russians hide their worrying much better. To them, our cooperation appears to be a procedural exercise. Each day they show that they have the wherewithal to transport an amphibious expedition and trust that the team will be brought ashore. Their schedule leaves plenty of room for error. Perhaps we are too tight and expect the impossible, too anxious for results, too confident of our abilities. Boyarsky is determined to lead us, on the way back, past the most monumental locations of cultural-historical importance under his charge. Imitating the underappreciated Kravchenko, some Russian colleagues speculate about re-enacting the wintering and the subsequent return voyage to gain a better understanding of De Veer's descriptions. "But not this year," they add, laughing. Thank God because I still have a few things to accomplish in my life. Minor frictions like these reflect the differences between our cultures.

The Russians are much better players and have learned to conceal their plans until the goal has come well within reach. The intense boredom may at any moment give way to excessive activity that puts us in a cold, hard wind on Novaya Zemlya. Half past five! I'm feeling miserable, after another day in cramped quarters under a fluorescent glare, sleepy but not tired, on the small bench or in my cot. The sheets are printed with small purple flowers. We have a dull headache from lack of exercise and breathing fuel vapors in unventilated spaces. Up on the bridge, one can hear the stationary engines humming far below, pacifying sounds of available power, power at rest, resonating through the steel decks of the vessel.

Wednesday, 23 August 1995 – Last night at eight o'clock, it was anchors aweigh! We were having fried rice when the Captain's voice on the intercom interrupted the MTV video: 'Bootsman op de bak!' [Bosun on the bow! it's centuries-old Dutch ship jargon]. Everyone jumped up to stow gear. Pressure valves sprayed water, the engine's hum reverberated throughout the ship, and all of a sudden the coast started to move. Steep, scoured cliffs surrounded the undulating landscape. The clouds were low. We were underway, and the very notion released a great feeling of enthusiasm. Two hours later, we were informed that the Kara Gates were 'boisterous'. At a quarter to midnight, Sascha, with whom I had played dominoes in the mess, returned from the bridge and said: "I am sorry to inform you that we will enter the storm within half an hour." Exactly half an hour later came the start of a hellish night.

The first jolts sent items flying through my cabin. Cockroaches ran up and down the walls. I could hear the galley's inventory clattering around, and when I got up to see if help was needed, I was tossed around from wall to wall and had to be careful not to get injured myself. The vessel danced across the waves. The noise was incredible. All over, beams were creaking and improperly closed doors were slamming. Konstantin, in his underwear, went to investigate the origin of a pervasive diesel smell. The Captain rode the cyclonic storm, intending by venturing deeper into the Kara Sea to launch us on a trajectory to the Saved House. North of the cyclone the seas would be calm, but first we had to cross the angry waters: again, the loss of a precious day. All day today I have been on my bunk, bobbing and dozing. The greasy food congests my body, and I need exertion soon. After tea around 4:00 p.m., Dr. Maat explained the blood pressure and ECG research to which we are being subjected. In the Arctic, one appears to age more quickly, and it was a shocker to find Henri lying on the top bunk looking like a dead cat. I brought him a piece of bread. "Henri, Henri... Are you OK? You've got to drink some, hear? Take some water, buddy." "No, no... I can't drink anything now," he stammered weakly.

Kiriev sails on towards the horizon, propelled by a tailwind. Our transit through the grey void is estimated at sixteen hours; thus, arrival at Ice Harbor will be tomorrow night. All afternoon, splendid transparent turquoise waves rose and fell behind the ship's stern. Walls of water rolled toward the vessel and crashed on the gangways. Every time the bow met another wave, there was a smack of water on steel. Deck water turbulently poured out the scuppers. Great brown skuas stayed with the ship for some hours, then vanished in their empty world. Moments after feeling the cold waters of the Kara Sea splash on my face, I found myself in the ship's sauna. *Kiriev* has to manage its fresh water supply carefully, but once a week we can take a shower, and on that day the sauna is open for an afternoon. We make a list and form teams, because the chamber has room for four people. The sauna is in the most stable spot aboard, the center of all motion: at midship and below the waterline. Starkov keeps his cap on; he says it's good for the hair.

Night has fallen – with sunset around 9:00 p.m. and overcast sky, the Arctic twilight is rather darker than I would have expected. Drops of seawater outside the portholes reflect the cabin lights. All doors are open. Eugene is reading in bed. Konstantin sits reading on a chair, clad in his purple warm-up suit. The ship is humming towards its goal. Jerzy and Bas are asleep. Henri has come back to life and is seated next to René. Some crew members are sitting together in the mess, watching a pirated Arnold Schwarzenegger video. In the back, as Herre and I play dominoes with Sascha, George has finally gotten up and headed for bed.

Thursday, 24 August 1995 – The day of our arrival at Ice Harbor has dawned: our sixth day at sea, our ninth since departure from Amsterdam. All night long, the ship was able to proceed at full speed. As the sea became calmer during the night, our speed increased to 12 knots or so. I slept well and was awakened at 7:00 a.m. by the girls mopping up the companionways. The weather was fine and the sea calm as the ship cut its way through the light blue waters. Beady-eyed and exhausted, I went on deck for the first time in days, squinting in the fierce sunshine. The wind felt cold and crisp: a polar wind. There was still no sea ice in sight, which we hear is rather exceptional. Karl Ernst von Baer, in 1837, dubbed the Kara Sea 'the ice cellar'. His observation followed on several unsuccessful attempts to identify the landforms and capes named by Barents, and establish the exact size of the island. The east coast that we could see in the distance was charted not even 90 years ago! We progressed unhindered, storm clouds, distinct from the cyclone trailing us, still visible on the southern horizon. The Captain's maneuver was outstanding. If conditions remain favorable, we will reach Ice Harbor just after midnight and land immediately. And then we'd have to get settled in a mad rush and prepare for foul weather. On the aft deck, I found René and Henri testing the satellite phone and the wind-powered generator. A serious problem had come to light during the first test, five days ago. The specifications for the wind generator show an unexpectedly large peak output, potentially fatal for many instruments. The gasoline generator's

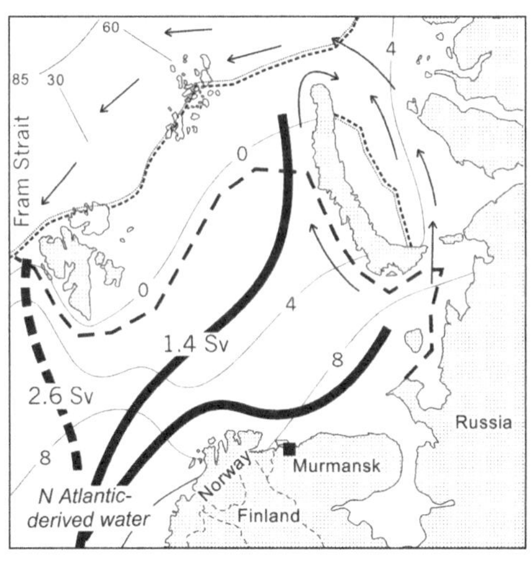

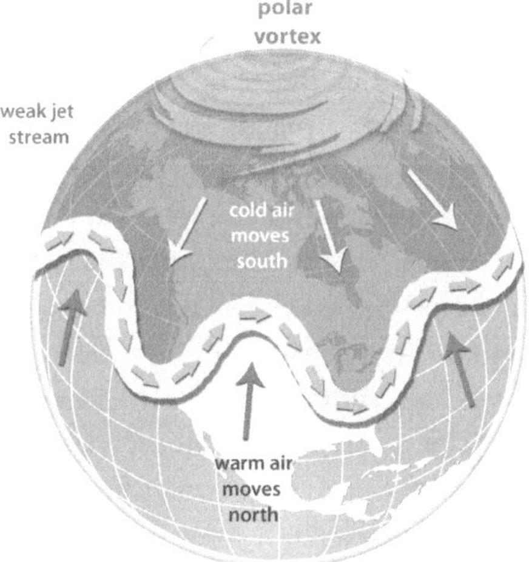

(A) The Barents Sea climate was in two alternating phases during the twentieth century, related to the influx of relatively warm Atlantic water (in Sverdrup or 1 million m3/ second). This pump is controlled by the force and location of the jet stream. (B) A weak polar vortex invites Atlantic depression systems to circle up north, like Katrina, 'Walking on Sunshine' (image by NOAA.gov 2021). When the pump is full 'on,' the inflow of the Gulf Stream nearly doubles, pushing the summer and winter sea ice limits north (from Zeeberg 2001).

transformer was equipped with a surge protector to prevent such overloading. *Kiriev*'s radio engineer proposed using an incandescent bulb as a fuse to protect the instruments during peak voltages. René was trying to remember his high school physics: Voltage increases as the rotations increase and 60 Watts divided by 12 Volts would give us the required 5 Amps. "That's it, eh?" he asks Henri. "A 60-Watt bulb would do, right?"

The engine room is a pounding inferno. Carefully I glanced inside the steel door, and a stream of hot air smelling of oil hit my face. Rasputin, seated in a soundproof office, waved at me to come in and look around. The engineer can hear from vibrations and hums anywhere in the vessel, whether we are doing all right. The heart of the vessel occupies about one-third of its length. Near the entry is an enormous yellow engine block. Through the steel grating that I entered on, I could look down three stories between pipes and conduits, colored blue, green, or red to indicate the various fluids they transport. One heavy stainless-steel shaft runs aft from the engine. This shaft turns the propeller and rotates fast, but not particularly fast. Its sound is imposing. Seven transparent glass tubes on the steel engine drew my attention as they filled with oil, emptied one by one, and then refilled. This tiny set of tubes in all its simplicity seemed to keep the entire power plant working. Our engineer can often be found in the small machinery room opposite the engine room. Into that room are crammed an obviously much-used workbench, covered with steel shavings, and metal lockboxes with tools: wrenches, pliers, hammers, files, fittings, bolts, belts, wires, clamps, filters and many other items whose applications I would not even know. Spare parts packed in cardboard boxes are stacked along the walls. He can improvise anything here and has already produced two beautiful brass battery clamps that we forgot to bring.

The winterers roasting a fox in the Saved House during the long Arctic night. This monumental plate from the German (Hulsius)-edition shows the steam bath, bunks, Gothic clock and copper kettle. When the clock froze on 3 December 1596, the hour glass was used to keep the time (see the Epilogue of this book). Next to the fire, one of the men lies ill with scurvy. A 11 cm-tall gunpower shell was hung by Willem Barents in the chimney when house and ship were abandoned in June 1597, containing his folded and rolled up letter of apology.

First day stamps traditionally issued by the Russians on board of the expedition vessel.

Full speed ahead of the storm: at three o'clock, fog banks started moving in. Fog forms readily in this quiet, warmer summer atmosphere over the cold Arctic waters of the Kara Sea. In the distance, dark masses lay spread across the sea, glistening silvery under the sun, brownish-grey and fearsome everywhere else. As we penetrated the thick mist, the minute vapor drops diffused the sun and temperature decreased noticeably. The light grew dimmer as the fog thickened, causing some unrest amongst the Dutch. We filled small plastic containers with gasoline from big rusty barrels on the foredeck. The weapons have all been inspected and oiled.

The landing on the beach at Ice Harbor will take place within hours, so we held a final meeting to discuss potential difficulties – and polar bears. Bears can be curious, if not aggressive. When they are rolling their shoulders, they are getting ready to attack. "Don't run!" urged Boyarsky. "If you run, he will come after you for sure. Bears swim better and run faster. Should you be stalked by a bear, throw him something smelly: a hat, for instance. He will stop to sniff it, because polar bears rely primarily on their sense of smell. I myself once scared off a bear by producing certain bodily gases when I did not have anything to throw." Translator Yuri Mazurov added, "Yes, Dr. Boyarsky has a lot of experience dealing with polar bears."

"If you are surprised by a bear, fire shots into the air, pelt him with rocks, shoot your flares at him. Wherever you're going, look around you. What looks like a snow patch may well be a polar bear. Look for something to hit or stab with, something sharp and adopt a threatening pose to create doubt within the animal. Show him, that you are not regular prey. Bears always need a few seconds to come to a decision: scram or attack! That will give you just enough time to kneel and load your gun. If a bear enters the camp, you are entitled to kill him." Bas opted to mark a security zone around the camp, because the flat terrain and fog may affect our estimation of distances.

Under the present circumstances, certainly after the last couple of days, which most of us spent in bed, it is hard to imagine that tonight we will be by ourselves in polar bear country. The bears wander this world that we have gradually penetrated. The unforgivable Arctic environment has in just 10,000 years produced a breathing creature that exists in harmony with its bleak surroundings. An adult polar bear annually kills fifty to seventy seals along the margins of the pack ice. The ice is farther north this summer than it has been in the past fifty years, likely because of the intense cyclones. Consequently, most bears are north, and the land-bound animals are underfed, seeking to build reserves for the long winter. *Ursus maritimus*, the 'sea bear', can swim 200 km and delivers its young in caves of ice. The hairs in a polar bear's pelt are hollow, like glass fiber, to transport the sun's energy to the skin, which is black for optimal heat absorption. How could anyone justify killing an animal of such splendid power and grace? We are not hunters, like the nineteenth century 'sportsmen' who shot bears by the dozens. We grew up in cities. The closest I have been to a wild animal was during a summer on West-Greenland, four years ago when I was face-to-face with a musk ox, that had forced me to take refuge on a big rock. Primitive as that beast appeared, with its Ice Age hair and horns protruding like tusks and eyes rolling, it didn't have sharp teeth and claws. Flyers and posters from the Norsk Polarinstitutt warn visitors to Svalbard: "It attacks without warning." George and Bas, to be forewarned of approaching bears during their stays on Amsterdam Island, constructed trip wires connected to small explosive charges around their camp sites. Bas Kist: "So, that doesn't work, does it?" George Maat concurred on the spot: "How often I walked through one!" he says. "Then I immediately had to hit the ground because I could hear my colleague cock his rifle." The men shared an anecdote about a Canadian researcher who, upon leaving his tent one morning, came face to face with a polar bear. "The bear backed away and, without even glancing down, stepped neatly over the wire." The polar bear in his habitat is not easily outsmarted. My great admiration for these animals notwithstanding, we will have to defend ourselves if a bear refuses to be repelled. We carry the Remington and concomitant high-velocity ammunition, as well as Russian rifles with the Brenneke, a 16-mm cartridge with a lead projectile and torpedo tail that, as George puts it, will "knock a steel door off its hinges." Our Doctor Labutin loads these cartridges himself, continually experimenting with the amount of gunpowder. If the percussion cap doesn't quite fit, he'll just tap it on the table a few times. The Russians also use rough-sized buckshot that, like the Brenneke, is effective up to about thirty meters.

Forty kilometers from the landing zone, two hours before arrival time, we encountered continuous fog. Bears will be able to 'see' us using their formidable sense of smell, but we won't be able to see them. They move fast and silently and are quick to arrive. It is up to the first group to establish a safety perimeter. The Russians have exchanged their training suits and slippers for camouflage garb. Jerzy sent us to our bunks to get some rest, but instead I went over my gear, polished my boots some more, and filled my canteen with water. I was feeling somewhat nervous, somewhat overheated with fatigue and adrenaline. I checked my watch every fifteen minutes and when I saw it was time, I got up. We continued at full speed, which was not a good sign. On deck, my dark suspicion was confirmed. Our landing had been cancelled because of the thick fog and a slight swell. Oiled and shined and ready to go, we paced through our cage of steel beams and cables, surrounded by impenetrable grey sky and light blue water. Back in the Netherlands, I had put the coordinates of the Saved House in my positioning system. When I activate the GPS it still needs a few minutes to 'lock in' on three satellites and calculate our position. Fulmar sailed centimeters above the rolling water surface, making steep turns to avoid wave crests. Immediately after finding our position, the GPS flashed the alarm and instructions to bring the ship around 222 degrees. We had passed our goal. The distance to the Saved House was less than 3 km, but increasing. From the beach, the gargling sound of the vessel passing through the fog would be quite audible. I am wide-awake. This is the moment when the action should have happened. Tomorrow at 6:00 a.m. we'll reach Ivanov Bay. Then it will be the turn of George and Pieter, numbers Three and Four, respectively.

Thus, at the end of this day, the expedition has divided into its two subject groups. George, Pieter, and their Russian colleagues have a few hours to prepare for their landing at Ivanov Bay. Within the next week, they may discover the grave of Willem Barents. The Ice Harbor group, meanwhile, can do little else but wait until *Kiriev* brings them back to the vicinity of the Saved House.

Chapter Six

Ashore in the Bay of Strangers

Friday, 25 August 1995 – 'Bootsman op de bak'. The Captain's command over the intercom, in Dutch maritime language aroused me from a deep sleep. Henri, jumping from his cot above mine, rushed out to film the action on deck. Soon the muffled rattling of the anchor chain reverberated throughout the ship: we were dropping anchor. Where are we? Slowly, I got up. Fleetingly, ever so fleetingly, I noticed a wave of revulsion and I tried not to think about what was outside: a fog-shrouded, ice-cold sea that had rolled and tossed us for a week now – and a huge, empty island. I glanced at my watch: 7:15 in the morning. Through the porthole I could see a calm sea, light blue under a low, grey sky. If this was Ivanov Bay, the grave search party would go ashore. Otherwise, who knows where on earth we might be. I got dressed and hurried outside. In the light, drizzly mist that engulfed the ship, Jerzy and Bas were siphoning gasoline into lemonade bottles from a big, rusty fuel barrel on the foredeck, using a rubber hose. It was +4°C. Novaya Zemlya was just a dark strip of land, the elevations above ca. 80 m disappearing into the low clouds. There was little snow.

Inside, on passing I noticed that the breakfast table had been set, but there was no time to eat. The landing of the grave-searchers was busily being prepared – before the sea would roughen again. Only George, with aristocratic unconcern, sat sipping a cup of tea in the otherwise empty mess room. The corridors teemed with foot traffic. The hum of electric motors resonated through the steel vessel as the deck crane deposited a huge stack of wooden beams and planks from the hold into the landing craft. To be protected against bears, the Ivanov Bay group will be constructing a hut for their stay. On deck, the atmosphere was frenzied and tension was palpable, with good-byes amid the din of cargo handling. Freed from all its cables, our landing craft, a red steel barge five meters long, danced merrily atop the waves. Once the entire Ivanov gang had climbed down the rope ladders, the droning *plashkot* sailed rapidly into the haze. Bundled up in gear as if ready to go ashore myself, I stood in a light rain atop *Kiriev*'s bridge and followed the progress of the landing through binoculars. A trio of long, rust brown walruses glided by the red craft through the pale blue sea. It was easy to distinguish their bristling snouts, which spit out a spray of condensation and water when the animals were surfacing. "Of reddish color and two teeth sticking from their mouth, up-down, elephant-wise," wrote Jan Huyghen van Linschoten – four hundred years ago.

By 11:15 a.m., the Ivanov group was ashore. The landing craft delivered a second load of wood and was hoisted aboard. *Kiriev* raised anchor but would not sail towards Ice Harbor. It had been decided to seek shelter from a new storm in Inostrantsev Bay, on the west coast of the island. Excitement swept over the ship when, at noon, we saw the first unobtrusive iceberg float by: the entire voyage along the illustrious east coast of the island had not provided this many sights. The silent flotilla of blue sculptures grew by the hour, indicating the proximity of calving glaciers. This is the coast where Willem Barents breathed his last, and was buried with one other crew, who died at the same time. The men had watched the icebergs of 'Ice Cape' as we did now: "Gerrit" he said, weakened and bleeding internally from scurvy to his writer and shipmate Gerrit de Veer, "are we about the Ice Cape? Lift me up then, I must see that cape once again." We sailed past the glaciers that had clearly receded back into their fjords, with black moraines stretching out to sea, no longer forming a closed 'ice cape'. Our arrival in Inostrantsev Bay was estimated for 3:00 p.m. The plan calls for a reconnaissance sortie with two groups along the beaches of the bay, to search for cairns. Boyarsky requests that we be specifically alert for objects indicating the presence of the ancient Pomors and the Nazis, who operated in greatest secrecy on these shores. To have weather stations in the Arctic was strategically important. We know that the Nazis hid an automated weather station on northwest Novaya Zemlya, but it hasn't ever been found.

The approaching landing put us back on the alert. Bas Kist, our curator and arms expert, distributed ammunition for the rifles and reviewed the arms discipline. "Should a polar bear come after us and we decide to fire at him," he instructed us, "we'll follow our firing range routine. The shooter kneels down and someone else counts the bear's approach: fifty meters... forty meters... thirty meters... Don't stare at the bear but focus on his chest or on his shoulder. There will be three cartridges in the magazine. For reasons of safety, do not keep a cartridge in the chamber. Remember, the second man keeps additional ammo at the ready."

Self-sufficiency is imperative for one venturing out in the Arctic and it was high time to get my gear in order. ("Coming along?" Anton, our film director, would tell the viewer.) What do I need? Everything! Light clothes to move and warm pieces of garment for when I stand or sit. The unpredictable weather changes from quiet to severe in half an hour and there is no shelter nowhere. The land is barren. I packed the thin, reinforced Gore-Tex cover of the Navy-issue sleeping bag, my borrowed oversized down jacket, the small *Whisperlite* gasoline stove with a one-liter bottle of gasoline, some packages of instant soup. There would be sufficient meltwater on land, but just to be sure, I filled my canteen with the ship's chlorine-rich water. I checked my waist belt, carrying a black dagger and a pouch containing flare gun, GPS, a set of waterproof-packed batteries; and another pouch with a notebook with waterproof paper, and a pencil. I took some extra rolls of film and decided where to stow away all these items I needed to keep track of.

The sea was calm: smooth as glass. The landing craft glided over in fifteen minutes and at 4:00 in the afternoon ground onto the steep, gravel beachfront. The sailors kept the engine running hard, to maintain a solid lock while we disembarked. In clouds of smoke and steam, we climbed the steep ridge of loose gravel. Then, after reversing the propeller's motion, the plashkot quickly retreated into the fog.

I looked around. A steep bluff, tall and dark, disappeared on either side of us into the mist: the Edge of the World. Gigantic whale vertebrae lay scattered across Novaya Zemlya's black, undulating beach. Large blocks of transparent ice swung in the surf with the regular fizzing of wet shingles. The group split without losing time and would walk in opposite direction: a group of five men had started off toward the northwest. We gathered the life vests in stacks, then covered them with heavy boulders and lengths of driftwood. Jerzy, Yuri, Dirk, Herre and me, we spread out over the ~200 m wide beach, walking southeast. The steep bluff denied us a view into the interior, and I quickly considered how much it would take to conquer the obstacle. As I approached the slope, over the flattened pebbles and weathered rocks of the beach, I discovered that it is barely 50 m tall. Each step lessened the elevation; the ground seemed to be falling away beneath my feet. As I reached the cliff edge and saw inland, my elevation above sea level was approximately

15 m, and I began to see the dimensions of this world. The land I saw was flat and barren, some dark undulating ridges dissolving in the very low clouds. No bear. Most people would find this environment intimidating, but I felt liberated. However, down on the beach, the expedition's leader Jerzy Gawronski, the Amsterdam archaeologist, already called and gestured and I came running back. "No more of that puppy like behavior!" he said angrily, as I, panting, resumed my position. One must feel the landscape. Fine, grainy debris was fanning across the plain. The ground consists of sharp, slaty sandstones, characterized by thin smooth plates and shiny slivers, which break down to sand-size fragments. The circles and some geometrical lines of patterned ground showed that there is permafrost: half a meter down, the ground remains frozen all year long. Repeated summer thaw of the upper soil has caused flat slabs of rock to sink and stand at odd angles, like headstones in a graveyard. Patches of bright green moss, which needs phosphates, form around decaying whale bones or large bird carcasses. They stand out in the otherwise dull landscape, adorned with thin little flowers. One such patch was rectangular and had the approximate dimensions of a burial. Jerzy assembled the metal detector and surveyed the moss. No signal. He shrugged and we moved on. We tossed each other an oversized rubber wader to cross a stream.

After walking for two hours, we arrived at a promontory and in awe observed a blue glacier tongue loom through the fog. The calving front was like bright blue marble, rising from the sea a sheer fifty meters. Every now and then, large slabs would collapse from the glacier with a roaring noise. The ice mass breaks and with enormous buoyance scatters and sinks into the water, spreading large rippling waves that spread throughout the bay. This process had filled the bay with larger and smaller icebergs, which, in the absence of wind, floated around randomly. Jerzy nodded, "If you, sailing along the coast, arrived here, and wanted to bury somebody... where would you do that?" We looked around and spotted a collapsed cairn nearby. The stack of rocks was about 1.5 m across and could easily cover a grave. To our surprise, the detector gave a loud and clear signal. There was a metal object underneath the cairn, which might well have been put together by Norwegian or Russian hunters. It could be a button, or a bullet. Often, those building a cairn would leave a message in a pewter can or inside a soldered bottle. Unfortunately, we ran out of time and within a half hour would have to move back to the landing zone to meet the plashkot. The GPS measurements came through and I read the coordinates to Dirk.

While the others prepared a quick sketch of the cairn, I had another half hour to explore the beach and joined the two Russian geologists who had caught up with us. They established the limits of a rock outcrop marked on the geological map. We walked further up to the glacier. Skeletal parts of marine animals were spread all over the place. I stumbled across three enormous polar bear skulls, one with a bullet hole. Water rose to my ankles in a muddy stream where I photographed a heavy wooden construction that must have washed ashore during a storm. A steep-sided moraine, possibly indicating the glacier's extent in Barents' time, stretched inland. Along the high-tide line lay unimaginable numbers of beached aluminum and plastic floats, shampoo bottles, cleaning brushes, plastic detergent containers, polyethylene rope, nets, crates, and other fishery material; the garbage that is carried on the poleward-flowing Gulf Stream current, like some mad oceanographic experiment. I expect that Ice Harbor will get less detritus. Mud and standing water everywhere; the black mass of rock, fragments, and clay that made up the wall of moraine was saturated: water percolated through, turning the surrounding area into quicksand. Just as

I was considering where to climb the moraine, and step onto the glacier, just to have reached that distant goal, my teammates called and we had to go back. We tossed each other the big rubber wading pants again and moved back across a small stream. The feet of these pants are square and thick so your boot will fit in.

"Shall we go?" said Jerzy when I returned to the cairn and found them zipper up to head back. "We'll come back later for this one." The clouds had lowered, and a fine rain swept across the beach. In a chilly dusk we started walking back.

Back at our landing site, I was thoroughly soaked by the continuing drizzle. The north group had returned earlier. It is a raucous gang! I had no desire to leave the peace and quiet that we just found and with great reluctance moved forward, observing the party. The ship's doctor was experimenting with his home-made cartridges, shooting at boards and crates set up by his assistant, blowing them to pieces. The experimental gunpowder created a huge cloud of smoke with each shot. Another man was firing green flares into the clouds to attract *Kiriev*'s attention, but I found it hard to believe that the vessel, anchored about a kilometer offshore, could see the fireworks. He then took a wide-barrelled handgun, pointed it at the sky, and with a loud bang and an enormous, yellow flare climbed up and bathed the layer of fog in a threatening glow, before arching into the sea and a flickering death. The Russians were very amicable and again liberally poured vodka around a big fire. The drinks hit mercilessly. Tired and chilled, I could feel my cold, damp shirt stick to my back. Snowflakes mixed with the rain. For this absurd beach festival, we abandoned our research of that cairn, for which neither cost nor effort had been spared. I was a step away from standing on the Novaya Zemlya ice cap. We stuck to the rules and came back at the agreed upon time – it's only a decent thing to do – and we pay the price. The doctor finally blasted the case to smithereens. So much for the firearm discipline, too. The spectacled Badyukov brothers, geologists Dmitri (Dima) and Daniel, then asked if I knew the joke about a Dutchman, a Frenchman, and a Russian on an uninhabited island, and I let go of my resistance. We must just go along as things have been going here for centuries.

"A Russian, a Frenchman, and a Dutchman are stranded together on an uninhabited island," the joke began. The vodka was stinging in our mouths. "They had to find means to survive and walked along the tide line in search of anything useful. The Frenchman found a bottle of wine; the Dutchman, a bottle of whiskey. But the Russian found a rare jar. They decided to open the jar first. As soon as the Russian pulled the cork, a spirit appeared, who said 'I am the spirit of this jar' and invited all three to make a wish. The Frenchman looked at his watch and said 'Now that it is six o'clock, I would like to be with my wife.' And he disappeared! The Dutchman thought for a few moments and then asked the ghost to whisk him off to a grand hotel. He, too, was gone. Now, it was the Russian's turn. He looked sad and said to the ghost, 'I just had two buddies and two bottles to empty with them.'" Daniel, who was presenting this joke, paused contentedly, and stared into the flames before continuing: "'And now,' the Russian said, 'I have only this empty jar. I wish that they would return!'" The brothers laughed uproariously.

"So you see," says Dima, "it won't help to wish yourself away from here."

The toast caused a brief intermission in the fireworks. Soon enough, that flare-shooting man resumed his effort to draw the ship's attention. Each flare went up with a frightening firecracker bang. It was making everyone jumpy. Not a moment too soon, Jerzy tossed his cigarette on the ground and pulled a radio from his pocket to call in the landing craft. Half an hour later, at 10:15 p.m., our salvation emerged from the dusk.

The return to *Kiriev* was ice cold but indescribably beautiful. People were silent, tired and intoxicated to the point of exhaustion. The fire on the beach rapidly turned into a small orange light and then vanished into the fog. The sea was a light blue, with widely scattered icebergs, silent and still. It is difficult not to see all kinds of images in the melted, clear blue or crystal-clear ice shapes: knights on horseback, gruesome figureheads with mute, frozen screams on their faces, grotesque monsters, gargoyles, and dragons. Pieces of transparent and molten ice floated past the sides of the plashkot, crackling sharply like ice cubes in a glass of lemonade. The deckhand hung across the bow of our barge, signalling port or starboard to the helmsman as we manoeuvred through the bergs. *Kiriev* continued to remain out of sight. Four hundred years ago, on 26 June 1597 off this same coast, the two sloops of the castaways rowing and sailing back to civilization, fired muskets to find each other in the dense fog. Our helmsman got on the radio several times to find out where we are headed. Because the vessel could not see us either, I assume he received directions based on *Kiriev's* radar. In any case, a weak glow soon appeared in the fog.

Kiriev turned on all lights: a magnificent show. We were silent; I was struck by size of our ship. Our safe, warm base appeared terribly small, yet an ingeniously composed steel craft, floating on the vast sea under that great, impermeable sky. After a good fifteen minutes, which seemed endless, we docked alongside the vessel and climbed aboard by a rope ladder. In heavy weather, as we noticed on another occasion, the crew drops a large mesh alongside, which you must grab onto at the crest of a wave. To counteract the waves, the ship will turn into the wind like a mother swan of steel. The crew works smartly and fully focused, and as soon as they can grab you they'll hoist you aboard in one swift motion. When all had boarded, the crane lifted the landing craft onto the deck, cargo and all. In the mess room, it turned out, dinner was waiting. Anton sat across from me.

"So..." he pushed his chair closer, "a delicious soup!" He rubbed his hands, grabbed the spoon and carefully slurped the yellowish, salt water. The kitchen staff was already setting out the next dish: potatoes and black fried liver. The soup gone, Anton looked at me.

"Marvellous, right, all those frost-shattered rocks?" While he was talking, I thought of Pieter and Dr. Maat. How are they doing? They are sitting like princes with Eugene, Konstantin, Vitali, and Nicolai in their small cabin, surrounded by silence. Meanwhile, I worried about the time I would get on the island. Every day spent at anchor is critical. Now the schedule is also being nibbled at from the other side: Starkov, the Representative of the Academy has to be back in Moscow on 14 September, to catch the monthly flight from Moscow to Spitsbergen. He expects us to drop him off well before that at Amderma, on the North Russian coast. This puts us under enormous pressure. Starkov too looks grimmer by the day, and we'll have to use our time at Ice Harbor to the fullest to get the work done. Thus, it becomes almost impossible to journey inland. This is quite a blow, but better not piss and moan about it, for I, too, will have to strain to complete my tasks.

Saturday, 26 August 1995 – After some five hours of sleep, I awoke at 7:00 a.m. and dressed for a landing near yesterday's find. Instead, I soon found out, we will lose another day. Our chief, Pyotr Boyarsky doesn't want to risk our getting stuck on land if the weather suddenly deteriorates. The Russians have denied our survey ashore. This I am not sure about. Are they trying to keep us away from something? What is their agenda? Paranoia is not uncommon in these parts and for a good reason. Even the sailing to Ice Harbor is being delayed and we apparently wait out the arrival of a storm in the confines of the bay. "Just get some rest," Jerzy said comfortingly. "When the action comes, it'll be fast." I hung my waders to dry and rubbed them free of Novaya Zemlya's glittering black sand in one of the ship's corridors. As the heavy steel door clanged hermetically shut behind me, I sauntered whistling to the mess. The Captain, just coming down the stairs, put a finger to his lips. Embarrassed, I covered my mouth with my hand. Lore of the sea says that whistling aboard ship invites calamity. In the mess, I found Dr. Labutin and when he saw me, he jumped up and signalled me to come along. He's quite a character! George told me that Labutin is almost 50 years old, but he looks like a caricature of the Russian medical student: tufted hair; horn rimmed glasses; threadbare, checkered shirt with even the collar buttoned; and a brown knitted pullover. I followed him through the narrow corridors. Last night, bored, I had glued one of the paste on kid tattoos that were sent with the packages of batteries onto my chest. Once you're under his care, Dr. Labutin won't even look you in the face. He'll pull your T-shirt out of your pants and has eyes for what the meters indicate. But now, when he pulled my T-shirt up to place an electrode over my heart, he read "Kiss me" and a grin appeared across his face. Weight: 71 kilograms. Blood pressure: 130/75 ("Only if you see a girl walking down the street can it be somewhat higher," says Dr. Maat). Heartbeat 60 beats per minute. And then he signalled me to get on the bicycle again. The porthole was open and I could see icebergs. A good sized, blue berg lazily floated by, scraping the side of the ship. I thought back to Amsterdam; the city hadn't defeated me. I had only been there a short while and lived in a deserted warehouse on the quays of the IJ River.

At nights, when I had trouble falling asleep, I would walk into town. Outside, further down along the dark building, I would see the outlines of girls in high heels, a purse across one shoulder, against an endless stream of headlights. Some nights, there were a hundred of them 'working' and when I came home, they asked for cigarettes. Mind you, they are not all girls, you notice when they speak. Because of the solitary smoking and drinking, I wasn't in such great shape two months ago, when I entered Gawronski's basement office. But my strength quickly returned, entirely to the credit of my youth. When I had pedalled enough, Doctor Labutin gestured again and I sat up straight to look at the dial indicating my pulse. He was satisfied with the result. I could go now.

The wind had turned to the northwest, so that Ice Harbor on the other side of the island would now be in the lee. But would this be a stable situation? At night the weather forecasts from Dikson, Murmansk, and a German station still contradicted each other. The clouds had lifted somewhat, providing us with a better view of the Inostrantsev Bay or the 'Bay of Strangers.' Through binoculars, I observed the landscape that we had traversed yesterday. The plateau slopes towards dark mountains of ~300 m, behind which lies the ice cap; still hidden in clouds. In the southeast, the calving fronts of glaciers rise from the waters of the fjord. At the dark horizon of the Barents Sea is a number of small, rocky islands. I urged Jerzy to get us ashore in Ice Harbor at any cost. In my opinion, now that we have come so far, we should risk a bit more to go farther. This crew is restless and murmuring.

Working in the Arctic has a frustratingly low effort-to-yield ratio, and most days are spent waiting and watching. For this, we invested years of our lives; I see the stack of scientific papers we've carried along, know the methods and instruments at our disposal. More people have been up Mount Everest than on

Cape Spory Navolok, the wintering site on east Novaya Zemlya. We are prepared and standing by. In the afternoon, Jerzy called his scientists together to give them an accounting of this totally lost day. It is insane that we have been killing time lying at anchor in a flat sea and calm weather, only a stone's throw from our once-remote goal. Why did they not allow us ashore? "We've all been somewhat frustrated by today's events," Jerzy started. "The ship's lying at anchor is the Captain's decision. Here we have a good anchorage. Off Ice Harbor, *Kiriev* will have to cruise under difficult circumstances. That will cost fuel, fuel that we need to wrestle our way back to Archangelsk. We didn't schedule a landing today because we can ill afford to have five men ashore for five or six days. The point is: our barge is unstable if the swell increases. This morning, we were all ready for it, but I declined to congregate on deck in full gear because this would be much more demoralizing, especially if we have to repeat it several times. Should the situation remain unchanged, then we can say back home in the Netherlands that we were ready but unable to do anything. We are now supporting the Ivanov group. They will have to work for us. Looking at it this way, we have made pretty good progress in the ten days that we have been underway: the search for Barents' grave was landed and we were able to investigate the west coast. We are still working towards our schedule. By midway next week, that will be different."

"Then we will be working off our schedule," Bas grinned.

"Any questions?" – no questions. Just tired faces. We discussed the possibility of landing a small team tomorrow morning: Jerzy, two Russians, Herre, and me. At least, we could investigate what triggered the metal detector. Even while we were anchored offshore of Novaya Zemlya, our destination seemed farther away than ever.

With *Kiriev* still lying at anchor, engines shut off, I was on deck and gazed at the walls of ice, black rock formations, and inert blue icebergs that surrounded us. Two majestic glaciers, one left and one right, I could see coming down from an inland ice dome the whitest of whites. An eerie pewter-grey overcast made the blues stand out brilliantly. There was no sign of life: the vast bay appeared frozen in time. Rough Inostrantsev Bay, what may all have been here? The bay is 14 km wide and a 130 m deep, large enough to hide a submarine. The remoteness and desolation of the Arctic is a thing of the past, wrote one of the scientists of ice station Alpha in August 1958, after the surfacing of nuclear submarine *Skate* in a nearby polynya. It's captain, James Calvert in his 1960 book 'Surface at the Pole' quoted the base commander as saying: "Watching that periscope come slowly up in the centre of our little lake was the eeriest experience that I have ever had in my life." The submarines lower themselves silently into the deep Arctic Basin, crossing the pole in less than four days. Down decks I shared a weird concoction with Herre, Vadim Starkov, and Victor Dershawin, who brought it with him. A genuine Che Guevara poster decorates the wall of Herre and Victor's hot cabin. The pungent odour of perspiration, garlic, and booze is made bearable only by Herre's constant stream of rolled cigarettes. Jerzy came down earlier and told us that a strong cyclone is approaching and we must wait for it to pass: perhaps three days. We accepted his announcement without any reaction. Later on, lying pensively in my berth and feeling tired and not too good, I heard the anchor chain rattle throughout the vessel as it was being hauled in.

"They're hoisting the anchor," I said to myself, sitting up. "What are they up to now?" I looked into the cabin across the hallway. Starkov shook his head, saying in halting German that it couldn't be the anchor. Yet within a short time, the ship was buzzing with activity and the engine started. The vessel

had awakened! The decks were vibrating again. The hydraulic system was pressurized, and water fell clattering along the decks. The Captain's commands echoed through the corridors and sailors ran to duty. I stowed such loose items as drinking glasses, clothing, pens, books, and cassette tapes, and then hurried topside. As *Kiriev* began to move, a blackish sky hung over the clear white dome of the ice cap. It was beautiful with that light blue sea. The wind was blowing past the ship as if sucked from a northerly direction. I learned that forecasts from three weather stations had differed, leaving a 'window of opportunity'. Jerzy, Boyarsky, and the Captain decided that it was all or nothing now and shook hands for success. We can outrace the depression and will not waste one moment more. The course around north Novaya Zemlya will take approximately eight hours. It is 10:15 p.m. In the middle of the night, we will sail past the Ivanov Bay.

Sunday, 27 August 1995 – Six o'clock in the morning and awakened by the sun, which shone in my face through the porthole. A calm sea, and the ship was slicing through it at full speed toward the south. Not a cloud in the sky. The landscape of northeast Novaya Zemlya showed as a vast, light-brown expanse, slightly undulating and moulded by glaciers. It is a low lying land, with hardly any snow. The ice cap, some twenty kilometers inland, is undistinguishable through the haze on the horizon. Nothing can stop us now, I said to myself. I couldn't keep still and moved around excitedly. Two hours later *Kiriev* decreased speed. Just after 8:00 a.m., the vessel on which we left Archangelsk dropped anchor in the wide semicircular bay christened 'Ice Harbor' by our countrymen 400 years ago. The calm sea sloshed against a narrow edge of land fast ice along the shore. Cape Spory Navolok is a low and virtually flat headland. Feverishly, we gathered crates, boxes, our instruments, and backpacks on deck.

"I told you!" said Jerzy proudly. "I told you! When the action comes, it comes fast!" Then, the first man climbed down the rope ladder into the plashkot. Boyarsky at the railing blessed everyone going overboard with a good-luck kiss.

"Dawai!, he called out hoarsely, "Dawai!": Let's go, let's go!

"Just focus on Jerzy!" Anton yelled out to his cameraman, his voice breaking, as the barge drifted away from *Kiriev*. To add to the show, I fastened the Dutch banner and the blue Russian Navy cross with duct tape to a red and-white surveying pole. As we gathered speed and slid across the water, the banners unfurled and flapped in the wind. The ship's crew applauded and waved goodbye with raised fists. The high door of the landing craft limits sight, so I could not gauge our progress. I asked Hans Bonke, who was here two years ago, how wide the beach is and if it is easy to climb the plateau. "You just walk right up to it," he said. Suddenly, the shore loomed up close. Kravchenko's cross showed thin, in sharp contrast to the clear sky. Carefully, the fully loaded landing craft wended its way across the shoals that wrecked Barents' ship. Fifty meters to the beach.

The promontory's beach is an undulating field of dull brown gravels, about 150 meters wide and slightly inclined toward a low rocky cliff that blocks the view inland. The tide line was a few meters away when the craft almost came to a halt to keep from running aground. Seconds were passing with high viscosity. Then we heard the crunch of steel on rocks. Jerzy and I jumped into the surf, and I made my way across the beach. "This is it," I said to myself, "this is it." I came ashore at Cape Spory Navolok on 27 August 1995, at 10:00 in the morning. There are shouts behind my back and sounds of excitement, with the gentle swash of the sea on the shingles. I felt very comfortable all of a sudden, now that we have made it this far, and slowed down. I took in my new surroundings for a moment while the expedition's cargo stacked up along the high-tide line. Then, with my heart in my throat, I headed for the rocks. I could barely make any progress, strapped into the life jacket and rubber waders, which I had better taken off. But there is no time for that now. Gasping for breath, I struggled against the escarpment.

As soon as I could peer over the edge, I searched the flat, grey terrain for polar bears. The landscape was empty. The beams of the Saved House didn't catch my eye directly. Behind the cross, now really just in front of me, stretched a field of small wooden spikes. This is the grid that was left behind after the excavations of 1993, I quickly realized. In the far distance, the hills of Novaya Zemlya shone in weak sunlight. Very much content, I walked back, freeing myself of the life vest along the way. We made it after all.

Chapter Seven

In search of Willem Barents

1995 Journal of Pieter Floore

Friday, 25 August 1995 – The sea was very calm and there was nary a breeze under the low dull sky. On deck, the crew was busy preparing the plashkot, the landing craft that would bring us ashore. The huge pile of lumber we stowed aboard in Archangelsk was destined for use here at Ivanov Bay. So much of it had to be brought ashore that the plashkot made two trips. On the first trip, the entire team searching for the burial site landed: Eugene and Konstantin, Nicolai, Vitali, George and I. Everyone coming had to get a life vest from the fo'c'sle. Fastened to the outside of each vest is a small light, soldered rather clumsily to a battery with a short, thin wire. I was wondering if such a contraption would really work if I plunged into the Arctic Ocean, but I soon realized that it wouldn't have to perform for long: if I fell into the ocean, I'd have only a few minutes before succumbing to the just-above-freezing water temperatures. Perhaps this was why, upon our departure from Archangelsk, we were given a tiny wooden bird with fragile wings made of slivers: it is supposed to bring good luck. According to Yuri, Pomors traditionally carved these relics from a birch tree.

Boyarsky was turning the departure into quite a show, adopting a pose as soon as anyone was ready to take his photograph. Then, suddenly, I was ordered down the ladder and into the plashkot

– so suddenly that I forgot the kite and the photo camera that we wanted to use to make air photos. I put on my waders, suspecting that we'd have to make part of our way through the water. A few days ago, everyone had to choose between rubber waders or some most peculiar long rubber overshoes and a long, green raincoat. It is all Russian Army chemical protection gear, and looks more like relics of 1950s science fiction. It had been packed in large crates between layers of greaseproof paper and richly sprinkled with talcum. It sure is not lightweight, but very solid. I lowered myself alongside our steel ship by rope ladder into the plashkot. Everyone was seated on the bottom of the craft, along its sides, with a big load of beams and hardboard in the middle.

In drizzling weather, we set out for the beach. The bosun with the thick black moustache stood, legs apart, in the back of the craft, the helm pressed tightly against one leg. A sailor, lying supine in the hatchway to the engine compartment, was keeping the small diesel engine sputtering by holding a wrench tight around an engine part. The red barge belched laboriously, emitting plumes of deep-black smoke. Slowly, through the light rain, we watched those remaining aboard our ship grow smaller and fainter. A few hundred meters away, two walrus heads emerged above the waves, just long enough to be seen but not long enough for a good look. The beach was fast approaching, a front of gravel with a white, foamy beard of surf.

"Just like Zeeuwse Uitkijk," mumbled George. "With the fog and snowflakes near the coast, it looks just like Spitsbergen." On the beach, Henri was pushed over the side and tumbled overboard, short legs and all. Jerzy, who had come along to help unload lumber, reached over to hand him his film camera. The loading door was not coming down, so everything would have to be carried overboard. However, well before Henri was ready to film, almost everyone was ashore. "Dammit, wait a sec!" he yelled at a Russian, who didn't even look back and continued to transfer cargo. He pushed another man in front of his camera, but that guy didn't understand a thing and, again, walked right off. "Bistro, bistro!" the bosun yelled, and together with his buddies, he pushed the beams frenetically overboard into the surf. All lumber was gathered on the beach, personal stuff stacked nearby underneath a tarpaulin, and the vessel departed for yet another load. It was 11:15 in the morning.

Just about 200 meters from the water, Vitali designated a place to erect our camp. We dragged lumber to that spot and began to sort it into various types. Meanwhile, the *plashkot* had returned with the second load of supplies. The sea had grown somewhat more tempestuous, and the landing craft had turned out to be a less-than-ideal means of transport. The last load of lumber was simply tossed overboard into the water. Luckily, Jerzy had also brought along my kite and camera bag. He threw them at me, and then the *plashkot* backed off from the beach and, groaning angrily, turned to wrestle its way back through the surf. The six of us remaining on the darkened beach watched the tiny vessel slowly disappearing in the direction of the mother ship, which lay hidden in the ever-thickening fog. I didn't feel quite confident about the plan to build a cabin, so George and I immediately set about erecting our dome tent. We shored up the guywires with some heavy pieces of the driftwood that lay strewn across the beach. Eugene and Konstantin were also erecting a tent, a large and venerable object that fluttered in the wind. Feeling smug, I stood next to our small *North Face* model and said to George, "If they have to sleep in *that*, we'll get all four of them visiting us tonight." However, it turned out that the thing was intended only to store supplies and materials in somewhat drier conditions. In the meantime, Vitali was erecting the antenna – several meters tall – for his transmitter.

When the tents were up, we immediately started to build the cabin. It soon became clear to me that this was going to be our home for tonight. If that didn't work, I thought, at least we would still have our tent. The Russians conspired to do something totally unexpected. At home, Vitali had fashioned a complicated scheme to put together a shelter using three kinds of beams. Calmly, he started hammering a window-frame together, and with help from all of us, the south wall, containing the windows, soon lay ready. Next, the slightly taller north wall had to be built. Two men kept those walls erect while Vitali hammered the sidewalls together. After only a few hours, the edifice was already beginning to take shape. By evening, when the beams supporting the roof were being installed, my faith in Vitali's abilities and his building was growing stronger every hour. Even George had grown enthusiastic, although he continued to think that it would perhaps be better to sleep inside the tent tonight. Everyone was working strenuously to make sure the cabin would be finished tonight.

Since everybody was so involved in construction, we forgot to watch regularly for polar bears. When someone reminded the others of that, one person would briefly stay on alert until all hands were needed again. Luckily, the polar bears didn't show. When, at last, the last beams were placed on the roof, we had run out of long nails. Almost half the roof had to be fastened down with short tacks. Afterwards, we tightened plastic sheets across the roof to close all the seams. A canvas tarpaulin held in place with leftover wooden slats now covers the construction. Very solid it is not! Let's hope there won't be a storm with gusty winds, or we may lose the whole roof at once. We dismantled two old tents and fastened them against the cabin's exterior to minimize drafts. The house won't have a floor. We did, however, search the beach for four large beams to serve as a platform for the berths. There will be a low bunk, about 30 cm off the floor, along the entire length of the north-facing wall. At half past midnight, after Vitali hung the door, we brought our gear inside. An hour later the berths were ready, and we christened our shelter 'Saved House No. 2'. Everybody was dead tired. The platform with its thick sleeping bags looked enticing. Too bad I couldn't go to sleep yet! Just before bedtime, we had put together our guard-duty roster. George and I drew the first watch, from 1:00 to 4:00 a.m. Outside the cabin, I approached the still-burning fire every now and then, trying to stay warm. I took my duty as polar bear guard seriously, but the only creature moving around was George, dragging more firewood. I circled the cabin, of which I was now quite proud.

Our shelter had turned into a nice, compact little dwelling with a sloping roof, light brown in its canvas wrapping. George and I kept busy gathering firewood, yet those hours seemed to last an eternity.

North of the cabin is a meltwater stream coming down from the ice cap, where I filled the first kettle. It's 600 meters or so and during my small outing, I carried a Geiger counter to measure the radiation of the ground and the mosses. Although in 1993 no increased radiation was found near the Saved House, fallout from nuclear tests conducted on Novaya Zemlya before 1990 may have descended over this region and may continue to descend when glaciers melt. The counter's needle didn't budge: just a small beep caused by background radiation. I assume that if the surface is clean, the water cannot be that contaminated either. And even if it is, what can I do?

To my utter amazement, on the way back and on the smooth ridge straight behind the cabin, I stumbled on a cairn, which, at first sight, resembled a grave. How could it be true that we had built our camp barely 200 meters from our goal? The pile covered a rectangular surface that had the measurements of a double grave: about 2 x 1.5 m, with two headstones and the other end clearly pointed towards the coast. In short, it had all the characteristics of the graves at the whaling station cemetery on the island of Zeeuwse Uitkijk in Svalbard. Besides, it would have been an easy walk from the waterline, approximately 350 m across a flat, gravel pavement. With this discovery resonating in my head, I called George, because the cairn was easily visible from outside the cabin. Tomorrow, we will look further.

Saturday, 26 August 1995 – All awake at 8:00, we spent the entire morning making improvements to the cabin. The Russians like to cook on a bottled-gas stove. The gas bottle remains outside the cabin, and Vitali has nailed a shelf for the stove to the inside wall. While George and I protested – because the cabin is damp as it is, with six men in a few square meters – he finished the cooking corner with a piece of tarpaulin, without bothering to provide drainage. Eugene and Nicolai were already starting to decorate the small kitchen. George tried to persuade the gentlemen to change plan, but his objections were dismissed. On the contrary, they contended, the stove would just make the interior warm and cozy. After sitting dejectedly on his cot for fifteen minutes, George took his knife, walked outside, and without a word, cut a small ventilation flap in the plastic window-sheet. Our colleagues good-naturedly shook their heads, but that was all. Well! That's apparently the Russian method of solving differences of opinion. I viewed the grey scenery outside through the opalescent plastic window. Rain drizzled down now and then, making the surroundings desolate and oppressive.

Our first objective is inspection of two burial sites discovered by Kravchenko. The 'BAR grave' must be somewhat to our west on Cape Petrovsky (which connects to Cape Varnek). The other possible grave is farther northeast, on Cape Vilkitsky; that one was adorned with the skull of a polar bear, according to a drawing made by Kravchenko. The spot I discovered last night then is our third possible grave. But first we must find these other two. George and I have fifty kilometers of shore, from Cape Petrovsky to Cape Vilkitsky, to inspect during the next week. Vitali and Nicolai will remain near the cabin. Nicolai doesn't have to venture far from camp for his botanical research. He is compiling an inventory of the mosses growing from the shore to higher elevations. On the first day, he has already discovered a plant not recorded before on this island.

In the morning, the four of us walked over to Site No. 3 behind our cabin. We decided to photograph the cairn and return tomorrow to sketch it. George and I then walked on towards the west, towards Cape Petrovsky. As we were walking along the edge of the coastal escarpment, George suddenly spotted something on the beach below. He tumbled down and I followed.

"What a hunk!" he exclaimed cheerily. Frozen in a small, icy puddle lay the skeleton of a polar bear, its skull half sticking out of the ice and its teeth in a frozen grin just above the surface. Slowly and carefully we tried to pry it loose with a pioneer's shovel, but it was stuck too deeply in the ice. Novaya Zemlya is hanging on tightly to this treasure. A few hundred meters further, we spotted a cairn high on the promontory. This solitary pile of rocks is the only sign so far that others have ever been here before us. Vitali and Nicolai joined us to review the pile, which has partly collapsed. If it signifies a grave, it is not large enough to hold two bodies. Before we moved on, I turned on the GPS to establish the coordinates of this marker.

The elevation of the escarpment was increasing, so we decided to stay high and cross the plateau, expecting to see Ice Cape come quickly into view. From a distance, I could already spot the glacier, with its moraines-massive piles of debris-along the bay.

The extent of these moraines suggests that at one time the ice tongue filled the entire fjord. During Barents' time, the glacier fronts formed a more or less continuous barrier over a distance of 30 km so that one could rightfully speak of an 'ice cape'. Icebergs released by the calving glaciers are depicted in the map of north Novaya Zemlya. From the plateau we descended to the beach. Screeching terns circled above the ice. My first encounter with a glacier was magnificent! The glacier is wonderful. Is this Ice Cape? At the mouth of the bay, we found a three-legged wooden beacon, and next to it, another cairn similar to the one we had discovered earlier in the afternoon. This cairn stands one-meter-tall and is clearly a navigational mark.

The clouds lowered during the afternoon, and by day's end, we were thoroughly soaked. My Gore-Tex jacket is not as waterproof as advertised, water has penetrated my underwear, and my shoes are sopping wet and cold. Nothing I am afraid dries inside the cabin. The temperature is +3°C, and a piercing wind is blowing from the northwest. Still no polar bears. I did see reindeer tracks near the wooden beacon and footprints of a descending polar bear in the snow along the foot of the escarpment. But if you ask me, those are not very recent.

Sunday, 27 August 1995 – Again, I stood the 1:00 to 4:00 a.m. watch with George. Each night, Konstantin and Eugene have been working the 'dogwatch' from 4:00 to 7:00. We offered to stand that watch too, but they said they didn't mind it. Tonight, turned out to be a pleasure; I had imagined I would have to drag myself through these three hours again. Instead, I made small talk with George, gathered some firewood, and walked the beat, the rifle slung across my shoulders. I have had enough time to update my diary (Friday and Saturday's entries). There really isn't much time or room inside the cabin to do this during the day.

After breakfast, at 9:00, Vitali contacted *Kiriev* via radio and learned that the first group may at last be able to land near Ice Harbor around noon today. I hope they are still in good spirits and have sufficient time to finish the program. We spent the entire day at Site No. 3, which lies 200 meters behind the cabin on the beach berm. The longer I look at it, the more I think it really is a grave. I assembled my kite inside the cabin to make some air photos of the undisturbed site before we begin to excavate. Outside, while I maneuvered the behemoth around, a gust of wind snapped a cross-member. Luckily, I had a spare one with me, but it had better not happen again, because that would end the aerial photography.

The wind was a bit too strong for kite photography, but if I didn't fly it now, I wouldn't get a chance to record the unopened grave. Already, I had had to stop Eugene and Konstantin from marking the spot with tape measures and stakes, thus marring the picture. When the kite was finally aloft with the camera attached, the line ran off the spool so fast that I'm not sure precisely what happened. I tried to hang on to it barehanded, but too late! The kite dove rapidly, and the camera skipped twice across the rock-hard ground. "Now you've done it!" I thought. I trudged toward the camera and noted that it was damaged. I felt terrible and I hadn't even started! Then I also noticed that the kite string had burned a deep cut in the palm of my hand.

In spite of its wounds, however, the camera appeared to be functioning as required. The remote control effortlessly triggered the shutter. I hope the scratches on the lens won't be too distracting. On the second try, the kite soared as expected. I handed the reel over to Nicolai; he's the biggest in our group and if anyone can control the kite, he's the one. The two of us maneuvered the kite over the grave, with Nicolai holding the reel tightly in his arms. His chubby body was lifted a bit at every step. I took pictures from 40 m straight up over the grave. When all was completed and I was stowing my gear, I was shocked to discover that the ASA setting was wrong: 400 instead of 100 as indicated on the roll of film. In all the commotion, I had forgotten to check the film speed. Again, all for naught!

After lunch, I flew the kite once more, this time with the correct camera settings. Then, it was finally Eugene and Konstantin's turn, and they drew the grave to scale. They used a marvelous method: in chalk they drew auxiliary grid lines over the surface, and *voilà*, the drawing was done in about an hour. In the meantime, George used a compass to locate the spot in relation to the beacon and the cabin on the beach. We numbered the rocks, so that they could be returned to their original locations. The excavation covers an area of 2.5 x 2.5 m, which narrowly encloses the rock pile. Together, all of us took turns digging, but the masses of pebbles made it slow going.

Of us all, Eugene was working steadily and quietly, and he didn't want any help. According to George, he's difficult to get along with, because he doesn't believe in much consultation. Konstantin is his asistant. Vitali was taking measurements of the elevations, using a level, and taking photographs. For the rest he stayed away from excavating. To my surprise, the soil below the rock pile still was undisturbed. We dug to a depth of 75 cm, but each scoop diminished our hopes of finding a grave. No one has ever dug here before. Eugene strictly followed the prescribed Russian archaeological procedure, making a drawing of the empty area. Around 7:00 p.m. the job was finished and the cairn restored. Everyone was pretty much tired out by the work, and we decided to hit the sack early.

Today, the weather was pretty good: the occasional drizzle and a temperature of +3°C. I had hung my jacket outside last night and found it completely dry this morning. Inside the cabin it remains cold and clammy, and of course it gets even damper every time we boil water. Nicolai has collected all kinds of mosses and other tiny plants. He has installed a shelf in the cabin on which to dry the seaweed he collected along the high-tide line. Tonight, George and I are standing watch from 3:00 to 6:00 a.m. I've used the opportunity to hoist the university flag on the three-legged beacon a short distance from the cabin. It does not flutter much, because there is hardly any breeze. Now a soft drizzle has started again.

Monday, 28 August 1995 – Got up at 9:00 a.m. The wind was coming from the southwest, and it was dry: a good day to investigate the long stretch along the northeast coast. We set off at 12.30, right after lunch. George and I carried our backpacks with some food and the necessary gun. Two meltwater rivers discharge into the northeastern part of Ivanov Bay. The first one, about half a kilometer east of the cabin, is easy to cross. The last two days we have been taking turns hauling drinking water from this stream. Quite in keeping with nineteenth-century tradition, we have named this 'Van Veen River' after our business director. Soon after we came to a much larger river that, according to our map, originates directly at the ice cap. This river even has a name: Snezhnaya River. Tree trunks and, farther inland, even large iron buoys for fishing nets or something akin can be found washed up in this river's valley. On the riverbanks I picked a few small plants for Nicolai's collection. George thought this a good spot to try out those heavy-caliber *Brenneke* cartridges the Russians gave us. This cartridge contains a leaden projectile that can stop large game with one shot. I had never shot such ammo and needed to practice its use. I selected a heavy steel buoy as target.

The target shooting went very well: I was off by about 20 cm, George by about 5 cm.

"He's 5 cm low," he states, as if nothing is wrong with his marksmanship. Such a large-caliber gun imparts a powerful recoil to one's shoulder. It was a weird sensation to see the bullet ricochet heavily and hear the sound echoing as it died in the valley. We felt like two pranksters, as if we were doing something illegal. We even lowered our voices. Yesterday, George cleaned and oiled all three rifles. The Russians had just left those weapons outside, and after two days they already showed considerable corrosion.

Then I donned my big, rubber wading trousers. Because I am taller and heavier than George, I would cross first and seek a way through the wild stream. I tied a rope around my waist. The first steps into the river were OK, but then the bottom dropped rapidly. Suddenly, I slipped sideways and found myself submerged in the frigid, roaring water. Water everywhere! I couldn't feel the cold – I couldn't feel anything – but the river angrily dragged me along. George managed with the rope to get me back on my feet. Moments later, sopping wet, I stood shivering on the side.

"You capsized big-time!" George burst out laughing.

"Sure, laugh!" I said, panting. "I was a near goner, idiot!" Quickly I emptied my backpack and video bag onto a small rise near the river's mouth. Water gushed out by the bucket. Luckily, it was sunny, so that the contents might dry. I am worried about the small video camera that Anton van Munster gave me to record important events. It has gotten damp, and in some tapes I have seen pearls of moisture. Anton would have liked to come along himself, but Jerzy opposed that idea. Recording the investigations near the Saved House remains our first priority. I hope that the film was not damaged, because in the past few days I have already captured a few things on videotape. Half undressed, I sat atop a big mound, with dollar bills spread out around me to dry. These were our emergency funds: just enough to pay for a helicopter flight to Dikson in Siberia, for even in case of emergency, *Aeroflot's* slogan is 'no pay, no way'. We certainly learned that in 1993. George, meanwhile, was searching for a fordable place.

"How goes it now?" he grumbled. "You are supposed to tell by the water surface where you can cross." It took him a good hour of crisscrossing, with a long stick and great concentration, to feel his way through the river. Once he had figured it out, it took us barely ten minutes to cross.

We finally set off again at 4:00 p.m. Our goal was Cape Vilkitsky, where Dmitri Kravchenko in 1979 discovered a circular cairn. It had a height of 1.2 m and sat atop a rectangular disturbance measuring 1.8 x 2 m, 'like a double-grave,' according to his report [1983]. In front of the pile, shows a drawing, there is a bear skull. Upon closer inspection this skull showed a bullet hole, which, according to Kravchenko, had exactly the same size (18 mm) as a shot from a musket, for instance (it is suggested) a musket carried by Barents' men. That site was at the top of my list. Unfortunately, with all the setbacks, it was getting late and I doubted if we could finish the 15 20 km we still had to go. Nonetheless, it was a splendid trip along the coast. To my left, the Arctic Ocean stretched to the horizon. The beach was getting narrower, and in some places it extended only a few meters to the steep rock escarpment. Eventually, we climbed onto the plateau looking for cairns. The ground was very even, a compact layer of neatly sorted pebbles. The few large rocks could already be seen from a great distance. The sun's low angle caused every irregularity to stand out in contrast. Water seeps from the soil in deeper spots, so we found patches of moss and grasses in small depressions. Around these 'Novaya Zemlya jungles' we immediately spotted hoofprints and excrement from reindeer, but the animals themselves were nowhere to be seen. Toward the inland, I could see the black debris hills behind which the great icecap is hidden.

Up to Cape Marii, we had found only one cairn, at Cape Drizhenko. Eugene had explained that these rock piles are called *guri*. They were supposedly erected by the Pomors, the seafaring Russians living on the mainland coast. I think that the *guri* don't date back to the sixteenth century; otherwise, De Veer would certainly have reported them just as he described the Pomor crosses. Cape Marii provides a marvelous view of Ivanov Bay on one side and the two Orange Islands on the other. Both islands are flat-topped columns of pale stone, sheer cliffs that rise straight from the dark blue sea. It now became clear to me that if you sailed along the coast, you would have a view of these islands around the entire north cape. The grey landscape assumed a near-bluish tint in the clear sunshine, and it looked as though we could see infinitely far away.

The journey back from Cape Marii to our cabin took a good three and a half hours, and we arrived around 9:00 in the evening. The others were sitting outside in the sunshine. Eugene showed us some bear prints along the beach. Well, well! They are around somewhere. But how old are these tracks? From yesterday, or last month? One cannot tell. Tonight, all of us will be feeling somewhat less carefree as we sit around the campfire.

Our friends had waited for us with dinner. Konstantin has been taking care of our meals for the past few days. At dinner we discussed our experiences, and George presented a plan for the next two days. He intends to reach Cape Vilkitsky. We could stay overnight at the cape and start excavating the next day. Eugene does not think it is such a good idea to split the group. There is only one radio, and without radio contact he cannot take responsibility for the proposed project. "We'll just have to try and accomplish that in two trips," George said later. "Too bad. But if the weather remains like this, they will be great trips and quite a blessing after all that rain."

For the remainder of the evening, we sat outside around the campfire. It wasn't cold, because there was hardly any breeze. Bare feet close to the fire, I let my sopping-wet shoes dry out. Our watch tonight runs from midnight to 3:00 a.m. Just before midnight, with the sun low on the horizon and the sky clear, hoarfrost started to form. George deliberated collecting the bear's skull he had discovered on Saturday. Maybe tomorrow's weather would be worse, and we wouldn't have a chance to go in that direction. George left and it turned out to be quite a hike. After an hour and a half, he emerged from a thick fog, which had set in extremely fast. It was not altogether without peril, because in fog our polar bear friends can approach unseen. Sunrise was at 2:47 a.m.

Tuesday, 29 August 1995 – Around 9:30, finally, everybody was up and about. Vitali contacted Kiriev: everything's OK with the team at Ice Harbor. For today, we had planned to complete our route to Cape Vilkitsky. Eugene, however, made it clear he preferred to stick with Boyarsky's original instructions to conduct investigation of the beach between Cape Petrovsky and Cape Varnek, which lies in the opposite direction. We all agreed on that and departed around noon in a westerly direction. The weather, again, was exceptionally fine: nary a whisper of a breeze and partly cloudy, with excellent visibility, just like yesterday. Temperature at departure time was 7°C, no less! We set off for Ice Cape, following the curve of the bay shore. I compared the notes from our first reconnaissance trip, on Saturday, with the topographical map. It turns out that the bay with the ice tongue, Petersen Glacier, may not be the only 'Ice Cape'. Other fjords lie three times farther away and are several kilometers wide. They probably

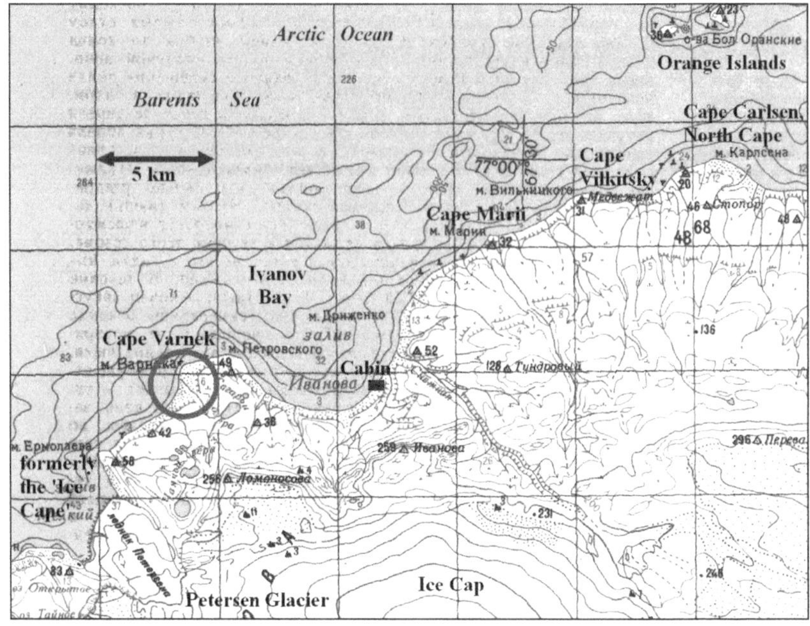

Official 1:50.000 topographic map of North Novaya Zemlya prepared in 1952. Circle marks probable location of Barents' burial. Block marks cabin on Ivanov Bay beach.

connected four hundred years ago to more of an ice front than today. Halfway to Cape Petrovsky, the beach is cut by an unnamed river, which we easily forded using waders. We christened it Boyarsky River. Just before we reached the river, George had found a second bear skull, half-buried in the beach and covered with a layer of moss. Nearby was the skull of a seal, and a bit farther away, that of a dolphin or porpoise. Along the beach at the foot of the steep escarpment there were plenty of bones of seal, walrus, polar bears, and whales. The old snowbanks that remained in the shelter of hillslopes and small valleys were melting. Underneath those, there are likely more bones, which may have been there for centuries. The beach was littered with whale ribs and vertebrae. You spot them easily because they contrast with the greyish gravel on the beach, overgrown with green mosses that feed on the phosphate released by the bone.

We crossed the river and proceeded along the rim of the plateau. We didn't find a thing all the way to Cape Petrovsky, where Eugene and Konstantin rejoined us. They had been walking way ahead of us, but suddenly stopped and hurried back in our direction. Mighty excited and terrified, they told us they had seen a bear. A bear? That, I'd like to see, too! Focusing my binoculars on the spot they were pointing at, I looked for a bear. And indeed! On a mossy spot, I saw a polar bear lying on its back taking a nap – like a puppy, with its legs spread out. According to the Russians, it was now impossible to go on. It's hard to predict the mood of a bear aroused from sleep. "Bear is mysterious animal," said Nicolai, "very dangerous." As far as he was concerned, this was it: we couldn't go on. George lodged a feeble protest: "After all, we do have guns, don't we?" But even he was not very much at ease. During his stay on Spitsbergen, he hardly saw any bears, so he doesn't really know the animal very well. Now what? We could not and would not be allowed to go any farther. During our retreat, high on the plateau of Cape Petrovsky, we stumbled on the remnants of a tent camp. There were cans, nails, pieces of electrical cable, a tent sail, and bricks. In the vicinity I discovered a pair of wooden skis. Eugene told me this was a land surveyors' camp. According to Eugene, the camp is forty years old and was occupied during the making of the topographic map that we are now using. I took a second to look around, but Nicolai thought I needed to hurry. Although there was little chance that the bear might be in pursuit, everyone remained on the alert.

In the evening, as we were once again comfortably seated around the campfire, Nicolai suddenly called out: "Bear! Bear!" Nobody could see a thing, so he raced inside to get a flare. It turned out to be a seal in the surf! Everybody cracked up, and also Nicolai appreciated the humor of it. Back around the fire, Eugene started talking about his fascination with the mystical aspects of archaeology: *Hyperboreas*: the mystic North, and the archaeological hunts during World War II by the Nazi organization *Ahnenerbe*, searching for proof of occult matters. In the same breath, he offered his thoughts on ethnicity. George said, "There's too much talk here about occultism and ethnic nonsense!" He was getting mighty annoyed and sneered: "That nonsense about determining ethnic differences via cranial measurements! He's shamelessly pronouncing ideas from the nineteenth century – and he's a scientist! Of course, these ideas were suppressed for years and only now are surfacing again. They simply continue where they left off in 1917. And we have to conduct explorations with such types." I couldn't get too excited about it. I rather like listening to Eugene. He can talk enthusiastically, and one anecdote follows the next. Eugene has really loosened up. One rarely has such a conversation about someone's interests, and quiet Eugene continues to amaze me.

Wednesday, 30 August 1995 – We woke to a terrific storm raging overhead, the wind pounding hard on the roof of the cabin. The beams were bending quite a bit and the plastic window sheets kept flapping violently. Then Vitali arrived to warn me that the *North Face* tent was about to be launched into space. The small tent had been semi-flattened, and the arched frames were having a hard time. Despite the driftwood logs that George and I had used to fortify the stakes, the wind was now so strong that the tent was almost completely flattened. The Russian tent, inflated by the wind and tethered to its last guy wires, was soaring about one meter off the ground, dancing up and down in short gusts. Frenetically we tried to salvage the tents and ultimately put them down. Afterwards, sitting down to breakfast, I could feel the shivers coming on and crawled back into my sleeping bag, feeling sick. George went back out into the intensifying storm to retrieve, as best he could, the remaining items from our flattened tent. He also reinforced the plastic windows with duct tape, for if the wind were to blow underneath the cabin roof, that would really cook our goose. Perspiring, I stayed in my sleeping bag. By 2:00 p.m., the wind had completely ripped the plastic off the roof. This morning, George had wanted to use the canvas tarpaulin we've been sleeping on to cover the roof. "No," our Russian colleagues said. "We'd better wait until the wind decreases." You couldn't chase them outside with a stick! They remained in their sleeping bags, resigned to observing the destruction of the roof.

There was something odd about this storm. It came over the hills straight from the ice cap, but it felt strangely warm. In the afternoon, the temperature inside the cabin climbed to 13°C.

"It's *Bora*," said Nicolai. What is *Bora*? The Spirit of the North? The Scourge of our Cabin? Nicolai couldn't tell me any more about it. Either he doesn't know, or he doesn't know how to translate it. At 5:30 p.m., the storm suddenly stopped. Now was the time to fortify the canvas tarps on the roof, but the damage had been done. Just when we were ready to step outside, it began to rain and the roof started leaking all over. Water poured down on the platform where our sleeping bags lie. Vitali and Eugene nailed the sail meant for groundcover onto the roof, and we cut up the torn storage tent for more roofing material. The installation progressed slowly. George marched around the cabin giving instructions, but the roofers ignored him. After almost an hour and much grumbling, the new roof was in place, fortified with additional beams and rocks. I hope that it will keep the interior of the cabin dry for the days remaining, but I don't have much confidence in those threadbare pieces of canvas tent. Everyone recovered after a solid and tasty meal of rice and canned stew with gyros spices. We sat happily, sipping coffee and discussing the Universe. Tonight, it has stayed warm: +7°C.

Our night watch tonight runs from 4:00 to 7:00 a.m. For the first time, we saw icebergs floating into the bay. Around 5:00, a dark object took shape on the northern horizon. At first, I thought it must be a submarine surfacing to inspect our encampment. We heard via radio this morning that *Kiriev* had encountered a Navy ship near Cape Zhelaniya. Perhaps they passed the word that we're out here? George and I took turns observing that object through our binoculars. After twenty minutes, George called me out onto the beach: "If you ask me, they're whales!" he said excitedly. "Look! Two of them! A small one and a big one!" I could already see with the naked eye that the object was split in two. The creatures were slowly changing position, and sometimes they submerged. We watched them for a while longer, but they were too far away to see any details. What were they? Even with binoculars we couldn't make out much. I didn't even see them spout.

Thursday, 31 August 1995 – When our watch finished at 7:00 a.m., George and I didn't feel like sleeping. We could thus take advantage of a long day and depart immediately for Cape Varnek and Ice Cape. I woke up Nicolai, who was snoring loudly. The Russians sleep in heavy, cotton sleeping bags with kapok filling. Apparently they're effective, because neither of our partners complains about being cold. Every evening, Nicolai hits the sack in a woolen Army nightshirt, his head covered with a leather flight cap. I told him of our plan and he approved, provided we were careful. As he put it: "Achtung! Because of bear, you know."

This time, I wasn't wearing anything heavy, just waders and a field pack filled with bread, sausage, and cheese. After walking for an hour and wading through the Boyarsky River, I spotted a bear in the distance; a big, yellow polar bear, messing around along the remnants of frozen snow below the escarpment where the beach curves out towards Cape Petrovsky. To be stopped again by a bear, that would be too much for us. We briefly put our heads together and worked out a plan. It appeared best to cut straight across the promontory towards Ice Cape, behind the bear, hoping it wouldn't get a whiff of us. George wanted to confront the bear and get it over with, but I was against this. At the first opportunity, we left the beach and climbed the plateau. The trek led towards Cape Jermolaev and right through the Gagarii Lakes, so called for the red- or black-breasted Arctic loons (*Gavia* sp.; *gagara* in Russian) that breed on a small island in the largest lake. It is late in the season now, and the birds have left. When we first reached here on Saturday, a week ago, Nicolai discovered a freshwater shrimp in these small bodies of water. It's puzzling where these shrimps came from. Were they left behind when the lakes were isolated from the sea? Do these animals evolve so rapidly, or did they get here some other way?

The going was difficult between the lakes, over streams of large boulders, so-called 'block fields', alternating with marshy terrain. Fully concentrating, I jumped from boulder to boulder. It was really slow and soon became terribly exhausting. At 12.30 we came to a rivulet that thundered down the plateau alongside a big pile of glacial debris and into the sea. Standing atop the debris hill [lateral moraine], I could see the Petersen Glacier before me in all its glory. In the sunshine, the glacier ice seemed to radiate blue light. These days the glacier tongue lies several kilometers inside the fjord, but at one time, it carved out this entire bay. The fjord is more than a kilometer wide. From here the coast bends towards the southwest. On the opposite side I could see a broad beach that could easily be accessed from the sea, but it was beyond our reach. We couldn't go any farther now. If we wanted to go to the other side, we'd have to cross the glacier, which would be extremely dangerous. Some of its crevasses are several meters wide. A glacier calving into a fjord. Is like a loaf of sliced bread with its sections falling apart.

From this westernmost point in our research area, we walked back along the beach towards Cape Varnek and then cross back to our cabin. The beach is very narrow in the fjord, and the cliffs of the plateau are almost vertical. The polished and stratified rock layers are awesome. Where a softer layer overlies a harder one, more erosion has taken place, and those eroded strata form excellent balconies for birds' nests, which, indeed, abound. It would have been nearly impossible to drag the deceased Barents and Claes Andriesz to the top of this plateau for burial. "Imagine! They'd have had to ascend that slope with two stiffly frozen ice dummies," said George. "That would've meant

Eugene and Konstantin surveying rock-pile (Site #3) on a 13 m-high beach ridge in Ivanov Bay. The shelter erected by the expedition can be seen near the water line (P. Floore 1995).

tackling and hoisting, and I don't think they would have had enough pep for that." Nodding, I looked past the cliffs. "If they buried them over here, it could only have been on the beach." That conclusion makes our search nearly a mission impossible, because the beach is covered with numerous pieces of lumber and rubbish, and big boulders regularly tumble down the slope. We kept our hopes up and continued on our way. For kilometers we walked along the beach without seeing anything of importance, not even a marker. It was only southwest of Cape Varnek, near a flat strand about a kilometer wide, that we were able with some ease to climb back onto the plateau. Here a braiding stream ran down the beach. At the widest of its channels, about 100 meters from the sea, we saw a log cabin. This one had been put together from tree trunks that washed ashore, the cracks between the logs sealed with mosses and clay. The south wall, seven beams high, was interrupted by a doorframe, and we found the door lying behind the cabin. It had been hinged with strips of rubber. Half the roof, made up of small, adjoining logs, was still intact. Inside the cabin, along its entire length, there was a bench to sleep or sit on. In the corner, to the right of and next to the door, we discovered a large pile of rocks, which must have served as a fireplace. In the fire pit we spotted an iron buoy like those so often found along the shore. A square hole had been cut out of it, and it looked as though it had been used as a small stove. Here and there we found modern wire nails driven into the cabin's wood. Everything indicated that the cabin had probably been used several decades ago, but we could only guess who might have used it. Perhaps some coast guard soldiers, pelt hunters, or Pomors? Or maybe the Nazis or the land surveyors?

The skull of a large walrus lay on the beach not far from that small cabin. A long ivory tusk was still pointing away from the massive skull. For the rest, all its molars were still present, but when we picked up the skull, they came falling out. They were flat, round bony pieces that were not deeply embedded in the jaw: perfect for cracking shells. The ivory tusk was more than half a meter long, heavy and splendidly formed. After our visit to the cabin, we climbed back onto the plateau to investigate the last kilometers towards Cape Petrovsky. This stretch didn't produce any new finds either. We cut straight across to Ivanov Bay and, again, passed the surveyors' camp. From far away, we could see rusted fuel barrels and wooden fences for the tents that once stood here. The area was littered with aluminum tent poles, wooden crates, tent floors, and rusted, metal tools. I even dug up a complete cot amid the mess. We didn't stay long there but kept moving, because this was the area where we had spotted the bear in the morning. It's also near the spot where one of those animals was sleeping two days ago. Near the Boyarsky River, we descended towards the beach. In the distance we could see our cabin with the red flag of the university flapping in the wind. Around 6:00 p.m. we arrived 'home'.

Vitali and Nicolai, as it turned out, had kept us well in their view this morning and were very much concerned. They had also seen the loitering bear. Then it caught a seal, and after this meal it fell asleep on the beach. They lost sight of it later in the afternoon. Just before we returned, Vitali had talked to *Kiriev*. He told us that the ship is now anchored off the Cape Zhelaniya polar station. Boyarsky wants us to stand by and is waiting for the appropriate moment to come in and take us off the island. Konstantin and Eugene aren't wasting any time and have begun to pack their equipment. Shovels and pickaxes stand tied together next to the door. After a second contact with the ship at 9:00 p.m., we learned that there had been a delay, and we can't expect the vessel until tomorrow morning at the earliest. It had been a clear and sunny day, with little wind and air temperatures around +5°C, but in the afternoon the weather deteriorated rapidly.

Friday, 1 September 1995 – Yesterday I didn't quite understand why we had to pack up immediately, while we still had a lot of work ahead of us. Today it turned out that very bad weather was forecast. Winds have increased towards Beaufort 6. It is raining, and as long as there is an onshore wind, the landing craft cannot collect us. Nicolai cooked up a really disgusting breakfast, mixing overcooked spaghetti with canned meat in a large pot. And he expected us to eat this greasy dish! Even ketchup failed to disguise its grubby, flat taste. George was about to throw up and avoided most of it. The others didn't want much to do with it either. Nicolai thought he'd do us a favor by preparing so much food that we would have our fill for the rest of the day. Meanwhile, the bread was gone and the thought of filling my mug once again with this pile of misery left me in a deep funk. There wasn't much to do, and indecision soon became the order of the day. No one had a desire to go outside in the driving rain. The cabin is somewhat cramped with six men, as there's less than a meter of walking space along the bunks. Four boxes containing our provisions are on the floor. During mealtimes, a board on top of these boxes serves as table. We sit next to one another at the edge of the bunk, where one's feet would be. Today I sat against the outer wall, with George, Eugene, Konstantin, and Nicolai next to me. Against the other wall was Vitali, with the radio transmitter next to him. Underneath the elevated floor we had stored things that aren't that necessary, such as a Russian-English dictionary. My clothes were still hanging on a couple of nails in the wall. On this desolate day we just sat next to each other, doing nothing. Nicolai was snoring in his sleeping bag wearing his coat, and Konstantin was chain-smoking in a corner of the kitchen. The entire cabin soon filled with a bluish haze.

At 6:00 p.m. we would get to hear if the vessel would arrive and, more importantly, when. However, we would probably be here for some time. I hadn't done a thing all day – just packed my possessions, cleaned up, and stowed the tent, and that's that. We had all spent the afternoon collecting wood for a big fire next to our cabin. Around the fire there were now three wooden screens, built to ward off the southwestern wind. A big drawback of this new construction is that it allows the smoke to circulate, and one cannot sit close to the fire without being troubled by it. The Russians don't think that's a problem: according to them, smoke is good and it keeps one warm.

Konstantin exhausted his supply of cigarettes several days ago, and now he was rolling something – I didn't know what – himself. Judging by the pungent odors, he seemed to either smoking pot or burning someone's rubbish from the yard. Then I saw what he was doing: he was rolling a small pile of tea (from the little boxes adorned with a small blue elephant) into a scrap of newspaper he had picked up from the floor. He tells me that he always used to do that with his buddies, years ago, when he was assigned to the border patrol. "Tea contains nicotine," he said; and thus, in his mind, it should be OK.

Dinner consisted of this morning's leftover spaghetti. I tried to improve its taste somewhat by adding spices, but that had the opposite effect. Later, when lying down on my sleeping bag, I suffered quite a bit of discomfort. Eugene returned to his favorite topic after dinner, launching into yet another lecture about ethnic differences and cranial types. He even mentioned the prewar theories about ethnic dispersion of the German archaeologist Kossina. This was like raising a red flag for George! He didn't want to hear about this and came close to starting an argument. Luckily, we were able to change the subject when, at 6:00 p.m. sharp, we heard that our vessel won't get here until tomorrow. All day, a storm has been raging from the south and southwest.

Saturday, 2 September 1995 – The weather grew even worse overnight. While George and I stood watch from 4:00 to 7:00 a.m., a strong wind blew in from the sea, carrying a steady drizzle. George used the opportunity to relax and photograph our cabin and its surroundings. Although the thick overcast produced little light, he was able to get something using a tripod and very long exposure times. I stayed up until 8:00 a.m., then decided I'd better get a few hours of sleep. This morning, for the first time, I was bothered by cold feet, because the wind was blowing straight at the door and creating a draft by my sleeping bag. The 'door' is more like a panel. We have to pull it closed and fasten it with a rope to a wooden reel. Its hinges were made out of two pieces of walrus hide that Vitali found on the beach.

I woke up at 10:00 a.m. I might as well have stayed put, for we're not doing anything other than waiting for *Kiriev*. Radio contact at 9:30 had brought the news that the ship's arrival has been delayed once again. The connection was very bad, so we were unable to learn the reason for all these delays. It's still damp inside the cabin. The canvas on the roof has clearly tightened shut, but water still drips without interruption on the sleeping bags. George brought along the waterproof, Navy-issue Gore-Tex outer bag, which has served him well. I left mine on *Kiriev*, and I'm very sorry about that now. Besides, George swears by Army and Navy surplus materials and won't hear a word about sponsored outdoor sports items. He had already suffered problems with defective sports clothing fifteen years ago on Spitsbergen. According to him, nothing has changed in fifteen years: it looks good but it falls apart quickly. The mood inside is still A-OK. The change in Eugene's attitude remains most remarkable. On board, he was gruff and very curt. It looked as if he didn't want to talk to you. But since our arrival in Ivanov Bay, he's been telling one joke after another, all day long. If he isn't doing that, he's singing or teaching George and me some droll Russian saying. Konstantin always hangs around and functions as comic sidekick for Eugene's zinging repartee. Nicolai, on the other hand, isn't talking much. He is by nature a man of few words, but he also has only a rudimentary knowledge of German or English. Often, too, he's unable to say anything because he has his mouth full of cheese, sugar cubes, chocolate, or anything else that's edible. When he thinks no one is watching, he will reach into a crate of provisions. Almost all the snacks and tasty morsels have vanished.

George has spent his time listing a few Russian habits. He's still bothered by non-Dutch solutions to Life's discomforts:

Peculiarities of Russian Habits

- An ordinary loaf of bread first gets cut lengthwise, then sliced: half slices.
- Ladling food from a collective pot.
- Eating raw garlic.
- Drying out over a campfire wearing wet clothes: burnt sleeves, legs, boots, etc.
- Purposely sitting downwind from a campfire = healthy, a lot of smoke is best.
- Going to bed in wet, kapok-filled sleeping bags without drying them.
- Drinking ethyl spirit diluted with water.
- Wrapping feet and legs in loose strips of cloth before putting on boots.
- Pouring very strong tea, which then gets diluted with water in one's glass.
- Cooking inside a cabin without ventilation or protection.
- Campfire: no picking up of ashes and no burning logs in half.
- Blind, slavish obedience to superiors.

- Brown, knitted long johns and leather flight-caps (World War I) in bed.
- Belt outside one's coat/jacket instead of inside.
- Extreme fear of 'polar bears', even when these are asleep.
- Much magic and swearing off.
- Still unsolved trauma (German) from World War II.
- Tapping one's throat with index and middle finger crossed = drinking vodka (lots!).
- Mustard contains lots of horseradish = very spicy and delicious.
- Navy cap with side flaps and laces.
- Drinking bouts with endless speeches (dialogues) and rounds of toasts.
- Tasty large salty/sour chanterelles; baked sprat with tail.
- Women and sex are almost never talked or joked about, not even after much drinking.

Nothing to do but wait, wait, wait for contact with *Ivan Kiriev*. Hundreds of times I've looked to see if it's 6:00. To kill time, I made a pot of pea soup this afternoon. Just cleaning Nicola's spaghetti dish off the pan was an hour's task. It's remarkable how inert we all become from sitting around waiting, with nothing to do. The afternoon was spent aimlessly wandering around outside or sitting near the fire. After dinner, George and I took another good look at the map, with Kravchenko's report at hand to compare. It turned out that we must simply have overlooked the wooden pole with 'BAR 55' on the beach in the direction of Cape Petrovsky. Perhaps we'll get a chance tomorrow to revisit that spot. Altogether, I think, we'll need four hours for that task, which would fit nicely into the morning. Nicolai thinks it's better not to decide now, but to wait and see tomorrow. We have to know what *Kiriev* will be doing.

Extra-long watch tonight, from 9:30 p.m. until 1:00 a.m.

George has had it with the water leak over his sleeping bag, and tonight he improvised a small cover from a remaining piece of plastic, fastening it between the roof's support beams with small wooden pegs. First, he patiently cut slivers; then, he danced around between the heads of the sleeping men to set up his tent. Once it was installed, we celebrated with his last bar of Cadbury chocolate.

Sunday, 3 September 1995 – When we woke up, the weather had turned foul: a lot of wind and rain! George's plastic cover worked splendidly: today I woke up dry. At the posted 9:30 contact time, we talked with the *Kiriev*. Again, they couldn't tell us any more – only that they would be doing their utmost to collect us. They're still anchored off Cape Zhelaniya. Vitali and Nicolai were sitting close to the radio and because the conversation was carried on in Russian, I didn't understand a lot. Vitali announced to them that our bread was gone. The reply: "I can't understand you. Would you repeat that, please?" For a good ten minutes we all sat around the radio listening to static and unintelligible talk. After these radio contacts, George and I always have a lot of trouble getting the entire conversation translated in detail. Vitali speaks only Russian, and Nicolai says nothing if we don't ask. In this manner, it is impossible to stay informed. After much questioning, I found out that the ship indeed would not arrive today.

"On previous days, the story went that the Captain was asleep, or that Boyarsky was asleep, or that he'd just gone ashore to the polar station," said George, annoyed. "The prevailing surf would not have presented a problem getting ashore with a Zodiac inflatable. At our departure from Zeeuwse Uitkijk [Spitsbergen] we were battling much more serious circumstances. "In low spirits, everyone sat down to breakfast: an insipid bit of yesterday's pea soup. To enhance the taste, we added portions of *sambal* [red pepper paste]. We'd brought large quantities of that stuff from the Netherlands because it adds pep to tasteless or failed dishes. The Russians, especially, are crazy about it. They add heaping spoonfuls to a bowl of soup and then down it without batting an eye. All day long we stayed inside. Outside, interminable rain: the most miserable weather one can imagine. Everything is wet and won't dry. The cabin most resembles a sheep's pen. The dampness exudes a pungent odor of people cramped together for too long. Again, we're waiting. Eugene is our translator for communications with Nicolai and Vitali. Konstantin talks a blue streak in German. He's a very warm man, totally without bragging and pretensions. For years already, he's been collaborating with Eugene in excavations and field investigations in the Russian Arctic. He told me that last year they excavated Eskimo settlements on the Chukotka Peninsula near the Bering Strait. The permafrost guaranteed optimal conservation, and they found frozen blood and seal meat hundreds of years old in underground supply depots, as if they'd only recently been interred. It was as if, by telling me this, he somehow wished to compel my good fortune; as if we still might have a chance to find Barents' grave. Although in the Great School of Archaeology we've been taught that a negative result is also a scientific result, a feeling of dismay came over me. Perhaps, naive as I am, it stems from my belief – since my discovery on the first day – that the grave was nearby the cabin. George had another take on it: "Look," he said, "Since we have thoroughly combed the shore between Cape Varnek and Cape Marii, no one would really have to come and look for it here. Then he won't be here, OK?" One more time, we grabbed the map and assured ourselves that we had thoroughly investigated the entire region along the coast. The only thing we are not certain of is the 'BAR' pole, which, according to Kravchenko, must be somewhere on the beach to the west of us. But there is a slim chance we will still be able to go that way.

All afternoon, Eugene whittled away at a small piece of wood he found along the beach. Hours later, he finished his work. It had turned into a sort of Irish Cross, which to me had the makings of a German Medal. Quite in keeping with his obsession for all things esoteric, he explained the object as an ancient, universal symbol for the World, Life, and so on. George shrugged his shoulders upon hearing this. I was pleased when Eugene presented it to me as a small gift. Later in the afternoon, we ate yesterday's leftovers. This would be our last meal today. The food locker's bottom is coming into view. We'll have to ration.

George has been taking care of the rifles. He already oiled them once at the beginning of the week, but everyone is so careless that they are already rusted. We have:

- Two 12-caliber Baikal Hunting Rifles (Bork System)
- One 12-caliber Hunting Rifle (Anson system, with rebuilt percussion arm)
- Two metal Flare Guns with many rounds
- Ten manual Flares (Russian-made: 30 cm long, cardboard container with metal caps: *Katyusha* they call them)
- Two flare-shooting containers (Western-made plastic with small flares)

After two hours' worth of polishing, George announced, in his pure Leiden accent: "It's all right now, spic-and-span. Let those white rascals approach!" The arsenal was shining as before. But half an hour later, two rifles again were lying in the mud.

At 6:00 p.m. we made radio contact again with our ship. The message was very puzzling. What I could gather from Vitali was that the Ice Harbor team was no longer busy at the Saved House, but back on board! I asked Eugene once again if that was certain, and his confirmation caused George and me to fall back on our sleeping bags utterly speechless. Would they really have stayed at Ice Harbor for only three or four days? Would we then be returning home entirely without results? I tried to imagine the somber mood that must be engulfing those men. I could hardly believe it. Meanwhile, Vitali had carved an entire Russian text on the inside surface of the door. On top was the name of the expedition: (MAK3) 1995 25/VIII – ∞. Under that he had carved our names. If he had an entire winter, I think he could turn Saved House No. 2 into an Orthodox cathedral!

As small consolation, the weather improved somewhat in the evening, so we were able to sit around the fire. It was a clear night, but noticeably colder. The mountains looming over the bay's beaches were coated with rime. It won't be long before the cabin's surroundings will also be white. Nobody's cooking dinner. The food is gone. We'll just go and get some sleep.

Monday, 4 September 1995 – At 1:00 a.m. I was awakened by Eugene, who clearly was three sails to the wind. When I emerged and tried to wipe the sleep from my eyes near the fire, he asked me if maybe I would like to go to sleep again. He was sitting with Konstantin on a tree trunk by the fire, smiling expansively to show the fun had just begun. Actually, I would prefer they go to bed rather than remaining there slurring. We are around each other all day long anyway, and I cherish the quiet of the midnight watch. They poured another round and offered me a full mug. The last few days, for lack of anything better, they have been drinking nothing but 'spiritus', medicinal alcohol diluted with ever-smaller parts of water. Yesterday I tried a swig, but the stuff was not fit to drink. My throat was raw! Eventually, I started to feel less and less irritated, and I choked up when they told me that their stay here had been an ideal situation for them. Tomorrow, all this would be over and then they'd have to return to Moscow, back to the same misery as always. And while nostalgically wallowing in the smoke, we cut up the last pieces of old cheese and Spanish sausage, which tasted excellent. Russian songs echoed across the frozen plains.

Our watch ended at 4:00 a.m. It seemed a good idea to me to visit Cape Petrovsky once more before Kiriev comes. We probably missed that section where the 'BAR' pole could be when that bear blocked us a few days ago. According to Kravchenko's report, the pole is some 400 m southwest of the cape. We got ready to leave in the direction of Cape Petrovsky. While we were busy checking our rifles, I spotted a polar bear leisurely sniffing the large flag of Amsterdam. Panic immediately erupted in the camp. Vitali, dozing by the fire, jumped almost a meter into the air. I ran inside to grab my camera and flare gun. The animal, spooked by the sudden commotion, made an abrupt about-face and quickly trotted off. This was very encouraging: the polar bear that annoyed us for days apparently appreciated our presence even less than we did his. We immediately set off

View across Cape Varnek's storm ridges (Photo's JJ Zeeberg 1998). A Nazi sea mine marks the spot of Willem Barents' probable burial site.

and heroically followed him, shooting flares. We chased that bear for ten minutes or so until he disappeared into the interior. The Russians stayed behind, deathly afraid of the monster, and we left them very much on the alert.

After a good hour and a half, we reached the spot described by Kravchenko in his 1983 report. The location, to my surprise, was close to the remains of the surveyors' camp. I looked around and (I'll be damned!) spotted a well dug-in pole, some 45 meters away from the camp. The pole, 25 cm in diameter, stood about 100 meters from the current shore. The top was cone-shaped, and a thick but modern wire nail had been driven into its tip. On a flattened side of the pole was carved: 'BpR 1955 г', or BpK, in Cyrillic with a damaged K. The г is clearly Cyrillic, the Russian abbreviation for 'год' (year) after 55. On the north side, a crude face had been carved. The surveyors had used this pole to calibrate their work.

There is no burial or anything in the immediate surroundings. How Kravchenko could ever not have understood this as a calibration pole is a puzzle to me. For sure he must have seen the camp and been able to draw his conclusions. I put George next to the pole and took a few photographs to prove Kravchenko wrong. Around 7:45 a.m., a bit disappointed, we got back to the cabin.

Our colleagues were intently waiting for radio contact with *Kiriev*. At 8:30 a.m. we got the news that the ship was underway and would be sailing into the bay within fifteen minutes! Now we immediately had to prepare our departure. We dragged all the packed items to the tide line. In the distance we suddenly saw the ship. The landing craft was already at sea and approaching. They sure weren't wasting any time now! Once they were offshore, it soon became clear that they didn't dare sail the craft through the breakers. The boatswain clumsily maneuvered the *plashkot* back and forth behind them. They were so close we could almost see the sweat on his brow. Repeatedly he tried to ride in on a wave, but when he saw the water crash against the bow, he'd quickly turn around. His attempts grew ever clumsier. Both deckhands moved hastily from stern to bow and back again. It was clear they were in a panic! In a last desperate attempt, one of the deckhands was put overboard in a small dinghy they had towed along. The poor soul was barely seated, his oars ready to push through the breakers, when his dinghy filled up in one fell swoop. The second deckhand held a towline in his hands and helplessly watched his buddy row like a soaked cat. Each wave made the situation more desperate and almost hilarious. Wearing our waders we walked as far as possible into the water to drag him ashore as soon as we could. The intention was to make several trips to the landing craft with people and gear. The Russians stuck with that plan. The dinghy was quickly bailed out and filled with mattresses and sleeping bags. Back in the surf, of course, the dinghy again got flooded, and our sleeping bags were floating around the Ice Sea. Eventually, the crew in the craft decided to reel in the dinghy and discontinue the evacuation. We remained ashore, downcast, with one thoroughly drenched deckhand and some equally drenched sleeping bags. To make matters worse, someone put a dripping sleeping bag on top of my camera. When I picked it up, water poured out of it. Just this camera with photographs of the 'BAR 55' pole. All for naught.

We returned to the cabin defeated. Half the crew was soaked. We dried the clothes over the still burning fire. Konstantin helped Stas, the deckhand, to disrobe and set him down near the fire. His body was giving off steam. For quite a while, I nursed the hope that they'd make another attempt this afternoon to get us off the island. This turned out to be too optimistic. We'll have to spend another night at the Saved

House No. 2. Vitali again raised the radio antenna and tried to establish contact with *Kiriev*. No reaction. The red flares we launched didn't elicit a reaction either. The entire crew must be aboard. Surely someone would notice us. With my binoculars, I couldn't see a soul on deck. What was going on there?

Only at the stipulated time of 6:00 p.m. did we make contact. It then turned out the ship could see no chance at all of retrieving us. Whereupon Boyarsky proposed that we all hike to Cape Zhelaniya. Nicolai and Vitali have no problem with that and without even scanning the map to see how far it might be, they start filling a backpack with the most needed items: Nicolai his plant samples and Vitali his radio.

"Death March," Eugene said, "but I think we can do it." I looked once more on the map. It's a distance of more than 40 kilometers, straight across mountains and block fields, through rivers and fissures filled with molten snow. Very unfamiliar terrain! Konstantin sat next to me wearing his rubber boots. He would accompany Eugene unconditionally, but doubt was visibly eating at him. He looked at us. George and I refused categorically. After a long discussion, everyone recognized that the plan was insane. The Russians decided that if we wouldn't go, then they wouldn't either. We could have hugged them; apparently, our sojourn has created solidarity. Stas, the deckhand, doesn't have proper footwear; some of us have injuries; in short, it probably wouldn't have ended well. Now a new situation has arisen. With small hope of any help from the ship, George and I discussed the possibility of using the emergency funds to charter a helicopter from Dikson. In the end, we decided to await contact with *Kiriev* at 11:00 p.m. George asked if he could use the radio, and he made it clear that we will review the weather and, weather permitting, will expect another attempt by the landing craft. At the other end of the connection, luckily, they had been thinking similarly. I asked if I could talk to Gawronski, because we were told that the group from Ice Harbor had boarded. After breaking radio contact and another laborious translation by Eugene, I finally understood that everyone was still camped at Ice Harbor. The news perked us up and drove the feeling of resignation from the cabin. We could go peacefully to sleep now. The Russians crawled into their soggy kapok bags and Stas, who was walking around in a mélange of borrowed clothing, decided to stay near the fire all night. He refused to come in. I fell asleep, dead tired, around 11:15.

Tuesday, 5 September 1995 – Everyone went straight to bed yesterday. Thus, no one stood watch, but Stas was outside all night. He is dead tired. Finally, at 8:00 a.m. Eugene managed to talk him into a still wet sleeping bag, whereupon he immediately fell asleep. Last night it snowed. The entire bay and mountains are covered with rime, and odd, lens-shaped clouds hang over the landscape. Eugene says that in 1993, around this time, a thick coat of snow already covered the entire north coast.

During the 9:30 a.m. radio contact, we were told to search along the coast, in two separate groups, for a suitable landing spot. Eugene and Konstantin set out in the direction of Cape Petrovsky, and Nicolai and Vitali disappeared in the direction of the Snezhnaya River. I remained inside the cabin to pack the last items and to drag boxes and bags outside. After yesterday's debacle, I packed the most vulnerable items in water-tight plastic. An hour later, Nicolai and Vitali were back. Near the river, half a kilometer northeast they found a suitable place. All baggage must now be brought there. George searched for a long pole, so that we could carry our bags and crates between us. Our Russian colleagues took only their personal items and left sleeping bags, tools, and cooking utensils behind, so that we can board quickly.

As quickly as we were dropped here, eleven days ago, we were picked off the island. Aboard *Kiriev* I surrendered to the suffocating heat, still wearing all my stinking clothing. We ate something because lunch was served and then I retreated to the sauna to sweat and wash. After that, I spent another hour in my cabin, door locked, to regain my composure. Only then did I have the time to question some people about what precisely had happened at Ice Harbor. The excavating crew was supposed to be working until today, but no one could tell me anything about that because there has been no radio contact for five days. It took *Kiriev* almost a week to travel a distance that she would cover, under normal circumstances, in twelve hours. The bad weather had caused the ship to remain hove to off Cape Zhelaniya for four days. One day later, they had a medical emergency on board. Coincidentally, the Russian Coast Guard's patrol cutter *Irtysh* was passing by. The patient was transferred and had his appendix removed aboard that vessel.

At dusk, while in Boyarsky's cabin toasting our safe return, we sailed past Cape Vilkitsky. It's pretty clear now that we won't be setting foot on land there. Could Kravchenko have been right? Might that mound with the bear's skull on Cape Vilkitsky be Willem Barents' grave after all? And will we ever get another opportunity to find out? Tomorrow, if everything goes as planned, we'll be back in Ice Harbor. I'm burning to know what's been going on there.

Chapter Eight

The House on Shore

Sunday, 27 August 1995 – "We've landed. We're here!" Jerzy excitedly called out on the phone with Henk van Veen's office in the Netherlands. "We're here under a blue sky and radiant sunshine at two degrees above freezing." From the northern tip of Novaya Zemlya, one can barely contact a communications satellite. The big 1 m-sized satellite dish stood vertically, its signals skimming the bare, deserted grounds towards a satellite just above the horizon. Shots could be heard in the distance as the ship's doctor and his assistant were spending a couple of hours ashore hunting duck and geese. Dirk is a whole-hearted admirer of our feathered friends, but alive and in flight, and with each shot he let out an angry curse. One by one, during unpacking and setting up our tents, we looked over to the remains of the Saved House. The historical site lies in deplorable condition. The four beams have largely rotted away. "The site is considerably worse off than in 1993," said historian Hans Bonke. "Apparently there's been some digging, probably by tourists hunting for souvenirs, and the beams have rotted quite a bit more during those two years. Good thing the expedition wasn't postponed another year, or we would have found nothing." There were big puddles of standing water, which we drained immediately. On first inspection, I quickly found several cast-iron nails, shreds of fabric, and bits of leather, loosened from the soil by rain and wind. Hans and Victor didn't waste another minute and immediately got to work.

They collected all the loose items, carefully documenting each find. A shallow ravine cuts into the plateau just twenty meters away, its edges smooth and rounded from long exposure to the harsh climate. This must be the "clift of a hill near a stream of water" where the carpenter ('Of Purmerend') was buried on 24 September 1596, three weeks after their arrival and probably working relentlessly to get the cabin constructed. Only a trickle of water flowed in its channel, draining the inland ponds. No human remains anywhere: the 'burial mound' seen in the aerial photo appears to be an artifact of the stereophotography. In reality, it is a rocky outcrop. The area is bereft of snow or ice. Even the perennial snowbanks, which may survive for centuries on end in the shadows of the escarpment, have melted or ablated.

Cape Spory Navolok reveals an eerily smooth landscape. The panorama is stark and expansive: rocky, but in places soft with a yellowish mud. The vegetation consists of dark mosses and an occasional dwarf birch spread hard against the surface. There are some shallow ponds in the immediate interior, a few minutes away from our camp, but you can't really scoop a bucket of water from them and along the muddy shores, I found many traces of reindeer. As we approached, a large flight of terns and gulls exploded into the air. Their excrement dots the surface of the lake. While our camp neared completion, we needed to find a source of drinking water for the fifteen expedition members-two less than sought shelter in the Saved House (including the carpenter, who died, as said). The doctor's assistant, holding his gun and a small, dead duck, joined me and together we set out for a survey of the cape. Half a kilometer away from camp, the sounds of sawing and hammering died out. Then at last, amid the gently rolling terrain, there came a distinct feeling of remoteness. The landscape is wet and thawed. Through depressions and in between ridges, numerous drainages run to the sea. In some of the soft yellowish spots, you sink into the mud, often more than ankle-deep, until you reach the hard surface of frozen ground or permafrost. We approached the wooden beacon that marks the southeastern edge of the cape. This rudimentary lighthouse, about ten meters tall, consists of an electric light and batteries which have long run out. Stacking sea ice has partly demolished the construction, and the glass prisms lie shattered around the rock outcrop. Crew from the now abandoned polar station at Cape Zhelaniya, 70 km to the north of us, maintained the beacon during the 1960s and 1970s. The caterpillar tracks from their vehicle can be traced throughout the landscape and miss the Saved House by only a few meters.

Two walruses surfaced nearby in the sea when we rounded the cape to return to camp over the beach. They seemingly were passing by but held their pace and we saw their beady eyes and bristly snouts, with long whiskers, loudly exhaling as they stood on their tails to observe us. They are very large animals, probably twice as big as a cow. On they went, off to nowhere. The beach with its regular wavy ridges appeared flattened, by time, thousands of years of snow cover and gravity. About halfway back, there was a small body of crystal-clear water between two ridges. I kneeled to taste the water: it was fresh, snowmelt or water percolating through the beach shingles, and a pool large enough to assure our supply of drinking water. Back at the Saved House, the bustle of camp construction had ended as Russians and Dutch shifted their attention to the excavation site. A pan filled with potatoes was simmering on a driftwood fire. Dusk had fallen over the area, and this was a dusk that was to last all night. To record weather conditions during our stay, I unpacked and set up my meteorological instruments about twenty meters away from camp. Out in the open I managed to drive a pole into the stone-rich ground and deploy the big metal cylinder of the anemometer. Inside the steel casing is a roll of recording paper on a squeaky, spring-powered mechanism. Another container box holds a hygro-thermometer and several glass-tube, minimum-maximum thermometers. Next, I unpacked and tested the theodolite and found that it had weathered the trip in excellent condition. The day closed after a dinner of potatoes and fire-roasted chicken at 9:00 in the evening. We burned all waste and food leftovers so as not to attract bears. "Now we have to set up the night watches," said Yuri, articulating clearly in a conspiratorial tone of voice. He eyed the group as he let his remarks sink in. "I'll do the first watch. Who will be second?" We drafted a schedule and turned in. I am sharing the tent with Herre Wynia, and while he was still outside, I looked across the dark blue of the Kara Sea. The comfortable warmth of the sleeping bag quickly enveloped me. Very softly, as I began to relax, I felt the ground sway and roll: my body is still attuned to the ship. And I fell asleep to the loud whir of the gasoline generator recharging batteries for Henri and Anton, our TV crew.

28 August 1995 – I woke up with bright sun on my tent and found my watch: it was 4:00 a.m. Outside, Jerzy the night watch was moving noisily around packing and unpacking crates, and the excitement of being on Novaya Zemlya fired me with a burning curiosity. I would just as soon have started to work, but I forced myself to remain lying in my sleeping bag for another couple of hours. The team rose at 7:00. Yuri had sliced bread and cheese and offered 'special Arctic jam'. The weather is fortunate: a cloudless sky and a mild southwesterly breeze. Once again, I let my eyes scan the austere, beige-brown landscape. The morning sun provided a clear view of the round hills of Novaya Zemlya, much farther inland and some lined with perennial snowbanks. They are six to ten kilometers away. Behind those hills, I could distinguish the giant dome-shaped icecap from the pale sky, but only through binoculars, which bring out the meltwater channels that accentuate the curving ice surface. The ice margin is about twenty kilometers distant: six or seven hours of hiking through mostly level terrain.

Shortly after breakfast, tripods and red-and-white range poles appeared in the Arctic desert as we began organizing, plotting and measuring the wilderness. I set up the futuristic-looking theodolite in the corner of the research area, on a barely perceptible stone ridge. When I uncrated my gear, I discovered imprints of big paws in the clay between the pebbles: a sure sign of the great beast that owns this world. Kneeling people marked the excavation site in the distance. A long way behind those, expeditionary ship *Ivan Kiriev* lay offshore on a smooth sea. Each time I looked up, she was sitting at a different angle, swinging around the anchor chain. Someone took a few steps outside the camp: Yuri, our chief of camp for today, emptied the small pail in which he had washed potatoes. To the right I could see René Gerritsen manipulating his two-meter-tall kite, preparing to take advantage of today's abundant sunshine and light wind for some 'kite aerial photography'. The kite is a custom-made, lightweight carbon-rod *rokkaku* (Japanese for 'hexagon') with good soaring ability and a 100-meter line. For extra stability, the remote-controlled camera dangles away from the kite on a separate, 10-meter line. If the main line is at an angle of 45°, photographs will be taken from an altitude of ~60 meters.

Fellow geologist Dmitri Badyukov and I quickly measured a profile of the altitude of the terrain to be assured of the most basic data. Elevations are established by positioning a reflector of fixed height (1.5 m) at various distances on the ground. The man with the reflector essentially fills in the map, by choosing positions and densities on landmarks we wish to draw. The entire area is systematically covered by shifting the transect. The operator behind the machine targets this reflector in the cross hairs of the theodolite's powerful telescopic lens and then measures its elevation and distance by sending an infrared signal. The first transect we made was from sea level to the highest point we could find. The low ridge that I was standing on is 14 m above the sea. The Saved House lies at an elevation of exactly 13 m. The edge of the escarpment at 11 m is four meters high; the beach starts at 7 m. As Dima and I prepared to shift to the next transect, we were alerted by loud cries. "A bear!" someone yelled, and we all hurried to the edge of the escarpment. A polar bear was ambling along the water line. The white predator appeared just as bizarre as we do in this empty land. Every five paces he lifted his nose and sniffed around deliberately. The nasal cavity in a polar bear's skull is widely branched and lined with mucous membranes that enable the animal to smell and track its prey kilometers away. And they found us. Our first bear was a small one, bleeding from its right shoulder, wounded perhaps after an encounter with a larger competitor.

1 September 1995 – September has arrived. Sixth day ashore. We are working long days and there is little time to write. *Kiriev* has been gone one day now; she departed yesterday morning to support the Ivanov group. A huge cyclone is passing and we're on the trailing edge of it. A fantastic wind has been blowing, making the propeller that drives our electricity generator emit a wailing noise. When thick clouds darken the sky, the rugged canvas tent that covers the power station emits a bright light from the light bulb built into the wind generator's transformer as a fuse. The wind dominates your ears and ultimately your entire head. Air temperature is +5°C, but the wind chill gives a sensation of sub-zero temperatures. My clothing is effective (warm coat + raincoat, long-johns, woolen gloves with cut-off fingers), so I'm not bothered by the weather, but at the excavation some are suffering stiff limbs and painful, swollen hands due to cold and moisture. The weather makes a dramatic panorama all around us. In the wake of the storm, a thick, wide band of clouds, like a giant bridge to nowhere, blocks all sun, and everywhere around us along the darkened horizon cumulus clouds glisten like pearls. The sea is white, with tall waves that are blown to spray by short wind gusts before they break, and 'water devils' chase each other across the surface. When a patch of sun glides over the sea, it colors the otherwise dark waters aquamarine blue, like in a painting. Brief, colorful rainbows sparkle above the whitecaps; it is a very dynamic scene, and we watch it in awe. Today, the 'total station' stood on the edge of the terrace overlooking the beach. Our priority is to finish surveying the area around the digs; subsequently we'll complete the beach and assist in the ship search.

A drizzle started to come down during the afternoon and after a few hours, everything became so saturated that when you throw off your coat, your clothes give off steam. Paper curls. Condensation settles on metal and glass. I hesitated to switch on the total station and risk a short circuit that could destroy it. The humidity here is so great that things won't even dry. At night, you put your head on those wet clothes and go to sleep. The days are long. You are an island, alone with your tasks and thoughts. In that monotony, the world has shrunk to a small circle of bleak landscape with clouds of vapor from your breath in front of you. Shreds of thoughts whisk through my head and because everyday sensations and troubles are fading, memories and associations merge and take the center stage.

With dinner, our Russian friends miraculously produced two new bottles of *Moskovskaya* vodka. The drinks broke the tension of another day of hard, concentrated work. Bas described a 'conflict' in the Dutch East Indies at the beginning of this century. Dirk, Hans, and Jerzy discussed the strategy for the final days of excavation over a photocopy of Gerrit de Veer's text. Each followed his eloquence and thus we ended up together in this cabin. I enjoy listening to them talk and being part of it. And if I do it for anything, then it's for everything I had to leave to get here. As I jumped into the surf – six days ago now – I envisaged in my mind's eye a sweetheart and a place I could call home, not the seedy dump I was going to return to and cleaning the mouse droppings off my stove every day. Hold on, I am not there yet: I also miss having a purpose in life, a place in society, and sometimes going see a movie. But my place had to be the entire globe, and the most inhospitable parts of it, nonetheless.

"Over at Bert's [Haanstra, the famous film director], there always was that special atmosphere," Anton announced cheerfully tonight. "Every Friday night we made music at his house, and for thirty years, my flute and I were part of the party. While Bert was assembling a movie in his studio, we were merry making music."

This morning, the excavation revealed a piece of lead showing some scratches: "Barents" I made out. Here, I assumed, the man himself left his name. Perhaps, as René remarked jokingly, to mark his possessions: "This box is mine, I'm putting my name on it, and everyone else had better keep his fingers off it." Hans patiently explained that medieval handwritings do not translate so easily and need a specialist's interpretation. The black soil contains many other small surprises. Indeterminate nodules of clay and humus are untangled to yield buttons, two lead bullets connected with a wire, and coins with the Dutch escutcheon. Today I tried my luck with the metal detector and – what do you know – found one of these coins, still shining when I cleaned the soil of it and entirely similar to today's *stuivers* that I would carry in my wallet, except for the year on it: 1579.

[Stuivers remained until the introduction of the Euro in 2002]. The soil also contains reddish-brown beard shavings, perhaps dating back to the day that the winterers, by suggestion of Van Heemskerck, groomed themselves for the return trip [19 May 1597]. I kneeled down a few meters from the excavation, where tar was boiled to caulk the Saved House. The tar spot is still wet, and the tar clinging to your fingers spreads the characteristic strong smell that must have pervaded the House.

2 September 1995 – The surveying equipment went on the blink. At first, I refused to believe this was really happening and ran through the whole procedure anew: install freshly charged batteries, switch the machine on, select manual operation, rotate once around both axes to enter the 3D orientation web into memory. Nothing doing. The instrument remained dead: a useless lump of expensive electronics. Now what? Earlier, I'd lost a good many measurements, which I was about to round off, when the computer froze during data downloading. This I found irritating, and I was embarrassed to break the news to Dima, who has better things to do than walk around with that reflector. A morning thunderstorm increased the tension. The first flash through the fog found the archaeologists sitting up like a colony of rabbits, letting the fearful rumble wash over them. Anger and panic! I scrolled up and down the menus in an attempt to bring my sturdy machine back to life. As if quite by design, the failure that hit it is not listed in the manual. After considerable searching in the instructions, I found – in small print – this helpful note: "In all other emergencies contact the distributor." Now, this called for improvisation. It took me a while to straighten myself out and decide that condensation inside the steel housing was the most likely culprit. Anton had learned about that problem with his cameras and amicably brought out a hair dryer.

Miserably wet, soaked with rain I sat on the hard, cold ground in our small equipment tent pointing the hot air blower at all parts of the compact apparatus. The atmosphere was permeated with the smell of wood smoke from our campfire, which had been blowing between our tents for hours. Only when the wind changed direction did the plume drift across the dark terrain into the fog. “If looking gloomy could have helped it would have gone better all right,” the Dutch said to each other four centuries ago. Anton called for a moment to see how I was doing and advised me to establish warm-air circulation in the half-opened casing of the theodolite. “That will draw the moisture out,” he assured me with confidence and a supportive smile. I felt a rush of gratitude welling up, which I hastily suppressed, because we have yet to see whether it will work. But indeed, when I switched the machine on after half an hour of heating and another fifteen minutes of letting it adjust temperature, it sprang back to life. I spend another half hour constructing a protective cover from a transparent plastic sample bag, leaving only the seeker and directional controls exposed. Amid the fine rain, I continued working. Strong gusts caused the heavy yellow tripod to stagger about. I was overjoyed to be able to continue my task and owed it all to Anton. He helped me to save face, and the entire Dutch team as well, because the Russians would ridicule us forever about those swank, inoperable machines on Novaya Zemlya.

Even though we come from such disparate parts of the world, cooperation with the Russians has been close and without problems. I have no idea how the tasks are divided at the digs. I see the archaeologists' kneeling silhouettes in the fog. Everybody works in a disciplined manner, and the workdays are long. A much smaller team excavated the floor of the Saved House in 1993. This time, the digging is concentrated on the tenuous mossy mound that surrounds the House. The archaeologists intently shift through one-square-meter cells, searching for items thrown away and investigating the composition of, as Gerrit de Veer wrote, the 'filth' the winterers threw out. After four hundred years, what would still be visible of the presence of sixteen men in a scant sixty square meters? Each morning, it is uncertain how the day will develop. There could be a dearth of findings. Many things could go wrong. A blown fuse for which we have no spare… What didn't we think of? A cable runs from the wind generator to the transformer in the generator tent. From there, power cables run to the equipment tent, where I enter my data in the computer and make a backup disk. The camp is a mess of guy wires. No one knows how much time we still have, whether we'll be able to work tomorrow, or the day after tomorrow, and so on. Radio contact with *Kiriev* is impossible because she's out of reach these days. When the ship returns, she'll greet us with flares and that will be the signal to re-establish contact. Boyarsky will decide the best moment for departure. After that we'll have less than two hours to stow our gear and get ready because the seas may roughen again and prevent our pickup. That would keep us on the island another week or so. Not bad from a science point of view, but if the vessel can't make it back to port by 15 September, that will open a Pandora's box of bureaucratic hassle. It's not the ice that forces us back, but our busy time schedule and the silly routines of our lives. However, in light of today's hard winds, the possibility of our getting stuck on Novaya Zemlya has prompted the expedition leader to begin rationing of our food supplies.

Every now and then, a polar bear ambles along the beach. I take notice but have no time for it. We work all hours; I have hardly been able to observe my surroundings. From afar the animals observe the hustle and bustle; then they pass onward along the shore. Two days ago, a bear threatened to approach too closely: a humongous beast that left the waterline almost exactly opposite the excavation. The bear acted as if he didn't even see us. With Victor Dershawin I knelt down by the foot of the escarpment, while above us the usual panic erupted. "For fuck's sake what are you doing down there?!" I heard Jerzy calling. I was fully alert, but, strangely, felt no fear. Victor kept the black steel Russian flare gun at the ready and gazed in awe at the bear. It was a splendid animal, tremendously powerful and moving with a grace that only the largest of predators have. He smelled our traces on the beach gravels, softly placing his massive paws as he came ever closer. Eye-to-eye with the bear you feel totally charged up. You sense the danger emanating from him. Adrenaline spreads through your body and, eventually, my heart was in my throat. Apparently, proximity to such a powerful beast arouses primitive sensations. When the animal was less than fifty meters away, we decided to repel it, because this hunter must be kept from attacking. Once you enter into a confrontation with the beast, only a bullet can stop it. I pulled a flare from my hip-pouch, but where to aim? Do you point at the bear, potentially provoking its aggression? Pop, pop: a few flares already sailed overhead. The animal closely followed the sizzling lights that still shone bright in full sunlight. Did we chase him towards us? The bear waddled to the nearest flare, smoking in a reddish glow on the beach, and turned its head to see where that strange substance had arrived from. On the crack of a new salvo, however, it took off in a slow gallop that shook its hindquarters – but no farther than ten meters. There, he cast one more disturbed look before moving in a wide arc around us, straight through a swirling cloud of gulls and terns. After this encounter, everyone was irritable for as long as it took the adrenaline to be lost from the blood.

About two hours ago I took over night watch from Dirk van Smeerdijk and went down to the beach to collect firewood, the blocks of driftwood that Dirk sawed from a log earlier today. The sense of being alone in that peaceful black and grey world sends feelings of euphoria through my stomach. But not for long. In a thick fog, I saw a bear rounding the promontory barely 100 meters away. It moved right into my view. The team was asleep and I was alone with the bear. Was this the same bear we chased off two days ago? There was a straight and empty line between me and the bear. The gun lay on the table in camp. At first, fear streaked through my mind. Then I got a grip and reasoned that he couldn't smell me because I was standing downwind. What to do? The next thing I knew, he was ascending the black cliff as if it didn't exist and continued to approach, out of my sight. Noisily and breathing heavily, kicking loose some rocks, I climbed the escarpment too, to warn the others.

"What a dog!" Dirk softly called out as he readied his binoculars. "Binoculars? The gun! Get the gun!" I screamed without sound. We decided not to sound a general alarm. One wailing blast of the air horn and in no time this place boils over with nervous Nellies. The polar bear glanced balefully from afar, with a stare black and piercing like a shark's. The notion that polar bears have poor eyesight is a fable. I believe the animals see us as soon as they round the cape. At a distance of 100-150 meters from us, they will halt. Some lie down for a while to observe what opportunity may arise. Eventually they have all continued, and that's what this one seemingly did, disappearing into the mists.

My turn to stand watch, and I like it because in the quiet of night I have plenty time to take in the environment and write. The landscape has not changed since our forefathers walked here. Those men vanished from the earth, the language that they spoke evolved beyond recognition, and the world that they knew has largely disappeared. But this land is still just as the

Dutch with their halberds observed it. The House was built at an advantageous point: between two drainage channels on the edge of a vast plain, 13 m above sea level, with an unobstructed view in all directions. When winter set in, the land was soon covered by snow and ice. The four-meter-high escarpment was smoothed by snow, and the hills that surround the House in the engravings were likely snowdrifts. The frozen sea merged with the shore, and to a considerable extent, the scenery must have been defined by the impressive formations of stacking sea ice. You would be blinded by it in sunlight. The 150-meter-wide beach emerged when Novaya Zemlya rose out of the sea, freed of the weight of the massive glaciers that had covered the island during the Ice Age. With their regularly spaced gravel ridges and terraces, the beaches on both sides of the island Novaya Zemlya resemble each other. The highest elevation of the beach here is about 7 m above the sea level, compared to 10 m at Inostrantsev Bay, so I read in my field notes. Both remarkably low, if one considers that beaches on Svalbard have rebounded 30 m and more.

Ice Harbor during night watch, with a polar bear on the beach.

The bear is still spooking around the camp. Yesterday, Bas hammered a few 'security stakes' into the ground to indicate a 30 m perimeter, because estimating distances is hampered by fog. With binoculars, I observed an immense chunk of pack ice float by at a distance of some 10 km. I could see the Arctic pack on the horizon. It must have been drifting towards us in these last days, ever since the direction of the wind changed to north. After some hours outside, I quietly returned to our communal tent to prepare breakfast. By their sounds, I can tell that my partners are still sleeping peacefully. The last watch has to wake the others and make them breakfast, so I cut the bread (which is growing tougher by the day), fill a platter with cheese and boiled sausage, and make tea and coffee. Meanwhile I wonder if the archaeologists in Ivanov Bay have made any progress. I figure we would have known it by now if the discovery of Barents' grave had been made. But I can also imagine George and Pieter keeping it quiet to complete their research in full concentration. I picture a peculiar tableau: a man with dirty hands on either side of the grave, one holding our national flag. No one would be smiling, exhausted from days of hiking and hard labor. Besides, they would be stunned by their discovery. The water for tea and coffee doesn't boil easily. The kettle has been on the griddle over the campfire for hours, but the water cools faster than it heats. It would be better to place the kettle directly into the fire, but the construction leaves no room for that. Finally, I decide to ignite the gas stove.

Our daily routine is that after breakfast each morning, three men get drinking water and walk across the beach carrying pails. Another group collects driftwood and hauls the wooden blocks of the beach. Nature's call is answered: dig a small hole below the escarpment, do your thing, cover it with a rock. Some insist on the daily routine of washing. The Russians are especially thorough in this regard. Among the Dutch, Anton washes up very well. Every morning he joins breakfast, cleaned and shaved, wet hair slicked down. "Fantastic, eh, that cold water. It sure dilates your blood vessels something fierce!" he'll say. Today I worked throughout the morning, then suffered a bout of fatigue and went to sit in the tent for a mug of chocolate with Bas, who had camp duty. "OK, look here," Bas started in an irritated voice, "being sleepy and taking a nap I can understand, but loitering and not doing a thing, that's not very agreeable." I pulled my dagger and helped peel a minuscule potato waiting for the water to boil. I was getting dizzy with sleep. Bas laughed out loud when I mentioned that I don't like the rationing of chocolate. "Don't take too much, OK!" He also pronounced it miserably: "chuck-o-lad." On top of that, I purchased chocolate for thirty days for twenty men – a whole box, damn it, filled with six hundred bars – and I would really like to have one now. This made Bas laugh even harder: he was shaking all over and truly convulsing. But from today on, chocolate is part of the emergency provisions, and that box is locked. "You are just like those men of Barents, they also wanted to eat everything at once." Now that does it.

"It sure is blowing up a storm, isn't it?" said René as we were seated around the potato soup, listening to the ominous fluttering of the plastic sheets that cover our improvised cabin. In its most vulnerable spots, the construction has already been reinforced a few times with duct tape.

"Stormy," Anton mumbled.

"You said it."

"No, really," Anton continued, unfazed. "'It's blowing tremendously, but that's because you're so open and unprotected here, see? That's called *Stormy*. Force 4 winds, maybe just about 5 on the Beaufort Scale." A grim-looking Russian warship, possibly Coast Guard, dropped anchor in Ice Harbor.

From the beach, down by the waterline, I looked up and watched the tall, weather-beaten wooden cross put there by Kravchenko. I saw smoke from the campfire slowly pass over the terrace, backlit by the evening glow, and I tried to picture the squat cabin that stood there; a dark, geometric object, a monument to a new phase in our cultural evolution.

"You can't take a picture of it," yelled Herre, standing between the tents and looking up into the glowing night sky. Splendid, towering cloud formations sailed on by, into a transparent, deep-blue depth, shrouded in pearly veils and feathers and illuminated during the lengthy Arctic sunset from beyond the Earth's curvature. In my tent, I organized all the clothes and hardware, laying the 'total station' to rest for the night between my sleeping pad and Herre's, with the lid of its large orange casing slightly open to allow moisture to escape.

"Herre Wynia, are you coming into this tent too?" I call out.

"I'm coming, Japie." His head appeared through the tent flap.

"I sure would like to call home," Herre said, while René was using our bulky satellite-phone to talk to the newspapers. "Well, that's what you get when you start opening up a channel like that," I was thinking, but I kept it to myself. His girl is expecting, and why not make a quick call from the North Pole to find how everything is back home? We were asked not to make personal calls because we are on a tight budget. An important skill to be out in the field is the skill to be alone. People reject silence. There are field operations where the participants bring along their 'partners' or have them come over just because it makes a nice holiday, or to be comforted after another dispute with a nasty fellow-researcher. I leave it to the imagination what situations that might lead to. On these Antarctic research stations, all the boys and girls pair up within the first couple of weeks, and you'll be the sucker playing computer games all day.

"You'd better forget it, buddy," I said. "You're now on Novaya Zemlya and you're with me," I continued jokingly. "You can tell me anything you want. Fire away!" Herre climbed across his stuff, shoving some of it aside to make room to lie down. "Haw, haw, this is where my half begins," I gestured, drawing an imaginary line through the middle of the tent.

"But it would be nice to speak with one another and to hear that everything's OK," Herre sighed. I tried to relate. Herre's kneeling all day, looking at a frigid piece of earth and, possibly, grappling with the same thoughts as I am. The work is monotonous: you are left to yourself, and when it gets quiet the only noise is in your head. Endless associations of cozy situations, like a sunny winter Sunday morning long ago, or walking down a quiet, empty street on a hot summer's day, or people that you have altogether lost sight of. That's what I think of while working in the fog, peering through my telescopic sight, and hearing the optics in the instrument click. You hope that simplicity and contentedness will return, even though you called it boredom, and that the miserable grey mess surrounding you was nothing more than a weird narrowing of the senses. And you intend to be much nicer to everybody.

"Isn't there anyone you're thinking of," Herre asked, wriggling to find a good position, his sleeping bag zipped up to his neck.

"Funny you should mention it," I answered, laughing. "Yes; but that bird has flown."

3 September 1995 – Few hours after we all turned in, I woke up because the camp was restless. It was just after midnight and I got up. Jerzy was at the excavation, and I could see him moving around, repositioning beams. His hectic motions resembled a ritual dance. Sometimes he would stand still to contemplate the new configuration. The first-shift night watchers, René and

Henri, were sitting in front of their tent in a bleak light. The sun was just below the horizon.

"He suddenly jumped up and was gone," said René. "He must have thought of something." I stood and observed while Henri and René continued their discussion.

"So as I drive home, I say to myself, I'm late, I'm late, I'm late. She's not going to like it," said René. "And when I get home, what do you think is the first thing she says?"

"You're late!"

"That's right. And all of a sudden, I just don't feel like apologizing. Do you know what I mean?" We all laugh.

Meanwhile Jerzy had produced a tape measure and anchored it with a rock, quickly but carefully stepping over the rotted beams that remain of the Saved House. That night we witnessed the original and elusive process of inspiration. At last, he carried the freeze-dried roof beam into the new layout of the House and lit a cigarette. Then he walked back, deep in thought. When he had paced off the 150 meters, he said belatedly: "That south beam of 6.24 m has an intact corner joint. That indicates the maximum external width of the House. Five beams have been found, including the one 6.2 m long that was found two years ago [30 August 1993], which I believe is the roof beam. I've looked at all possibilities." He sat down with us, trying to ignore our teasing.

"No no, look here," he said, irritated by our incomprehension. He pulled out his knife and traced the layout of the Saved House in the trampled ground. "In the last century an Amsterdam ell measure, 68.8 centimeters long, was found at this spot. That's the unit they used to lay out the House." He pointed his knife across his shoulder towards the digs. "What we have outlined over there measures six meters and twenty centimeters, which is 9 ells, by ten meters and thirty centimeters, which is exactly

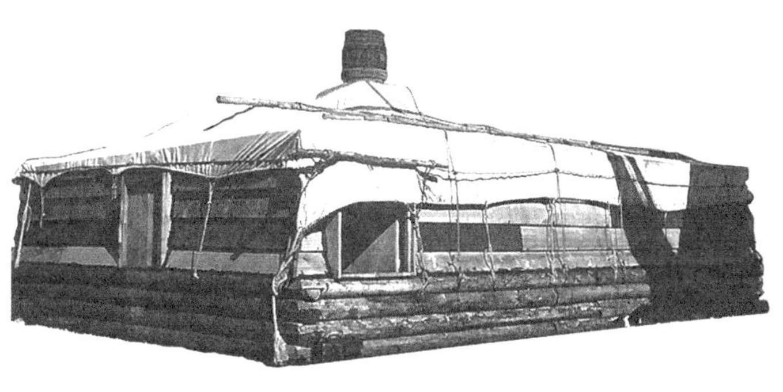

Remaining beams of the wintering cabin, the 'Saved House' and excavation of the cabin's surroundings. In 1997 a life-size reconstruction was build in Amsterdam. Note log-cabin construction closed with ship deck planks, covered with sails (Photo's JJZ).

fifteen ells – a ratio of three to five. That is the Golden Section: the mathematical building measure of the Renaissance. Do you understand?"

We were struck speechless. This insight breathed the soul into a mass of otherwise meaningless data. A design based on the Golden Section comes across as natural: it looks better and more reliable. "Those men became stranded in the unknown," Jerzy went on. "They could have stayed on board and pray to God to save them from the jaws of death. Instead, they took charge of their fate and constructed the Saved House. Now the cabin as we thought it was, until now, was too large. The entry was not attached, but enclosed: it was a small hallway, two ells wide. Everything's falling in place: it matches everything we've discovered up to now. The north beam is buried and weathered and probably in its original position. The south beam is 6.24 m long and lies on the surface. The cornerstones we find are 6.20 m apart. With that width, and a 3 to 5 ratio, the length of the House comes to a little more than ten meters, which is what Carlsen registered." He grinned in triumph. The entire construction can now be recalculated and arises virtually out of the ground. The height of the House is deduced from a worn upright of 206 cm long: three ells and a bit more for the runoff of water and snow, as De Veer wrote: "We covered our house, and made it somewhat higher in the middle that the water might run off" [5 October 1596].

"And something else," Jerzy continued: "The low pile of waste and excrement that we find on the south side was, of course, against the outside of the cabin, not inside. The find pattern shows three concentrations on the southside of the cabin, probably because that's where the doors were at. This is consistent with a fragment in the diary describing how they would be snowed in when the wind came from northern directions. What do you think of that? Where would the snow have ended up, then? In front, or in the rear?"

"Either way," I said, "but away from the wind in the shadow of the cabin is most likely." De Veer wrote: "And as there were three doors in our portal, and our house lay covered under snow, we took the middle door thereof away, and dug a hole in the snow that lay without the house, like the arch of a cellar, wherein we might go to ease ourselves and cast other filth into it" [5 January 1597].

"The Saved House was probably constructed using six by four uprights," analyzed Hans Bonke the next day, while we were sitting over soup. "These uprights were connected with crossbeams. If you are used to life on board of a ship, the House was spacious and offered enough room for seventeen sailors. Atop the roof beams, they seem to have place four beams as a frame for the chimney over the stove. An enormous amount of wood went into building this sturdy cabin. To close the walls, they would have need some 160 m^2 of boards and planks and nail it all together. Carlsen saw some of these and reported them to be 1.5 thumbs (~3.5 cm) thick and 16 thumbs (~40 cm) wide.[8] De Veer writes that this wood was obtained by demolishing the deck cabins of the vessel. Still, twice as many boards were needed as would have thus become available, and it seems that deck planks of the ship were also taken."

"Or did they bring some extra wood to construct a wintering cabin?" I asked, "and, perhaps for the same reason, those hundreds of iron nails too?"

"That is quite possible," Hans nodded kindly. You would almost believe that the construction of a shelter was part of the plan, bearing in mind the retreats that Barents had been forced to accept in 1594 and 1595.

Construction of the Saved House, offering protection against the elements and facilitating their daily routines during the long Arctic night, has been decisive in the survival of the shipwrecked expedition. Dutch shipbuilders adhered to fixed length-to-width ratios, which had been established after years of building experience. In the design of their wintering hut, the ship's carpenter appears to have fallen back upon another ratio, a geometrical ratio to bring order into Nature's chaos. Did he improvise? Surprisingly, the width of the cabin is similar to the width of the ship. Like the vessel, that was considered lost months before, the skipper only let go of the Saved House when the decision to escape Novaya Zemlya in open boats had been made. The Saved House was oriented towards the true north – not the magnetic north – by means of the stars. Through the chimney, the winterers would see the northern star and the stars of *Ursa Minor* that rotated around it. Before the northern side of the house, resembling its bow, was the sloop, upside down, as on the foredeck of a ship. Garbage was disposed of in its wake. So traversed these castaways in nine months by the gates of hell, always north, across the sea of time through the Arctic night.

Chapter Nine

We find parts of the ship

3 *September 1995* – An oak wood yacht of almost 20 m was wrecked before this beach and there must be more – much more – than the 4-m long piece that was recovered here three years ago. Fifty or sixty tons of wood and metal have sunk to the bottom. Add to that the cannons, cannonballs, and two large anchors of about 200 kg each. Stacking sea ice and currents may have moved part of the wreckage, but we assume that at least the heavy fittings and large skeleton remain in this area. The beach is undisturbed, with very regular undulating strandlines representing thousands of years of formation. Whatever there is must be around the high tide line or underwater. The tide at this location is 0.6 m but storms and storm surges may cause a violent run up. Storm waves and ice push accumulated a steep gravel-and-boulder ridge up to three meters above the sea level. In the trough behind this ridge, Jerzy, Bas, and Herre marked about thirty pieces of whitened European oak wood, as well as several points at which the metal detector gave a signal.

"Very little is known of shipbuilding techniques from precisely the times of Barents, when people began experimenting with larger ship types and new building methods," said Jerzy. "During the reclamation of the Zuider Zee, many wrecks of medieval and seventeenth-century ships were found, but the smaller sixteenth-century yachts are much rarer. Nor do any construction drawings remain, because ships were built by sight. It was only in the seventeenth century that basic measurements were specified for mass production. Where Barents' ship was built we don't know, and even the ship's name is not mentioned anywhere".[9] Our experts consider the etchings in De Veer's book realistic: the ship drawings in De Veer's journal appear technically accurate in every detail, which was novel for the time [Mollema 1947, Hoving & Emke 2004]. The ship's main characteristics, shape, size, and riggings are consistent in each drawing.

To add the location of each object we find along the beach to our map of the area, I put the total station on the escarpment and directed Jerzy who jumped around impatiently with the theodolite's reflector. It was a quiet and sunny morning. The metal detectors and magnetometer are capable of detecting metal objects buried by accumulating sea ice under a meter of gravel. With the mapping completed, Jerzy and Bas began to dig into the gravel to find the source of a signal. As soon as the detector beeped, Jerzy stepped back to swing the metal detector left and right and pinpoint the object. Henri hurried to kneel and place his camera close to the gravel. Henri was filming the investigations, with Anton directing across his shoulder.

"Here's something," said Jerzy. Carefully, he and Bas removed the pebbles. "I feel something. There's something here." Henri walked around and started filming from another angle.

"Is someone watching that bear?" Jerzy asked. In the distance, a bear was loitering.

"Aim well at those hands," said the director, while Jerzy uncovered the find.

"No more film," announced the cameraman. A pewter plate emerged from between the beach gravels.

"Pewter plate."

"Splendid, man," said Bas, cleaning the imprinted trademark of the Amsterdam manufacturer: a crowned rose. Bas being the museum's chief conservator, was truly impressed. "It's a fully intact Spanish plate: until now we just had fragments".

The filmmakers struggled to change the videotape. "Can we repeat this once more?" Anton brazenly asked. To my surprise Jerzy took the plate and buried it carefully, as Henri positioned the camera on his shoulder. A red light indicated that we were 'rolling' again. At the detector's first beep, Jerzy looked into the camera with an overly surprised expression on his face. Then he boasted: "I think I'll be finding a pewter plate here." Observing that this remarkable scene had completed, I announced, on behalf of Dima, who was doing kitchen duty, that lunch was ready. The camera crew immediately stowed its gear and walked back contentedly.

"You think you got good stuff?" I called after them. "Putting on quite a show, aren't they? But that's how those boys are." I looked smugly at Bas and Jerzy. Bas smiled and shook his head at Jerzy: "I can't believe you did that. How could you?"

"They asked me, didn't they?" Jerzy replied indignantly. "What should I have done?" Bas kept shaking his head, and Jerzy kicked some pebbles around. I inspected the pristine find. "Don't tell anyone yet," Jerzy said to me. "It should be a surprise. Look: it has the same mark as those plates that Carlsen discovered inside the House." Probably Carlsen or Gundersen or Gardiner dropped it, when carrying their catch into a sloop.

"Din-ner," Dima yelled from camp.

"What would the kitchen be serving this afternoon?" Bas wondered aloud as we walked back.

"They've been peeling potatoes all morning," I replied. "So it is my guess that it will be something with potatoes. And a touch of dill."

The question has arisen: are we looking in the right place? Ice Harbor in particular, beaches full with bleached trees, seems to be a solid trap for driftage. To search the beaches of Ice Harbor, I joined Dima and botanist Anatoli Kuliev, who set out in the afternoon to collect plant and rock samples of Cape Spory Navolok's northern extent. At the same time Herre Wynia and René Gerritsen searched the southern beaches of the Cape. While Dima investigated the bedrock outcrops in the coastal escarpment, and Tolya, silver cape flapping in the wind, disappeared from sight into the interior, I climbed across the hundreds of tree trunks cast ashore. Most of the trunks on the lower beach have cut ends and were most likely lost from lumber floats on the Siberian rivers. Higher on the beach lie the weathered and splintered remains of subfossil trees, some perhaps 5000 years old [Johansen 1999; Zeeberg 2001]. Drift-wood or 'plavnik' may remain floating with sea ice for a decade at most, and large amounts make it to the North Atlantic region. The wood is mostly larch (*Larix sp.*) and includes logs up to 6 m long. Imagine, the winterers hauled about 40–60 sledges of it, each sledge carrying four trunks, over a distance of three kilometers [Bonke 1998].

We had gone about three kilometers north of our camp when amid the flotsam on the shores of the bay, I noticed a remarkable piece of wreckage that looked like a ship's timber. I felt great pleasure and wonder. The wooden pegs and cast-iron nails indicated that this piece was truly part of the ice-wrecked vessel. I photographed its position and lifted it up to haul it off. It was a heavy piece, easily one meter long. When I triumphantly returned with the oak wood catch across my shoulder, more of it was already laid out in our camp. Herre had discovered four more timbers around the cape's beacon. Our experts tell that the retrieved items belonged to different parts of the ship's structure. They are small fragments, and it appears that the vessel was crushed by the ice, disintegrated, and sank to the bottom, perhaps within a year after the ship was abandoned. Ice shove and currents subsequently scattered the wreckage, washing pieces ashore around the entire promontory. It remains a possibility, however, that large parts of the vessel remained frozen into an ice floe and were carried away some unknown (but potentially great) distance.

4 September 1995 – Today I decided to return to Ice Harbor to see if I can find any more ship parts – and to recover my gloves. I must have taken them off while photographing the timber yesterday when I sat down to put a new roll of film in the camera. The day dawned bitingly cold, so I was determined to recover the loss right away. The wind was blowing straight from the north, I got tears in my eyes, and everybody was sniffing. The sky was calm, though, and a sharp-edged cloud, flattened and elongated by very high winds stood motionless above the island, darkening the landscape, and leaving the uncovered sky a deep transparent blue. I found Jerzy and signed myself out. "How long will you be gone then?" he asked grumpily, trowel in hand. "Bout two hours or so," I said.

"Well, take a gun, will you?"

Dima and Tolya cut across the cape during our excursion yesterday, but this time I decided to follow the shore. The surf bubbled quietly and while I was walking across the dark, pebbly beach, my feet crunching in wet gravel and pebbles, I recalled an amusing passage that Gerrit de Veer wrote about inspecting a bear's den at this very spot, in the snowbanks that accumulate each winter along the 4-5 m tall escarpment: "We went to the place from whence [the bear] came, to see whether she had any holes there, where we found a great hole made in the snow, about a man's length in depth, the entry thereof being very narrow, and within wide. There we thrust in our pikes to see if there was anybody home, and perceiving it was empty, one of our men crept into it, but not too far, for it was fearful as it was. After that we went along by the seaside [...] and saw that the ice was piled up in such manner that it looked like whole towns, with towers and bulwarks round about them" [15 April 1597].

When I rounded the promontory, the beach narrowed and suddenly the escarpment loomed so steeply that I had to sling the rifle across my back to climb it. Atop the 20 m-high cliff, I was able to stand and, upright, spotted two birds, moving in an uncontrolled (or very lazy) fashion across the dark blue water. In the blink of an eye the onshore wind had carried them towards me. It was a pair of big, golden-brown eagles with shimmering white tails (*Haliaeetus albicilla*). For a brief moment they whirled around me, while I struggled to ready my camera, and then they soared inland with the stiff breeze. From my elevated position I noticed the clear surf line 200 m to 1 km offshore, broken by occasional shoals. The breakers appeared to follow the edge of a shallow with roughly the same extent as the shore ice in the aerial photos. We are experiencing a mild Novaya Zemlya summer, as North Atlantic storm systems march into the Barents Sea one after the other. This summer Ice Harbor is ice-free, and neither is there any shore ice, which is exceptional. Shore ice or landfast ice usually endures through the summer, and it is visible around Cape Spory Navolok in the out-of-focus aerial photographs that our partners brought on my request. Without a doubt, Barents' vessel ran aground on the shoals that surround a shallow covered by ice, perhaps when they attempted to anchor [26 August 1596].

Kravchenko in 1979 and 1980 sounded the rim of the shore ice area and found water depths of 3 to 4 m. His theory was that the ship had been pushed inside the lagoon. In the *Nederland-USSR Bulletin* [1981], Kravchenko wrote:

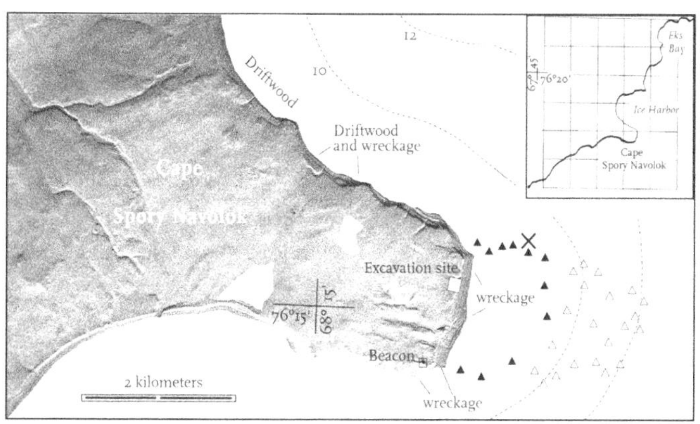

(Above) Map of Cape Spory Navolok with locations of drift wood and ship timber at the water line. Black triangles indicate surfacing rocks and the probable location of the ship's grounding (cross). (Below) Plate for 25 Oktober 1596 in the German (Hulsius) edition showing Jacob van Heemskerck (with long coat and fox-fur hat) and Gerrit de Veer fighting off polar bear around the vessel. Note fox trap next to the wintering cabin.

The more we thought about it, the clearer our idea became of where to look for Barents' ship. The journal of De Veer, which is very accurate, helped us a lot. My colleagues and I found the journal to be splendid! After careful analysis we concluded (because De Veer was eyewitness) that Willem Barents' vessel was trapped in Ledyanya Gavan' [Ice Harbor]. We collected proof for this theory. That part of the Harbor where the ship had been, was like a stone fish-trap from which, we found, it would have been impossible to escape. We reasoned as follows. In August 1596, the ship was beset in the ice and was transported with the ice. At [Cape Spory Navolok], the ice moved toward the shore. Suddenly it must have moved up and down with such amplitude that the ship was tossed over a rocky, submarine barrier. Now that it had left the rolling ice mass, the ship was trapped between that rocky shallow and the shore ice. We found that these rocks extended from the cape at a depth of less than 1.5 to 1.8 m. The ship had been damaged and slowly filled with water. Result: it became heavier and lay deeper. No force on earth could have rescued the ship from its entrapment.

"Well Yuozas [Kaziauskas], let's pay a visit to Willem Barents' ship," I said jokingly. When we walked along the beach, laughing, we came across the first frame... It consisted of oak wood and was corroded by the familiar effects of time and salt. We were there for only ten days, but still managed to salvage fragments of the vessel, together with metal parts and nails, from the water. To prove that these parts are from Willem Barents' vessel, we took a few nails from Barents' winter camp. Specialists have confirmed that both nails do indeed date to the sixteenth century. In 1980, during our third expedition, we hoped to rescue the remains of the sunken vessel. Although the lagoon was ice-covered and circumstances were difficult, we still managed to search the larger part of it. To be able to dive, the divers made holes in 1.5 m thick ice by exploding mines. From every hole thus made, they could explore a perimeter of 25 m. Lack of fuel forced us to halt this operation. In the summer

> of 1981 we intend to try, with the help of metal detectors, to find metal parts of the ship. I want to find the anchors, the guns, and possibly the lower hull of the ship. We found pieces of lead, which may indicate that the hull was lead-clad. Judging by the 80 timber fragments we have so far recovered, the upper parts of the vessel were destroyed. The lower part, heavy from the lead, must have sunk after the ice had cut through it [Kravchenko 1981, 17-18].

Dmitri Kravchenko and his diving team *Dolphin* from Moscow searched the lagoon, but they did not find any ship remains. However, the presence of shorefast ice and the draft of Barents' ship make it unlikely that the vessel ever entered the lagoon. The ship's draft was probably a little over 2 m; thus, it grounded onto the subsea rocks. The ship did not refloat, even when most of the sea ice had retreated under west-southwestern winds. The most probable location of the wreck when it foundered, then, is the northeastern edge of the shallow, where the sea bottom drops to 10-15 m. "We could not perceive otherwise but that we lay frozen right down to the ground, and there it was three and a half fathom [~6 m] deep" [5 October 1596]. Trapped in the ice, this sturdy wooden ship lay not directly in front of the House, but a bit more to the north, still almost one kilometer offshore. This observation may also explain that wreckage was scattered along the entire cape. And it implies that more wreckage may be on the sea bottom *outside* the lagoon. Unfortunately, we are unprepared for a search of the sea bottom. On the beach I found first one, then the other glove.

Work is progressing steadily. Sometimes the instruments malfunction, but I am getting quite handy at overcoming that. On the laptop's small screen, the map grows daily: a cloud of green electronic dots in a black field. The computer file contains the altitude and coordinates associated with each dot. Back home, 'Surfer' map-producing software will create a fantastic

3D wire structure that can be rotated inside the computer. Each day the excavation produces more finds. Five small, elegant pewter figures have emerged from the soil, each about the size of a thumb. They depict Faith, Hope, Love, a Scythian horse-rider, and a Venus figure: a remarkable mixture of Renaissance and Biblical symbols. Dig Master Hans records the location of each find on an accurate floor plan of the Saved House, and there's a continual flow of small plastic sample bags with shards, textile, bones, and special items. "Actually, we should sift the mess, but we don't have the time for that," says Hans. Two people do, however, minutely rework the long pile of black soil that has been carried out of the dig. The finds are described, photographed, recorded, and then packed. Aboard ship, the objects will undergo initial conservation before transport to Moscow. The metal objects in particular are now subjected to enormous changes of temperature and humidity and must be either dried or kept just moist enough to delay the process of corrosion. Compared with the finds from 1871, the wooden and metal objects collected around the Saved House in 1993 and 1995 are in poor condition. The activities on the site during the 1870s removed the protective ice cover, initiating a runaway decay by exposure of the frozen soil. Precisely in those years, the Little Ice Age, a centuries-long cold spell, was coming to an end, further increasing soil humidity and rates of corrosion. And now, more than a century later we see the last bits emerge from melting perennial snow patches.

In 1991, ten years after his initial surveys, Kravchenko discovered a plank (probably the mast-bench or standing thwart of a sloop) and a light-blue shirt that belonged to one of the winterers in the snowbank at the foot of the escarpment. These snowbanks have now altogether melted away, and on the same spot, three days ago, we found a grey woolen shirt in such good condition that Anton argued it is modern. Miloradovich in

1934 also reported: "Near the base of the escarpment, about 100-150 m of the water, lay several planks of a small boat, and nearby, a piece of a coarsely shaped paddle.[2]" According to Frans Heeres, Kravchenko's Dutch pilot, the mast-bench and the shirt were lost, probably disposed of sometime later in their journey [personal communication 1996]. This bench and these two shirts relate to the day that the winterers prepared their boats for the return journey. They had rescued two boats from their ship: the smaller *bok* (5 m) and larger *schuit* (6.5 m). "We turned the boat that lay by the house with her keel upwards and began to mend it and to heighten the gunwales, so that it might be fitter to carry us over the sea". It was a warm day, that made them take their shirts of while working: "The 4th of June it was fair clear weather and indifferently warm". But the weather changed, and the garments were left outside: "It was foul, uncomfortable weather with hail and snow, and inside the house we made all things ready: sails, oars, masts, sprit, rudder, leeboard and all other necessary things" [5 June 1597].

The amendments were not as sturdy as they would have wanted. On 1 July 1597, in the ice, "the sloop broke in many places, especially in places where we had added to it, like the mast and mast-bench." The wood needed to adjust the boats was taken from the Saved House. The winterers also disassembled the roof, and this seems to have quickened the collapse of the cabin. Its interior became encapsulated in snow, which endured until the mid-nineteenth century. The beach pebbles that now surround the site were spread on the roof on 29 October 1596 to stabilize the sailcloth; they probably came down when the hut was taken apart the following June. The sandstone rocks recovered in the Saved House, according to Dima, originate from the Permian outcrop near the Cape's beacon, because around the Saved House, bedrock appears to be of Carbonian age [Badyukov 1997], with little fossil imprints in it. The sandstones were probably collected on 11 January 1597, said Hans, Xeroxed copy of the journal in hand: "We went about a quarter of a mile to a hill, from whence we fetched certain stones, which we laid in the fire to keep us warm in our bunks."

All around us we see that the area is warming: no sea ice, big waves, thick moss, meltwater of melting permafrost pooling on the beach. The Saved House's remains wet and rotting. Average temperatures have gone up and down with a decade-long regularity ever since the 'Little Ice Age' came to an end. We're not even certain wether this climate episode had already begun when the Dutch entered the Arctic. Barents was able to round Cape Zhelaniya twice, indicating that the summer limit of sea ice was north of Novaya Zemlya. They had been able to sail through the Yugor Strait into the Kara Sea during their first journey, but the next year ran into sea ice. Russians encountered in the Yugor Strait in 1595 told that the strait freezes over at variable times, and on average remains frozen from early November until June [Van Linschoten 1601]. That is exactly the same as in 1959 [Arctic Pilot 1959], as yet the warmest decade in our century. A series of harsh winters occurred in northwestern Europe in the 1560s and 1570s, effectively starting a cold period that reached a first low in the 1590s [Bradley & Jones 1993; Buisman 2000]. Dutch summers were particularly cool and rainy between 1593 and 1597. If the 'Little Ice Age' had any effect on the Netherlanders, then it was that the harsh winters back home had strengthened their ability and preparedness to tolerate the cold.

To relish the quiet and solitude while it lasts, I volunteered for another night watch, my fourth in the past nine days. As the sun rose over the sea at 3:30 a.m., Victor zipped open the tent, pinching my foot; murmured something, and departed to get some sleep himself. Emerging from a deep rest I was disoriented and grappled to regain reality. Looking beside me I found Herre sound asleep. I quickly slid into my ice-cold clothes and crawled out of the tent. Outside I could feel the sleeping-warmth evaporate from my collar and buttoned up tightly. As summer gives way to winter, the soft soil freezes at night. Tonight the small puddles are iced over. The frozen membrane is sturdy enough to support only one step: leaving a grand star in the ice like that on the windshield of a car after a collision. The sun is glittering over the Kara Sea and orange light pours around the cape. Just to be sure, I climbed onto the improvised wooden table in our camp and used my binoculars to survey the surroundings for bears. Nothing moved. To get out of the wind, I went down the escarpment to the beach. Alone with that great copper sun, I am seated on a boulder writing, with my rifle on my knees. Alone, and yet not alone: the others are sound asleep. I lit a cigarette, which isn't really my custom, but Jerzy passes me a pack of cigarettes every now and then. He will work only with guys who smoke.

Arctic landscapes have a bare physical essence. The land reflects the forces and cycles of climate. It ages: you could say it lives. Because this world is so desolate and empty, you notice little things: you see the few flowers, a specific rock, and a distant animal. The pure atmosphere makes everything crystal-clear to the eye. You'll be lying in your tent listening to the wind, and when it drops off, you raise yourself to see what's going on. With the sun above the horizon in the east the landscape is all different from what we have seen during the day. The land changes as the light changes. A small bump in the middle of the day will assume serious dimensions at the low sun angle of late evening or early morning. Bas told me that during his solitary 1978 stay at Smeerenburg he'd wake up at 3:00 in the morning, and the landscape appeared unfamiliar with all the shadows reversed. Thus, I am now looking across a wildly undulating beach. I count a dozen (12!) pronounced beach ridges, not including the present storm ridge, which will be added in the future. The uprising of the land is gradual and viscous, then during a major storm event a ridge may disconnect and shed its contact with the ocean.

For a moment in time, this place was observed and watched, as we are observing and watching it now. It staged the wintering. For the vast remainder of time, this was a play before empty benches, a philosopher would say. At early age I was captivated by the Viking Mars-images printed in newspapers and magazines in 1976. A rusted landscape, bleak and weathered – billions of years old. It had never been taken in by any creature. It had just been there, forever. The distribution of rocks of every size is just right; perhaps an artist would be able to lay them down like that. We humans landed a camera in it (a fax machine, in fact). Images transmitted by orbiting spacecraft of the Moon and Mars have shown us that the density of impact-cratering is the same at any scale that you choose. Probes crashing into the Moon in the 1960s would relay their death flight carrying a television camera, showing the vast impact basins, expanding beyond the field of view as they approached. Closer up, there were kilometer-scale craters inside of those basins, and finally, in its last seconds before impact, the camera relayed meter-sized pits. (Under a microscope, even individual soil grains taken from the Moon by astronauts were seen to have tiny impact craters). The seemingly random distribution of rocks and craters, but also the 'fractal' geometry of coasts, reflect the math that includes our Golden Section. It famously is seen in the spiral of a nautilus as well as a galaxy, in the similarity between arteries and rivers, sand grains and boulders, the oscillation of atoms and sounds. A design based on the 'Golden Section' comes across as natural: it looks better and reliable.

5 September 1995 – For its last assignment, I set up the 'total station' near the surf, about 200 m away from Anton, who was by the escarpment, pants down around his knees, fumbling with a strip of toilet paper all tangled by the strong wind. While sweeping the powerful telescope across the beach, I caught him in the cross hairs of the theodolite. Judging by the patient grin on his face, I sensed that he, an experienced yachtsman, knew precisely how to untangle this knot. Further to the right, Hans was running after a sampling bag. For three weeks now we have shared our lives, and less than two weeks from today I'll say good-bye and probably never see them again. When I looked up, Dima handed me the reflector and started the computer. I sat down on the gravel to hitch my waders and then walked into the surf to measure the high-tide swash line. Dima manned the machine and after completing our task, we embraced each other and in a jubilant mood packed up the theodolite. In six days, we recorded more than 3000 data points. Dima understood from radio exchanges this morning that *Kiriev* may be back tomorrow. Time to stow gear and our turn for camp duty!

6 September 1995 – In the early morning of the tenth day, a shout from the night watch awakened us: "*Kiriev* is dropping anchor in Ice Harbor!" The announcement caused some commotion. In a short while, the camp was in uproar. Gawronski was assigning tasks, arms flailing expansively, and if something wasn't being done fast enough, he'd do it himself. Within the hour the evacuation was in full swing. Yuri Mazurov oversaw logistics. His radio contact with the ship confirmed that we had to go now, or we might be stuck here for days. We could see weather moving in along the horizon. The reverse of our landing process was taking place, with a line of people moving up and down the beach. At the prearranged time, the barge ran ashore and delivered our friends from Ivanov Bay. We greeted them as if they had been gone for a whole year. "No, didn't find a thing," they said, and their disappointment was palpable. Well, things will be better next time around.

"All right, pick up that marker," Jerzy said impatiently. Jerzy and I lifted the heavy marble tombstone from Terschelling onto a bed constructed by the Russians. Boyarsky was supposed to do the unveiling, and René would take a photograph. So it had gone, more than a century ago, on the Orange Islands, where the marker stone still lies. For the moment, nobody showed any interest in placing a memorial marker in Ice Harbor. The remaining party was taking a last look around the Saved House. Dirk and Herre pointed out those places where the most important discoveries had been made.

The sailors nervously urged everyone on. Jerzy deliberated briefly with Dirk and Hans, then made a quick decision: that roof beam will come along. Left here it would just rot, or someone else would take it. If it ever finds its way through Russian bureaucracy to the Netherlands, it will make a fitting monument in the Rijksmuseum. Four men marched it down the escarpment on their shoulders. At noon the last group sailed away from Cape Spory Navolok. The landing craft was cast off, and the distance from the beach increased every second. As our *plashkot* withdrew, we watched the remains of our small camp appear on top of the broad, flat plateau. Using the power of its motor, the craft slowly turned and set course for *Kiriev*. This would be the moment to remember once again the shipwreck of four centuries ago and the work of all our predecessors. I peered into the clear, shallow waters and watched our shadow move over the yellowish boulders on the sea bottom, hoping to catch a glimpse of some object still lying there waiting to be discovered. In the afternoon, our sojourn in the Arctic desert was like an incident that came and passed. As before, we rolled along with the ship. I lay sweating in my unventilated bunk. There was tea at 3:30 and dinner at 7:30: potato soup, baked potatoes, a bit of garlic and condensed milk with a slice of bread. The sauna had been fired up and Dirk, Herre, Pieter, and I took a bath. It was heavenly. I studied my face in the mirror: brown and dirty, but not filthy; bloodshot eyes, my skin red-hot from ten days of polar winds, my hair sticky, golden brown, and soft like an animal's. As fast as we had settled in, we got up and left. Only then it registered with me that in those ten days, the pulsating drone of the engines never left my ears.

Chapter Ten

In the Yugor Strait

7 *September 1995* – "Barents and his crew were gentlemen," Jerzy told the crowd gathered in the mess. "Take, for instance, this exquisitely shaped copper button. It shows that they were not a bunch of vagrants. They traveled in style. After discovering the Northeast Passage, Barents was to immediately establish trade contacts and therefore had bolts of fabric, among other things, on board. We have now found the leaden seals from this cloth near the Saved House." R/V *Ivan Kiriev* has embarked on its voyage home, and Jerzy presented the results of nine days of hard labor to the ship's crew. A selection of objects is exhibited on the mess room tables. The expeditions of 1993 and 1995 together produced 1370 itemized artifacts. More than a hundred soil samples were collected for analysis of plant seeds, pollen, and human parasites (fleas and lice). The survey has revealed the cabin's floor plan and given us a view of its interior and its Golden Section building structure. The objects that we recovered bear witness as to how the men gathered around the fire and mended their clothing, shoes, and instruments. Filling in these colorful details, we've completed the Rijksmuseum collection with the smallest objects. The prime example of these is the series of ten mythological figurines that were probably ornamental to cargo items. The commercial load represented a sample of the booming European cultures.

The expedition's finds are being processed at two tables in a laboratory room on the top deck of the ship. Some sample bags simply contain an amorphous mass of soil, held together by moss, which is gradually extracted to reveal diverse kinds of potsherds, nails, textiles, and bones. All the shards are then relabeled and sorted by color: orange-glazed shards are collected in bags with other orange-glazed shards, green with green, and white with white, etc. Objects are individually inspected, soil fragments are brushed off, and then the objects are repackaged. The iron nails are wrapped in wet toilet paper, then in aluminum foil, to delay corrosion. The pewter figurines, of which ten were found altogether, are being dried by immersion in alcohol. The mystery of the lead plaque showing Barents' signature has been resolved. The inscription is not a signature but indicates a '3 ons' weight measure. After the exhibition for *Kiriev's* crew, these fragile finds would be repackaged, to be opened, we hope, only at the Rijksmuseum's preservation studio in one of the turrets of the majestic building in Amsterdam. Conservator Ab Hoving, who holds office there, told me: "In my studio I experienced a major *historic sensation* from a small glass plate that I just couldn't rub clean. In the same collection of artifacts, I found three out of four parts of the frame that had held the glass, and suddenly I realized this had been a mirror. The corroded glass that I had been ignorantly studying a moment earlier once reflected the winterers' faces, and for a brief moment I felt their presence. It was as if they were looking over my shoulder in the remaining layer of mercury."

We're exuberantly celebrating the successful completion of the research activities, and tall tales abound. Our comrades from Ivanov Bay, by their own accounts, were put through quite an ordeal, and had almost been abandoned in that abominable Arctic land. They were indestructible, however, and we call them *Ivanova tarakan*: the Ivanov Cockroaches. Pieter and George told how the Russians who were rain-soaked or had fallen overboard would stand over fire "until they were steaming and their pants caught fire." Suddenly appear pickled mushrooms, a sausage, canned fish (called 'mass grave'). Boyarsky had produced a concoction of pure alcohol, Chechnian grasses, and some water. Another mix with red pepper burns you out of hell. Later that night, through the drubbing and howling of another storm, a feeble song was heard throughout the ship as Starkov, drunk but indefatigable, tried to remember some German opera. (But when he's on, the singing is splendid: Starkov's tenor with Dima's basso.) When, at last, the beer was gone, an alcoholic meltdown followed with the last vodka. "Those Dutch – they drink like Pomors," said Boyarsky. The kitchen chef was on the kitchen floor, dead-drunk. Sailors grinned as they stepped over him; they were working and hadn't touched a drop.

Shortly after midnight, when the celebration had ended, Jerzy pushed me on ahead of him, behind Vitali and Dima: "Hurry, hurry!" Dima has a brother, Daniel, and another brother who lives in St. Louis, Missouri, who resembles Jerzy, as he says, "like two drops of vodka." Tonight, all three of us are brothers, because we've stayed on our feet the longest. You too, Vitali – you are our brother, too. Embracing, we stumbled into Vitali's cabin. Vitali was wearing his *speznats* shirt – the blue-and-white stripes of the Russian Navy. He nodded amiably and stirred his heating coil in a glass of water that, indeed, started bubbling in no time. He had a plastic bag full of cookies and also offered us condensed milk with our tea. Then the door opened, first just a wee bit, and Anton entered.

"There you are!" he said. He had been listening at each door until he found us, I think; he had come back into the mess room and found everybody gone. Anton sat down on the bunk, dangling his legs over the edge. Since he was unable to lean now, he sat down bent slightly forward; it looked like he was broken. Vitali finished his hospitable household chores and proceeded to show us a picture of his small daughter, a cheerful girl of five.

I glanced once again towards Vitali, the charmer, and I could see little direct resemblance, but really, she is a beautiful child. The picture also affected Anton, who had been drinking and was a bit more emotional than usual. While Dima softly hummed a melancholy song and Jerzy plucked at his beard, Anton wrestled a photograph of his loved ones from his wallet. He peered at it and then, without taking his eyes off the photo, passed it on to me with a smile. I grasped the black-and-white print: a Dutch woman and a Dutch girl, smiling at the photographer. "They're coming to pick me up," he said, "they're coming to pick me up at the airport. Maybe you've seen them because they also saw me off." I handed the photo back to him.

"Hey!" said Dima seriously: "Why we have no drink?" He got up and with Vitali distributed the glasses and the vodka.

"Just a tad, OK?" said Anton, laughing but holding out his glass. "Yeah. Thank you very much."

"How's your movie?" Jerzy roared at him. Anton raised his glass:

"Good. Very good!"

"Anton," I said, "Did I ever thank you for your help when my theodolite didn't work? Did I ever thank you for that?"

"Don't mention it," Anton nodded, laughing.

"I really appreciated it, though," I said.

"It was entirely my pleasure."

8 September 1995 – We are belayed off the Russian mainland coast, near Amderma. *Kiriev* quietly rides the swells in the pale sunlight. Through my binoculars, I followed the descent of an Antonov-26 transport plane towards a landing strip on a sandy beach berm. The town rises on a slope about 15 m above the sea, and its seaside is one uninterrupted landfill of rusted junk and oil barrels. A small pilot launch was heading for *Kiriev* across the choppy waters. This black, smoking vessel was a steel container with car tires along its sides and a wooden cubicle just large enough for two or three men on top. Once it had come alongside, Starkov lowered himself via the rope ladder and was caught by one of the two men aboard. At 9:00 a.m., Starkov waved goodbye, standing legs apart on the galloping vessel, which lent a dramatic air to it all. Then they headed for the coast, where Starkov will board the Antonov-26 to Vorkuta and from there continue via Moscow to Longyearbyen. From Amderma back to Archangelsk, *Kiriev* will put another 1300 km under her bow.

Not even ten kilometers away we arrived at Staten Island, the name given to the island by the first Dutch Arctic expedition in 1594 in honor of the States General, the parliament of the Republic of the United Provinces. The modern name is Mestny Island or Ostrov Mestnyy, a 4.5 km long island just outside the Yugor Strait. Here the Dutch fleet lay at anchor in September 1595 with seven ships and about 180 men. This is a truly historical place even if there isn't the slightest indication that anything ever happened here at all. Seven wooden ships crept between the small island and the mainland, sheltering from the driving ice masses on the other side. It was a desperate shelter, following a do-or-die attempt by Willem Barents to enter the ice sea. Morale was already low when in full view of all the crew two men were killed by a polar bear, on the beach of the mainland, that we oversee from the deck of our ship.

Jan Huyghen van Linschoten: "Then came a large white bear, probably the same that we chased away from Staten Island the other day. It appeared to be starving and casually approached two of our men busy seeking crystals. They did not pay attention to what came so harmfully close. The bear caught one in the back of his neck and pulled him away, without the victim understanding what was happening to him and although he was crying for help, his companion, who had no other means, fled, stunned. The others hearing and seeing the event came running to chase away the bear, but in vain, because it had bitten through the cheek and jaw of the man, almost cracking his skull. And even though he was working at him for a long time with his knife, the bear sucked his blood on end so that this poor bootsman died. Several ships hearing the racket from afar immediately set out boats and rowed towards us but the disaster didn't end here. Before they arrived it was done and when the bear had had its fill of the first man, he turned towards the group that, although they resisted, seeing that it came running towards them furiously, fled, in short the one who couldn't run paid for it. This was the bootsman of our vessel, who was killed like the first man. Now at last with much firepower and clubbing [crew from Willem Barents vessel] killed the bear. They skinned it and inside him found halve heads and cheekbones of the men killed, without anything else. The bear was exceedingly large, more like a large ox. This horrible accident scared and angered the crews. The only thing we could do was inter the dead to our best ability with honor on Staten Island" [in: L'Honoré Naber 1914, p. 178]. A fine example of Jan Huyghen's juicy writing.

Jan Huyghen van Linschoten marked the burial site with a small cross and so, at 12:30 the plashkot put us ashore directly in front of the marked location. Standing on the beach gravels, George pointed out the different landforms that we recognize on Jan Huyghen's map, to assure everyone that we will be searching in the right spot. Capes, the beach across the water, and the various shallow, rocky inlets are easily recognizable on the very accurate map. So are the remarkable bands of peat, which seem to descend like glaciers from the center of the island to the sea. Van Linschoten's map shows the most obvious features as they would appear to a vessel approaching its shores.

Staten Island (Mestny Island, 4.5 km long) with the narrow strait that provided shelter to the 1595 fleet and beach, on the mainland, where two men were killed by a bear. Map and illustration showing the island's remarkable 'peat glaciers' and burial site from Van Linschoten (1601).

We didn't directly spot anything resembling a grave, so George proposed a bay-to-bay search. Finding the burial site would also shed light on a mystery created by a passage and plate in the German edition of De Veer's manuscript [Hulsius 1598], which claimed that five mutineers had been hanged and buried on Staten Island at the same location as the bear victims. As my boots grinded between the rounded cobbles and I heard the hissing of waves on gravel felt the strong sensation that Willem Barents and Jan Huyghen walked these same steps, separately, estimating their chances, shooting hare. On the highest, central part of the island we spot a wooden tower with a light on top. This lighthouse we found was powered by a thermonuclear battery of the kind that is used on interplanetary spacecraft, with cooling fins on the sides. Electricity was generated by heat and radioactivity released by a decaying strontium core, and our colleagues advised that we keep a minimum distance of 50 m.

Our search of the burial site yielded modern nails and a German cartridge from World War II. Over the centuries, the extensive peat 'glaciers' tumbling out to sea had probably pushed all away. "Peat lies meters deep along the shore," George said, disappointed. "What all may have covered up those 400-year-old graves? They can't be found."

9 September 1995 – Through a few threadbare holes in the cloud cover, golden rays sprayed across a dark world. *Kiriev* was sailing a straight line through Yugor Strait, a winding passage between Vaygach Island and the Russian mainland. Balthasar de Moucheron had wanted to erect his fort where the strait narrows to about 3 km, to close this entry to the Northeast Passage to competing vessels. It was with remarkable foresight, albeit a few centuries too soon and probably overlooking the Kara Gates to the north of the island. From the aft-deck, I observed the angular bend in the ship's wake from a sudden change of course. Ahead in the distance, I suddenly noticed a lonely settlement atop a plateau on the mainland coast. The ship was closing in on it fast, and I recognized wooden buildings on the beach, towers on the plateau, and then, through my binoculars, barbed wire-walls of barbed wire. I hurried forward along the gangway, where a few our Russian colleagues stared silently ahead.

"Khabarova," one said grimly: "Gulag."

Kiriev dropped anchor in Vaygach Island's Train Bay at 5:00 p.m. The landscape appeared liquid under hundreds of moving reindeer. The bay received its name from bags of train oil that were found half-buried in the beach gravels. Train Bay, now home to the small settlement of Varnek, was the first harbor to the Dutch fleet after their long journey past the Scandinavian coast, through hollow seas, making way against a cold wind blowing out of the wrong direction, from the north-northeast. In the bay, with ice racing past, they lay somewhat sheltered by the promontory called Idols Cape (Cape Diakanova). "We lay there as trapped," recorded Jan Huyghen. A yacht was dispatched to explore their chances, but it made it only halfway through the straight to the next bay, Cross Cape. August 1595 and to their great disappointment the fleet found the Yugor Strait to be full of sea ice. On the beach were the slaughtered carcasses of five walruses, half-buried sacks of skin with stinking train oil, sledges with fox skins and walrus hide. The sailors took some of those, ignoring the bartering system that the Samojeds had set up with the Russians: take some and leave some. Admiral Nay was inexorable and according to the mustering statutes that were well-known to each seaman, punished the theft.[9] He left one man behind on Vaygach Island and keelhauled another, tearing his body into two pieces, according to an image in the German edition of De Veer's journal [Hulsius 1598]. Men died while a thick fog enveloped the bay and the dead were buried on land. Spirits were low. Laying there in their miserable port, the crews started to complain, wrote Jan Huyghen, "secretly, that they would freeze with ships and all."

We are across the water from Khabarova, which a century ago was the last supply post – coal, dogs, and provisions – to the expeditions by Dr. Nansen and Baron E. Von Toll. It had a warehouse supplied by Alexander Sibiryakov,[10] "a large red building, with white door-frames, of a very homelike appearance," wrote Fridtjof Nansen. *Fram* sailed here, that sturdy three-mast-boat, and would have been right before our eyes on 30 July 1893, out on her mind-boggling journey. "There came a number of strange figures clad in heavy robes of reindeer-skin, which nearly touched the deck. They were fine, stalwart-looking fellows, these Russian traders who barter with the natives, giving them brandy in exchange for bearskins, sealskins, and other valuables, and who, once they have a hold on a man, keep him in such a state of dependence that he can scarcely call his soul his own. [...] Soon, too, the Samoyeds came flocking on board, pleasant-featured people of the broad Asiatic type" [Farthest North, p. 52].

As soon as *Kiriev* had dropped anchor, small outboards came racing past. The occupants waved, made a rapid turn around the vessel to come alongside, and quickly climbed aboard. Nenets, or Samoyeds as they had been called.[11] On *Kiriev's* deck quickly gathered a group of small men with weathered oriental faces. We kept our distance while the crew, tactfully but forcefully, confined them to the aft deck. They were after alcohol but received our, virtually untouched, stock of chocolate bars and some other delicacies instead. Invited to come ashore, we prepared the landing craft.

Varnek is a small settlement of wooden barracks. As we approached a pier, only children and a few elders were waiting. The kids didn't smile; they just stared. Villainous Orthodox missionaries and then the Communists attempted to break the Nenets' social organization by banishing shamans and by exiling clans from their sacred grounds. They were deported to Naryan Mar in 1954, when the Soviet military arrived to turn the region into a nuclear test ground. Varnek served as part of the Gulag and as home base for some dirty lead and copper mining on the other side of the bay. The town is a mess of broken glass and oil barrels. The young adults that we encountered were drunk. George explained that the Nenets lack the enzyme required to break down alcohol: thus, they remain drunk for days on end. He added that inbreeding is visible in their faces. It is terribly desolate, even now in summer, the most exuberant of seasons.

We hear that Varnek has about one hundred inhabitants, but many fewer in winter. The children stay for the summer with their grandparents on Vaygach and spend the other nine months on the mainland. Most of them live in Amderma and Naryan Mar, where the parents find work. On Vaygach, a 100 km long, mostly flat expanse of endless, fog-shrouded bogs and rolling terrain, a couple of families tend to their reindeer herds. The reindeer population, which numbered about 1200 three years ago, is rapidly declining: a trend associated with diseases that were better controlled during the Soviet days, when veterinary care was federally regulated. The community buys its tea, sugar, and vodka with the slight earnings it makes from the reindeer. Chartered icebreakers occasionally stop off at Varnek to allow tourists to buy a kitschy collection of fox fur, bear teeth, dolls, and reindeer skins. The older villagers surrounded us, cackling: "dollar, Amerikanski dollar." Henri explained to a woman that we were not from the United States, but from the Netherlands.

"Netherlands? *Ne panemayo* [I don't understand]," she replied, irritated. She walked off, causing a besotted old woman to fall down and stay down, cussing in Russian.

Sunday, 10 September 1995 – Across Yugor Strait on the Russian mainland is Khabarova, a small wooden village by a gravelly beach that was built over the old Pomor settlement of Nikolskoye. A narrow brook with clear tundra water comes from the brown-green hills behind the village. Vaygach glows in fall colors across the blue waters. Inland there is much old junk, just like at Varnek: mining tip-carts, antiquated tractors marked 'Made in USA', pieces of rail, a rust-encrusted fox trap, a zinc plate, big tuffs of white asbestos and an Art Deco spoon from the 1930s. We walked over planks between broken buildings and a few blossoming flowers. Eugene showed us a brick with the inscription 'ЧКЗ', the acronym for *Chelyabinsk Keramik Завод* (factory), indicating the brick was made in the southern Ural region. Most of the tombstones at the small cemetery were sagging. Coffins that were partially pushed above ground by repeated freezing and melting of the permafrost soil, have fallen apart. The exposed bones show that many children were buried here.

This dark past cuts right through the heart of Russian society. Khabarova was a prison camp between 1930 and – at least – 1943. Criminals and people who had fallen out of grace with the Stalinist system were sent here to die. Vorkuta was the gate to the hell of Siberia and Vaygach, the northern fringes of the *Gulag Archipelago*, so named for its geographic spreading. Inside the barracks at Khabarova, a dilapidated red flag with hammer and sickle bears silent witness to the oppressors of those days. The Russians have been very serious during our stay ashore. They would rather not talk about it, except to allow as how their fathers or grandfathers were imprisoned. Yuri bitterly rolled up the Communist flag. On the plateau that overlooks the barracks are factory sheds, either caved in or burnt out. There is a central field surrounded by the tall, barbed-wire walls we saw when we moved through the strait. A heavy door of steel grating that was torn off its hinges lies in front of an earthen bunker. Inside this sinister complex are five cells with wooden doors. Each underground cell has a barred window, which allows only a view of the sky, and a bracket in the wall for a chain. The prison has lost none of its oppressiveness in half a century. Outside, I took a deep breath. Prisoners emerging from this grave would see the frozen straits, the snow-white landscape, and its monotonous, treeless horizon... Atop a decayed wooden pallet someone has placed a human skull. The bone yards are covered by thousands of those small, white flowers that rustle in the mild breeze across the tundra.

"Russia shall rise again in two ways," said Dima that evening aboard the ship, "through Hope or by a Miracle. We hope Christ will return to Earth to help Russia out of its troubles, and it will be a Miracle if the Russians do it themselves." The dining tables were laid out with garlic in vinegar and dried fish. Tonight's movie was *Terminator Dwa*, a much worn copy this time. Despite feelings of relief and celebration, a pall descended over our merriment as we sailed within reach of Russian television and received word of the Bosnian War. Civilization was radiating in our faces as from a microwave oven. We watched F-18 bomber-jets spin above the battlefields like avenging angels. A confused, drink-induced mix of the Terminator, occultism, and nationalism took form. The Russians sometimes seem like a proud and wounded people searching to get even. Eugene entertained vocal (but mostly out-of-date) opinions about the Slavic race, which met with loud, mocking laughter from Pieter and "No, not again!" from George. Zenja, of the Russian People's Friendship University, Department of World History,

11 September 1995 – The landing craft moved full speed past the eroded cliffs of Cape Diakonov, the Idols Cape.[12] There was a cold breeze and the crashing waves sprayed us with droplets of seawater. All around, the sea swelled steel-blue as far as I could see, with countless waves rising and falling. Past the Cape, the *plashkot* brought us ashore on a gravel beach. Three Nenets from Varnek directed us to the sacred site that gave the cape its historical name, on the end of a bedrock ridge 3 km long and 25 m high. The sacrificial spot is a low mound of reindeer bones covered by grass and tall white flowers. Jawbones and teeth protruding from the soil and littering the beach below demonstrate that the Nenets brought and likely are still bringing offerings to their deceased in the afterlife. However, the idols – crudely carved sticks about 0.5 m long – are gone.

There were hundreds of them: "coarsely hewn, somewhat round on top, with a small bump in the middle for a nose and above this, two grooves for eyes, and below the nose a cut for a mouth. In front of those statues there were many ashes and bones of deer." Jan Huyghen counted 300 to 400 idols, large and small, that had been placed facing east. Some of the sticks were new, some decayed; he recognized that they represented human figures: men, women, and many children [July 1594, in L'Honoré Naber 1914, p. 76]. Some sticks showed multiple faces, representing a group of people who perished simultaneously. There are dozens of sites like this one on Vaygach Island. The Nenets believe that life is a cycle and that every death is followed by a rebirth. Children often receive the name of a recently deceased person. The idols preserve the soul and power of the dead to return in human form. To nineteenth-century missionaries, the Nenets were savages, and their idols, symbols of a pagan belief in nature that needed to be destroyed. Only two remote inland sites in north Vaygach feels emboldened in his convictions by the Russian Orthodox Church, and that he shares with his Yugoslav brothers. He and Konstantin declared that they bear no one ill-will, but if needed, they will go and fight for the Serbians. I was choking, trying to keep my mind clear. The Russians were getting all riled up and suddenly wanted to enter into debates, yelling insanely at the TV: "NATO fascists!"

"Dutch soldiers are fighting Serbians!" someone exclaimed, gesturing as if handling a machine gun. "Keep your cool, man!" I thought. Fighting – that's what the Dutch soldiers do with each other, in the barracks. We laughed about it and lit up our stogies, but the newscast warmongers cut clips of Hitler and parading Nazis into scenes of the Bosnian War.

The group laughed uproariously, smacking Bas on his shoulders. Great-grandfather Kist was the Dutch blacksmith from Archangelsk with whom Peter, "the Czar who slept at a blacksmith's," stayed in August 1697. The Czar visited shipyards in Zaandam and Amsterdam before establishing the Russian Fleet in St. Petersburg. This visit was arranged through the offices of the mayor of Amsterdam, Nicolaas Witsen. The Dutch Republic enriched itself more through its arms trade and military industry than through maritime trade with the Indies: the Netherlands sold armaments to friend and foe alike. Battle ships could be delivered within a few weeks, and in thousands of living rooms, nimble fingers worked to produce those favored Dutch muskets. The Czar recognized Kist when he arrived in Zaandam on a barge, and Kist in reply called: "Hey, Peterman!" According to our companions, this story is in all history-oriented Russian schoolbooks. Inspired by Dutch science institutions, Peter founded the Russian Academy of Sciences and proposed to introduce Dutch as the language for his court to make it compatible with other European states. History, however, took a different turn.

have been spared the destructiveness of missionaries and the collectors' madness of tourists and scientists alike.

Like our sixteenth century countrymen, we walked around the sacred site under the suspicious eyes of the Nenets: "They trust not strangers [...]. He that they called their King had sentinels stand about [...] that watched diligently on all sides what was done," wrote Gerrit de Veer. The oldest of the Nenets men pointed across the waters of the Yugor Strait to where German submarines would surface during World War II. Another man in a worn-out flight jacket wanted to know from me, "What color is the tundra?" "It has many colors," I answered, and he nodded.

Looking carefully, we could see a Pomor cross in the distance atop the next cape, Cape Stvorny, about 2 km away. The cape and its beacon entirely resemble the 400-year-old panoramic sketch of these promontories by the Dutch. Walking along the beach, it took us an hour to get there. The cross is 4 m high and made of beams 17 cm wide. Like other Pomor crosses, it has a 'roof' that forms a triangle with its horizontal beam. This triangle depicts the Holy Trinity: Father, Son, and Holy Ghost. Above the horizontal beam is a slat with Pilate's mocking inscription 'INRI' (*Iesus Nazarenus Rex Iudaeorum*). Into the pole is carved, in Russian Cyrillic script, 'To You, Christ, Whom we Adore'. A weathered, slanting slat on the pole shows a skull and the letters G and L in the Cyrillic alphabet: Golgotha, site of the execution. A detailed drawing of one of these crosses by Van Linschoten demonstrates that they haven't changed any over the centuries. Nobody let out a word when Eugene and Konstantin, with their rifles and bandoleers, kneeled to pray. These crosses marked the edges of the world, beyond which the Unknown began; a deserted and flattened expanse, empty valleys, waiting for something, something terrifying that would break the monotony – and where to take shelter then? The sun was low on the horizon and the sea reflected a blinding glimmer. Inland, not far above the horizon, a flock of geese moved in disorder. Eugene and Konstantin got up and put their caps back on their heads. As we marched on, descending along cliffs of eroded peat towards the beach, a dozen mirages appeared above the steel-blue sea on the bright yellow horizon. And so this journey ends, where many others began.

Chapter Eleven

Aftermath, a history

While I was getting familiar with Amsterdam and crossed the city on foot, it was not difficult to imagine our heroes walking through the streets: the narrow passages between the sixteenth and seventeenth-century houses, bridges, the Zeedijk and the quays of the Geldersekade. Amsterdam offered an historical sensation at every corner, and I was shown around by the experts. Like the 'fin de siècle' of 400 years before, the 1990s brought prosperity to Northwest Europe. Similarly, the immediate threat of war had ceased; borders opened and the new people brought, we said, 'multiculturalism.' Everything was being 'globalized' and surely, the world wide web unfolded. In the Old Church in the centre of town, visiting Jacob van Heemskerck's tomb, Bast Kist was telling me that he found the 'Nova Zembla wintering' to be a footnote with European history. I thought a footnote was very little. After all, Willem Barents, Jacob van Heemskerck, and Jan Huyghen van Linschoten, they are main characters in the becoming of the Netherlands as a nation. During the ensuing century, Holland was influential in the international playing field indeed. Bas said: "They are quite agreeable heroes, not yet associated with a colonial past. Perhaps exactly because so little is known of them, it is easy to remember them in a favorable light."

Within a decade after its original success, Holland's Arctic adventure disappeared between a multitude of travelogues from

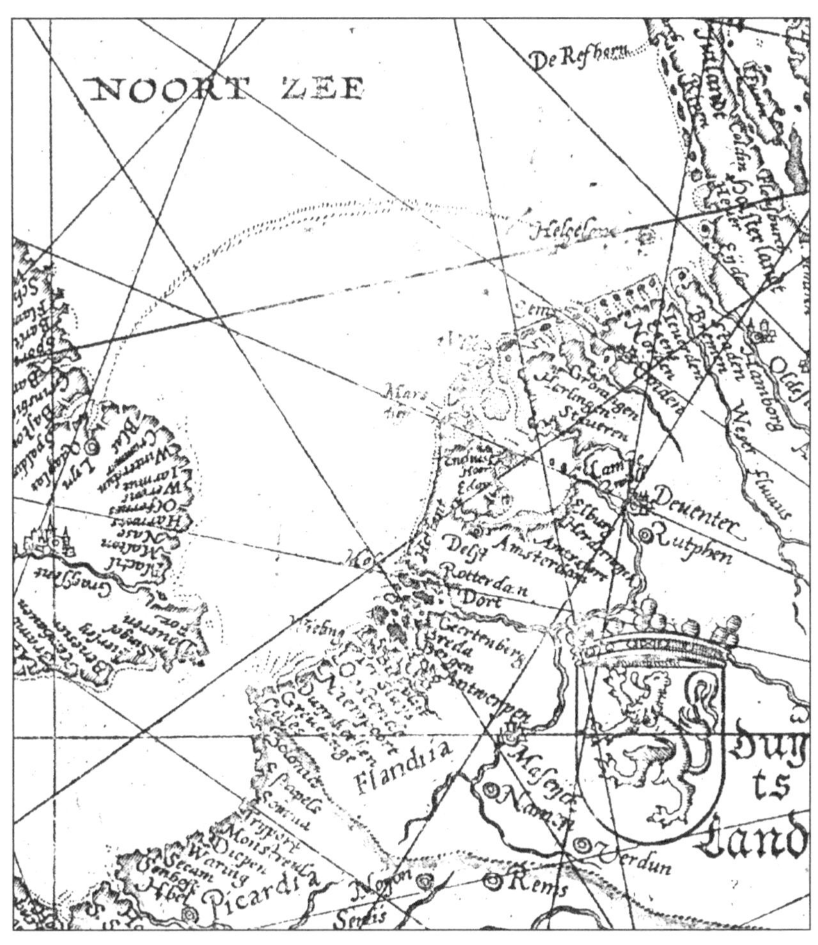

The Dutch Republic on Lucas Waghenaer's map of Europe (1589). You may notice the river delta outline of the country when holding the map upside-down.

all parts of the globe. The Dutch established a gigantic colonial empire and journals were published describing the wonders and peculiarities of Bali, Cambodia, Laos (the 'East Indies'). There were journeys around the world, like that of the large vessel *Love* reaching the Shogun's Japan; the establishing of 'New Amsterdam' (present New York City) and South-Africa. There were absolute horror stories like the stranding of *Batavia* on Australia's west coast; the onset of slave trading, descriptions of violent semi-military raids against Portuguese strongholds in Brazil and Angola, and several ruthless peg-legged pirates. For two hundred years or so, the memory of the wintering on Novaya Zemlya and its spectacular account faded and seemed forever lost. When early in the nineteenth century it was rediscovered, dusted off, and warmed up, it was because of its quiet and almost philosophical quality. Gerrit de Veer, Willem Barents' writer during that third, bold expedition into the Arctic pack ice, left a personal reflection and sharp observations of Nature, untrodden and in its most elementary form. The 'True and perfect description,' published in May 1598, was an instant success, with reprints in 1599 and 1605 and immediate translation into several languages. In his dedication to the second German edition (1602), Nuremberg publisher Levinus Hulsius explained that the first edition of 1500 copies had sold out, and that the demand for the work was still great. Books of travel, then as much as today, enjoyed great popularity, and this one recounted a journey past the entrance of Hell. "The Amsterdammers went home, and the others spent a few days in a hostel until we received our pay," wrote Gerrit De Veer dryly about the return of the expedition to Amsterdam, fox-fur hats and all, on 1 November 1597. "Afterwards, each went his own way."

The Climate changed: it cooled and the Arctic froze in all directions. Barents' wintering site for centuries on end remained solidly ice-locked under the spell of the 'Little Ice Age,' adding to Novaya Zemlya's mystery of wintering location. Early in the nineteenth century, following the war with Napoleonic France, the Arctic was again challenged in steamships, schooners, and with gas-filled balloons. When in 1853 London's Hakluyt Society re-issued Gerrit de Veer's journal, Editor Charles T. Beke acknowledged that public attention at the time was "painfully absorbed by apprehensions as to the fate of Franklin and his companions." The Franklin expedition departed from England in May 1845 aboard HMS *Erebus* and HMS *Terror* with 129 men. The expedition was to chart the Northwest Passage in the Canadian Arctic and had effectively vanished off the face of the earth. Beke expressed the hope that some of the Franklin crew might have survived, like Gerrit de Veer, to tell of their tribulations and final deliverance. "It is not known, however, whether any remains of the *Behouden Huys*, or 'house of safety', have ever been found," Beke wrote. In 1871, while Henry Morton Stanley in Africa was "finding" David Livingstone, the ice in the polar seas at last receded, and the Saved House yielded its treasure. Norwegian ice pilot and hunter Elling Carlsen dropped anchor on 7 September 1871, "close to shore, near Barentshavet, where Barents wintered" [Koolemans-Beijnen, Introduction to Beke, 1876: xlvi].

The direct connection between De Veer's account and the many objects collected from the wintering site was provided by Charles Gardiner who visited Novaya Zemlya five years after Carlsen. "Mr. Charles Gardiner [is] a passionate sportsman, who regards neither expense nor danger in order to gratify his love for adventurous hunting expeditions," wrote the Amsterdam curator J.K.J. de Jonge [1877] after receiving Gardiner's catch. The Englishman had collected several curious finds from the remains of the wintering cabin, most importantly an Amsterdam ell measure or 'yard stick' of 68.8 cm, which indicated the standard of measurement applied by the winterers. This object enabled deduction of the dimensions of the Saved House in 1995. The collection furthermore included 'powder cases' (for gunpowder) and a dozen 10 to 12 cm-tall brass tubes that had held the amount of gunpowder for a single musket shot. One of these had something sticking out and Gardiner pulled it. Out came a compressed roll of paper that lost bits and pieces. Gardiner brushed it all in a blue paper folder and wrote on it: "Fragments of manuscript found in powder-horn – Chs. G." Curator De Jonge, upon receiving the envelope, recorded: "In this paper folder was a tightly folded or rather compressed and fumbled piece of paper, some parts of which were sticking together, on the right-side turned green and yellow by copper oxide, the paper woolen and decomposed on the folds, in total very much damaged and of poor appearance. With this lay several smaller fragments." He carefully unfolded the document by exposing it for two days to a mixture of steam and spirit.

Thus opened a centuries-old letter, the 'cedelken' written by Willem Barents on their leaving Novaya Zemlya and abandoning ship. It is a 40 cm-tall sheet with a pattern of two folds and subsequent rolling up, to fit precisely in a gunpowder shell. De Veer documented that all men signed Barents' declaration and how Barents then put the "small warrant" in the gunpowder shell and hung it himself in the chimney: "een klein ceel geschreven en in een musketmaat gedaan, en het zelf in de schoorsteen opgehangen." (The 'powder horn' mentioned by Gardiner was confused in the Rijksmuseum's archive with the wooden 'horn' that was also found by him. However, as noticed by the Editor of this book, using the word 'horn' Gardiner probably refers to the cone or spout shape of the musketmaat). With the find of Barents' letter in 1876, De Veer's journal and all these objects littered around the wintering spot, the *'True and Perfect description'* proved to be just that: true, and perfectly accurate.

Stirring the melting pot

Amsterdam in the days of Willem Barents and Jacob van Heemskerck was a melting pot. Elsewhere in the country war was still going on, but the city had been liberated and had absorbed all the knowledge and skills that the refugees brought from occupied Antwerp. Before Amsterdam rose to the stage, Antwerp, 170 km south, had been northwestern Europe's center of action, the metropolis that had inspired Bruegels' painting "Tower of Babel." Amsterdam was amongst the northernmost towns of the Spanish Empire, located in a bog by the shore of a shallow tidal inlet, the Zuiderzee. Built by farm laborers and sailors, the city began to accommodate the southern entrepreneurs and scholars that would 'make our country great again.' De Moucheron, Brunel, LeMaire, Massa, LeCannu and Plancius: they chose to move their business north. Despite the religious undertones of the war against the Spaniards, the many different creeds found a place side by side in town and on board its ships. More than a decade after independence, the past as a Spanish city still resounded in its language and customs. The Novaya Zemlya expedition journals demonstrate the Catholic and Spanish origins: the explorers carried Spanish currency (reals), ate mazamorra (porridge), and named several landforms in Spanish (e.g. Capo Baxo, Capo Negro). The winterers in their Saved House celebrated Three Kings' Eve (the Catholic Holiday Epiphany, on 5 January 1597), Candlemas Eve (1 February), and Shrove Tuesday ("Fasten's Even," 17 February). Curator J.K.J. de Jonge in 1872 pointed out that in spite of the Revolution, the songbook recovered from the Saved House was Catholic, rather than Calvinist. The 'Low Countries' had been in a state of war for many years but shifts in the international power field (France and England having their issues with Spain) lifted pressure of the north. Just years before the ships set sail for the Arctic, towns in Brabant and Zeeland, just north of Antwerp, were recaptured by the Republic's forces. Indeed, Captain Carlsen, in 1871 wrote in his log that judging by his findings, the castaways had been equipped for war. Pikes and halberds lay around the place, but also the latest wheel-lock firearms of the period, musket rounds, parts of muskets, and 7-cm cannon balls.

Between Carlsen's finds was a leather-bound history book about the 'rebellious' provinces, written in part by Gerrit's father Ellert de Veer (1541–1599). "The chronicles of Holland, Zeeland, and Friesland until the year 1517," it is called, "and what has happened since the reign of Charles of Burgundy, Fifth Roman Emperor." It was published in 1585, when the independence war was still widening. The young nation was eagerly searching for sources of income to cover the crippling damages of war. The war against the Spanish in 1585 cost 3.2 million guilders, and expenses would quadruple in the following thirty years, carried by a population of not even one million people [Schama 1987]. Dutch exploration had one clear goal: economic growth, "...on the one hand not to give the other [Spain] advantage, on the other hand to satisfy the desire for gain (although insatiable)" [Van Linschoten 1601, in L'Honoré Naber 1914, p. 26]. The struggle for independence and subsequent expansion is reflected in the toponymy of the New World: at opposite ends of the globe appeared names like Staten Island, Zealand, Nassau Straits, the Orange Islands, and Mauritius.

International trade rapidly broadened the view of the surrounding world. The merchant fleet, especially, provided the eyes and ears of the new Republic. Willem Barents and Petrus

Plancius were Amsterdam cartographers, separating fact from fiction. The steady flow of geographical data generated by the expeditions invited frequent updates of sea-route descriptions and navigational handbooks. The involvement of Willem Barents with the early merchant-explorers is shown by his atlas of the Mediterranean Sea. The grain trade with Italy, generally tolerated by Spain to relieve grain shortages, had grown to involve 400 ships a year. These ships produced data and themselves needed charts with solar declination tables. Barents' collected these in his Caertboek van de Middellandse Zee [Chartbook of the Mediterranean Sea], which appeared in 1595. His actual Chart, a copper engraving (418 x 855 mm), is an almost unaltered copy of a coasting pilot or 'portolano' for the Mediterranean from the 14th century [Nordenskiöld 1889], demonstrating the passing on and collection of knowledge in Amsterdam.

The driving force in the positioning of Amsterdam as the center of new geographic knowledge was Petrus Plancius [Peter Platevoet, 1552-1622]. Plancius taught the seamen how to navigate and in return received information about the coasts they navigated. But there was another side to him. In his parish on the Oudezijds Voorburgwal, near the IJ River, Plancius spiced his teachings about the Earth and the Universe with an orthodox reformed worldview. (There is no trace, however, of the Creationist's dilemma that would put such pressure on notably the biological sciences, with the Almighty as the creator of All). In 1591, this 'combat preacher' was called to answer to the city council of Amsterdam for the turmoil he caused by his dispute with Jacobus Armenius, who questioned the doctrine of destiny. Arminianism would divide ranks for decades to come and eventually tore Dutch politics apart. Plancius did not end his life in 1622 with a scientific work but had started a revision of the Old Testament.

Because it seems that the men worked together, some of Plancius' militancy has also become attached to Willem Barents. "Willem Barents mind what you say!" admiral Nay stroke out on 1 September 1595, when Barents was pushing hard to lift the anchors. This brief collision, one of several that were sufficiently fierce to be recorded both by Gerrit de Veer and Jan Huyghen, provides a glimpse into the character of this otherwise elusive historical figure. Who then, was Willem Barents? The motto in the chartbook that he published in 1595 says he 'does not without God,' but then, no one did. In the notary archives of Amsterdam, Willem Barents' name is found on a sales contract for a house on the Nieuwe Zijds Kolk, within the estate of Gerrit Jacob Witsen, one of the city's most influential denizens who made his fortune in the Baltic trade. Through their contacts with men like Witsen, Plancius and Barents succeeded in having their voyage to Novaya Zemlya financed by the city [Floore 1996]. Of his homely conditions, we know that Barents was the father of five. His widow asked the General States to pay compensation to her and her children. The State forwarded the young family to Amsterdam's Admirality, because it had been their enterprise. In its resolution, the States called on the Admiralty and the magistrates to "show compassion to the petitioner."

Willem Barents was much younger than the image generally portrayed: being the father of five children, he was probably in his late thirties in 1596 [L'Honoré Naber 1917]. During the wintering he was at least ten years senior to most of his shipmates. The only confirmed portrait of Willem Barents was discovered by A.D. de Vries in 1882 in the collection of a prints dealer, on an engraving honoring the explorers titled "'s Lans Welvaren" (the Country's Prosperity) [De Vries 1883]. The portrait is 3 cm tall and De Vries puts forward the argument that it could have some likeness, because people that have known Willem

Barents were still around in 1613, when it was produced[13]. But he doesn't seem to find much authenticity in it, adding dryly: "The portrait would be more welcome if it demonstrated a more artistic treatment" [Toch zou het portret ons nog welkomer zijn geweest als 't van meer artistieke behandeling getuigenis aflegde.] Another image circulates: Barents and Gerrit de Veer appear to be depicted in Aert Pietersz's painting from 1599 of 'The Company of Captain Jan de Bisschop and his Officer Pieter Egbertsz Vinck,' a group of civil guardsmen. This painting in the Amsterdam Historical Museum shows two men pointing to the map of Novaya Zemlya, the senior one holding navigator's dividers. It was constructed in the years that De Veer's publication was a hit, which lends some credit to the senior man being Barents, albeit two years after his death. This figure has also been identified as Cornelis Claesz (c. 1551-1609), Amsterdam's maritime publisher. The younger man with little doubt is Gerrit de Veer.

Jacob van Heemskerck and the De Veer family

The image that exists in the twenty-first century of Jacob van Heemskerck is much sharper, although Van Heemkerck's fame was largely established by his death and is carried by street names and war ships. During the final months on Novaya Zemlya, while Barents was physically weak and confined to his bunk, Van Heemskerck provided ample authority. He was reluctant to relinquish his ship and the crew did not dare ask him directly to prepare for departure. Instead, they asked Willem Barents to do so on their behalf. Jacob van Heemskerck grew up in Spanish controlled Amsterdam. He was the son of an Amsterdam sail maker living in the Spinhuissteeg, an orphan at age fourteen. Barents and Van Heemskerck, as expedition leader and skipper, provided leadership together. They were open to suggestions, wrote De Veer, "because they would gladly talk things over," but

Willem Barents (1613)

Jacob van Heemskerck (1610)

J. van Linschoten (1596)

Petrus Plancius (1623)

Gerrit de Veer (1599)

then they would send the men away to make their decisions in private (9 May 1597). Van Heemskerck's command of the vessel allowed Barents to concentrate on charting the coasts of the northeastern seaway. This was Van Heemskerck's first mission as commander. The log later kept by Van Heemskerck as captain of *Gelderland* [*Gelria*, 1601-1604] provides some insight into his style and austere personality. Aboard the fleet, Van Heemskerck maintained discipline by emphasizing the importance of daily prayer, celebration of Sunday as a day of rest, and rejection of drunkenness and other perversions. "Pious and honest," according to a contemporary. Hugo de Groot (Grotius), who needed to justify the captain's 1604 privateering within (as yet unwritten) international law, found him to be "in face and clothes merely civil" ['in gelaet en kleedingh t'eenemael borgherlijck'].[14]

Jacob van Heemskerck and Gerrit de Veer both followed the navigation lessons given by Le Canu from his inn "De Leydstar" near Amsterdam's Haarlemmer Poort. Because they trained together, Gerrit de Veer likely was a year or two younger than Van Heemskerck, who was 29 years old in 1596. They were related because Gerrit's older brother Albert (1564-1620), secretary of the Council of Amsterdam, married a cousin of Van Heemskerck. Conversely, Van Heemskerck in September 1604 married De Veer's cousin, daughter of the burgomaster of the city of Haarlem. Van Heemskerck when he was not at sea lived in the house of Albert de Veer on the Oudezijds Achterburgwal. The De Veers were part of Amsterdam's regent circles – Albert became city attorney and was even knighted by the King of England in 1610. Father's influence is apparent in the lengthy, historical and philosophical rationale that Gerrit included with his own work. Father Ellert (1541-1599) was a pamphleteer and the history book that he contributed to was reprinted over the next century. However, Gerrit left no further traces after his famed publication. He seems to have been a thin or a small man because when volunteering to cross an unstable ice floe, Gerrit refers to himself as "the lightest of all" (17 June 1597). Tempers flared when Robert Le Canu expressed his doubt on the observation of the returning sun as described by Gerrit de Veer. "Do you, Master Robert, say that we have been mistaken in the time and erred?" Van Heemskerk brazenly told off his teacher during the debriefing in November 1597. Gerrit died sometime before 1627, because Le Canu in the letter describing the debriefing mentions that "he continued in his misjudgment until the end of his life" (Epilogue of this book).

War and pandemics

The mixture of religious resignation and at the same time resolve that characterizes the expedition accounts, reflects a society used to war and pandemics. Outbreaks of the plague and flu-like infections were never far away. Jan Hughen describes losing his brother and suffering high fever, 'being let blood three times' upon arrival in Spain. Both at home and at sea, death rates were high. The ships were suffocatingly small and vulnerable, medical care was minimal. For Barents' last voyage, men were selected "unmarried, as much as possible, to have a brave crew that would be less distracted by yearn for wife and children" [De Veer 1598]. Lambert Biesman, who accompanied De Houtman on his first voyage to the Indies, wrote to his father on 6 November 1594: "If I should safely return, then I am set for life, and should I die, well, what harm? For then I will be free of all travail through the Love of God." Four years later, sailing with Olivier van Noort, Biesman wrote: "Do not forget to reclaim my money should I happen to die underway... I was badly shaken up by that great epidemic in Zeeland and the great number of fatalities there, but against God nothing can be done. May he spare you from the plague" [Mollema 1943, p. 190–191].

Gerrit de Veer and friends. Section from 19 person group painting by Aert Pietersz (1599) commissioned by wood salesman Pieter Vinck. The Prince's flag, the colors of the Revolt, is prominently featured. Gerrit points at the Northeast Passage on the map of the world and has an arm around the shoulder of the man next to him: probably a prominent, however unidentified, historical figure.

Energy, guts, and curiosity – in combination with the context of time, having little to lose and much to gain – made these sailors step on board of their ships, in the face of overwhelming forces and poor odds, and travel into the unknown. "Now it is sufficiently clear that it does not please the Lord this time, to make us discover the passage," wrote Jan Huyghen [September 1595, in L'Honoré Naber 1914, p 176]. "We didn't find it appropriate to provoke him willingly and run our heads into the wall." As skilled and diligent as these seamen were, braving the seas in their oak vessels, they do not forget to acknowledge their God and at least on paper, placed their fate in His hands. De Veer's account keeps on repeating that things would go the way God wanted them to go. Selling his enterprise to the Dutch

State, Balthasar de Moucheron wrote: "God's Honor will be spread and Christ be known by those that still call on the Devil, to which matter all potentates and governments should be committed, and spare no expenses, trusting that the Almighty will compensate manifold." Here, Christian dogma's were put to good use. "Notwithstanding the expenses this will bring eternal profits and honor, and be to the Glory of God, spreading the Gospel and bless our Fatherland" [Van Linschoten, in L'Honoré Naber 1914, p. 207].

Riches of Asia

"Jan Huyghen van Linschoten presented the matter very favorably, in such way that the General State and Prince Maurits resolved [in 1595], to prepare and send out seven ships again, to discover the route and invite merchants to send over some goods and money," wrote Gerrit de Veer. Jan Huyghen represented the town Enkhuizen, north of Amsterdam. At the time of the expeditions, he was 35 years old (about the same age as Barents) and had already established name as expert on the 'East Indies' and 'the Kingdoms of China and Cathay' [Kitay]. He had moved to Sevilla in 1579 at age sixteen "to see and travel into strange countries, thereby to seek some adventure." In the streets of Sevilla strolled people from every corner of the vast colonial realm, even some "Indians" from Patagonia, "of large build with coarse arms and legs, in the growth of facial hair and color not unlike the Samoyeds of Novaya Zemlya and Vaygach or the Straits of Nassau." Thirteen years he stayed abroad and during the '80s lived in Goa, seat of the Portuguese government on India's west coast, as assistant to the new Archbishop. The young clerk diligently copied everything that passed by his eyes. He listed the best fishes and the best fruits, but also wax, indigo, tropical wood, opium, rubies and diamonds. Dirk Gerritsz Pomp, homeward bound after years in Japan, provided him with detailed information on the Far East. Jan

Huyghen's *magnum opus*, the 'Itinerario' that he wrote between 1592 and 1595 ('For the lovers of stranglinesses'), would be a work of reference for the century to come. When it was published, he had already turned his sight to the Arctic, "although I had only recently returned from the East Indian Countries, had barely completed the description of those, and had only briefly enjoyed my Fatherland and the company of my remaining friends" [Round by the North (1601), in L'Honoré Naber 1914, p. 27]. "But with newly invigorated enthusiasm, the desire started to grow to attend personally (putting all difficulties through blind diligence behind me), on the one hand to advance the prosperity of our country, on the other to somewhat feed my own desires and needs."

And this Jan Huyghen was not amused by that cocky reference to him done by some Gerrit de Veer from Amsterdam. In 1601 he published his side of the story. "Whether I made it more favorable than it was in effect, as those of Plancius claim in their Treatise, I leave to the judgement of the discrete and unbiased reader" [Preface 1595]. "Those of Plancius:" Jan Huyghen was not impressed with Plancius, who just to prove himself right, even sacrificed those sailors who entrusted their fates into his hands. "The route under the Polo, to be sure round by the north of Novaya Zemlya, is assured, totally certain, and without a doubt right," Van Linschoten wrote sarcastically, "but how this turned out to be is now known to everybody, after the unfortunate and last Tragic Voyage of Willem Barents, which was undertaken at the urging of Plancius" [in L'Honoré Naber 1914, p. 29]. The Ode that was added to the opening of his book, went as far as to compare the Reverend to the Biblical snake: "He chose the figure of a delusional Cosmographer [Waen-cosmograaf], spreading cold poison amongst the pilots, secretly hissing false images of streams never heard of before" (Directed to be sung to the tune of the 42nd Psalm).

White Sea Opportunity

Both Van Linschoten and De Veer note that the White Sea, a remote inlet of the Barents Sea, was frequently sailed on and fished at. This was a meaningful notion, because shipping concentrated on the Baltic and however profitable had been strictly controlled by the Danish. Archangelsk deep inside the White Sea was the primary port of the Muscovite State. The English first, followed by the Dutch in the 1570s, had build a commercial infrastructure around it. They traded with 'Pomors,' the Russian inhabitants of the coasts of the White Sea. The Dutch connection was first laid by Olivier Brunel (ca. 1552–1585). Not only can we trace the coining of the Dutch words 'Nova Zembla' to Brunel, but he also inspired Balthasar de Moucheron to investigate the northern searoute. "Olivier Brunel, who for some time stayed at Kazan and Astrakan, often assured me verbally that he was confident to sail to China once he had reached the mouth of the Ob River. He collected his information when imprisoned and serving a Russian gentleman, who was locally familiar," wrote De Moucheron [6 April 1595, in L'Honoré Naber 1914, p. 234].[15] During the 1570s Olivier Brunel was employed by the Stroganov brothers, Yakov and Grigory Stroganov, who were wealthy and influential men from the White Sea region. They were well connected with Tsar Ivan the Terrible, much to the disadvantage of the English that worked in the area. The English had landed Brunel in a Moscow prison, where he was discovered by these early oligarchs.

With the Pomors, Brunel arrived at the southern coast of Novaya Zemlya as early as 1576 [Unaddressed Letter 1594, in L'Honoré Naber 1914, p. 229]. Willem Barents was well informed in 1594 when he made his way south by the Novaya Zemlya coast. "Willem Barents guessed that this is the place where Olivier Brunel had been before, called Costinsarch," De

Veer recorded for 8 August 1594. [Kostin Shar Strait, which separates Mezhdusharsky Island from Novaya Zemlya]. In an embayment of the peninsula below the 'schar' Barents stumbled upon a small settlement, with three deserted wooden cabins, and graves with 5 or 6 coffins frozen out of the ground, filled with stones, bones visible [11 August 1594]. Nearby was a broken Russian lodya, with a keel 44 feet long. From sacks of wheat it was called 'Meelhaven,' presently and significantly called Bukhta Stroganova. Combining journal information reported by De Veer and Van Linschoten, it transpires that Meelhaven was a proper station used by the men they would meet on Vaygach. These Pomors came from Colmogory, just above Archangelsk. They explored Novaya Zemlya up to 76°N, which limit they marked with three orthodox crosses. Van Heemskerck and the others run into them again on the Novaya Zemlya coast, when they return after the wintering (the event was depicted in one of the plates).

Pelts, leather, train oil, minerals, caviar, and fish found their way to markets in Venice and Italy. Van Linschoten registered while the fleet was making way past Scandinavia's North Cape, through hollow seas, that on the horizon two vessels were sailing parallel with them. Destined for Venice, as it transpired on the roadstead of Kildin, the small island near Kola [Murmansk] that was used as rendez vous. "Let us note that the White Sea, on the northside of Moscovia, which is now trafficked commonly, has been discovered with trouble and danger. [...] Is this not the same long journey that it was before?" Gerrit de Veer rhetorically asked in the introduction to his work. "Yes, but the straight courses that have been found, cruising the sea from one cape to the next, if the wind lets it be, changed it from difficult to easy." Van Linschoten: "Who was it then, seeing the ice and cold, that didn't think it would ever be possible to start any trade there? And who is it now, now that awe has been replaced by experience, that gets business done there?" Who is it now, that gets business done there? At Kildin, to report their safe arrival they handed the *Iron Pig* a letter for Balthasar de Moucheron.

Jan Huyghen in his introduction fully credits Balthasar de Moucheron as 'general manager' of the expeditions. Like Plancius, the map maker, De Moucheron connected information and chatter he received from ships returning from the Baltic and White Seas. They probably did not mingle, because of their believes and cohorts, but together they provided the driving force behind the Arctic endeavors. Son of an influential French trader, Balthasar de Moucheron (1552–1630?) made his own fortune as shipowner. He represented the province of Zeeland, spread across islands in the Rhine's estuary, with a lightly populated harbor like Veere that was excellent for secret ship outfitting. He was 80 km from Antwerp, 200 km from Amsterdam, but by sea less than a 100 km from Den Haag, the seat of the General States of the new Dutch Republic. As early as 1584, De Moucheron send his brother Melchior and Olivier Brunel to set up the White Sea business (Spies 1994). For State support, he approached William of Orange [L'Honoré Naber 1914, p. 26], but the new Prince was murdered not much later. His enterprises would eventually send a thousand men across the globe.

The Yugor Strait, a new gateway to Asia

Seeing the war had entered a quiet phase, but nothing happening on the Arctic frontier, De Moucheron became restless. Competition on every side was growing. For years he had invested in further opening of the northern trade route – perhaps discover a passage to Asia. At long last, in December 1593, the head of state, Prince Maurits provided De Moucheron with a letter of recommendation, making him superintendent of the proposed expedition. De Moucheron would bear a quarter of the costs and have rights to one-eighth of the profits. The province of Holland (Amsterdam) protested the arrangement immediately. The Amsterdammers, at the instance of Plancius questioned the route, referring to the bad experience of the English in the 1550s and 1580. They chose to explore the route across the Pole, claiming that it would be free of ice during the long Arctic summer.

State attorney and 'prime-minister' Johan van Oldenbarnevelt [16] called a meeting in The Hague in March 1594 to discuss the expedition and solve the situation. Here was a chance to extend the young Republic's foreign relations. The meeting ended with the decision to try both routes: north by the coast of Novaya Zemlya, and south, through the Yugor Strait [Mollema 1947, p. 88]. According to a letter from an unnamed witness, the Zeelanders argued that Novaya Zemlya probably connected to Mercator's Arctic Continent, blocking the northern route[17]. The Amsterdammers replied that in their view Novaya Zemlya would connect to Cape Tabin and the southern route would be a dead end. Hence Willem Barents' experiment in the Yugor Strait: "for the ebb and flood here: I can find none."

De Moucheron submitted a written protest on 5 May 1594, but to no avail. Willem Barents received personal instructions from Johan van Oldenbarnevelt with explicit orders to investigate the northern route [16 May 1594, in: L'Honoré Naber 1914, p. 223]. "Willem Barents will go to Nova Zembla and survey by every means if the Tartarian sea named Mare Tabin can be entered. And in case the said Willem Barents would not be able to pass by Nova Zembla, he will be held to follow the other ships by Vaygach. Conversely if the other ships can't pass Vaygach or after sailing some miles would encounter ice, they will direct their journey to Nova Zembla, and follow the other vessel." 'Cape Tabin' returns in the all the communications and instructions. It was recognized as the most northerly cape of the Eurasian continent. Nobody knew how far to the east it would in fact be, except that it was past the Yugor Strait and beyond the Ob River.

First expedition 1594: to the North

On the longest day, 21 June, 1594, *Mercurius* arrived at the *rendez vous* of Kildin, a small, tall island in Russian waters, two days sailing past Waardhuys (Vardø) which had been passed to avoid Danish meddling. On the 22nd, the *Swaen* arrived, and on the 23rd Barents' two vessels. Jan Huyghen recorded: "The Danish [at Kildin] were very much agitated and worried, gossiping to the Lapps and Finns [ashore] that they couldn't figure out what we were up to, because the wind was favorable to continue our journey to the White Sea, and we didn't. In summary, they were confused and perplexed. [...] The [Russian] Boyar or the high official of the Grand-Fürst, formally complained that we set out fishing without requesting his permission, probably expecting that we would compensate him in any way, but we kept it off, pretending we didn't know, without hurting or upsetting anybody. When the Boyar found out, they deliberated and stole our nets [...] But one of us on watch and strolling on deck saw it and woke four of five sailors, and (as one says) head over heels they tumbled into a boat and rowed after the Russians. The Russians when they realized they had been discovered hurried to get ashore and started running, leaving the boat and nets. Our men caught up with them (even though they had taken off their fishing pants) and gave them a serious beating that they will remember. [...] The next day the Boyar came on board. He saluted us very politely, pretending that he felt very sorry for what the Russians had done [...], begging us to return the boat and fishing pants to his friends, who complained loudly to him about their loss. [...] In any way they left us alone although they continued to look at us badly" [translated from l'Honoré Naber 1914 p. 38-40].

After resting for a week, the expedition split and its two parts set out on their separate course, agreeing to wait for one another at Kildin till the end of September. As instructed by the States, Willem Barents went north. He sighted Novaya Zemlya four days later at 73°25', just above Matochkin Shar (the narrow strait that runs through Novaya Zemlya). The Amsterdammers then began to follow the coast, running into sea ice on 13 July. They continued by maneuvering between sea ice floes and ice bergs calving from glaciers. Six long days later, they freed themselves of the ice, and needed another twelve days to reach the island's north cape [now Cape Carlsen]. Opposite of the cape they came about the Orange Islands, flat and circular; steep cliffs filled with rows of black and white birds (*Uria lomvia*) and a beach packed with a hundred walrus. There, observing more sea ice "the crew became weary and refused to sail further." Before them lay the Kara Sea and to the southeast, the land dropped away. The farthest cape they could see in the distance, from which the jump into the unknown was to be made, was given the significant name "Cape Desire," Mys Zhelaniya in Russian. About 50 km out the coast, at 77°30'N they reached the edge of the pack ice and sounded depth, without finding the bottom (>200 m)[18].

This demonstrated that on top of the world there was a deep ocean – Barents wiped the Arctic Continent of the map. His anxiety two years later that ice or even land would block their passage is conveyed by Gerrit de Veer, when a crew of ten climbed the mountain behind Cape Carlsen [16 August 1596]: "When we saw open water to the southeast and east-southeast, we were much comforted, thinking we had won our voyage, and

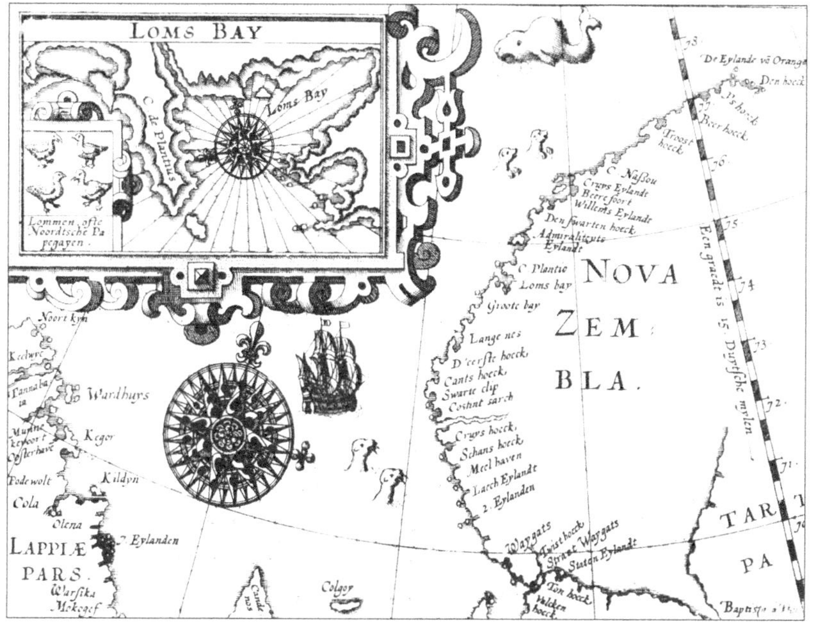

First cartographic map of Novaya Zemlya, produced by Baptista a Doetechum, drawn by Willem Barents during the 1594-expedition. The box details the bay with Atlantic puffin (Fratercula arctica) at about 74.5°N.

knew not how we should get soon enough back on board to certify Willem Barents thereof."

The other expedition had sailed east to collect information on what was believed to be the true sea route. On Monday 11 July 1594, Jan Huyghen van Linschoten wrote: "From our shelter in the sandy, eastern inlet of Toxar [Sengeiski] Island we watched three sails approach from the west, by the coast. We quickly sailed towards them with our yacht and saw that they were lodya's that together were headed for Pechora. We spoke to them and asked about the lay of the coast and rivers, and about Vaygach. [...] They said we could indeed continue to Vaygach, but there would be such an enormous amount of whales and sea horses [walrus] that ships could not go through and would be destroyed. This was a relief, if there were no other obstacles than that. Some had said we would find rocks, cliffs, and shallows, so it would be impossible to go through. The Grand-Fürst had in the past send three lodya's there, which had all perished in the ice and most of the crew was lost, the survivors telling of the news. We heard all these stories, understanding well that they were telling fabulations to keep us from going, or perhaps they honestly believed what they were saying [...] When it gets quiet here with no wind, there is such a torment of mosquitos that it is a real plague.

Jan Huyghen's report mentions that the first expeditions were not prepared to go much further than Novaya Zemlya. *Swaen* and *Mercurius* had hardly explored Vaygach when Jan Huyghen writes, just clear of the Yugor Strait [9 August 1594, in l'Honoré Naber 1914 p. 100]: "We certainly wished that we had been prepared to investigate and complete it once and for all, rather than return to the Fatherland. Nevertheless, we hope and trust that our Lord and God after keeping this hidden for so many centuries [...] will guide us through in the future as well." This southern group continued for three more days, about 300 km, through open sea. They ran into the very familiar looking sand-and-dunes coast of the Yamal Peninsula, with sandy shallows and beaches. Thinking the route to Cape Tabin lay open from thereon (the reader is invited to compare on a modern map), they returned.

When Barents arrived to rejoin the other two ships in the Yugor Strait, Jan Huyghen was jubilant: "Over the island we saw two sails approaching, thinking at first that they were two Russian lodya's. Then we noticed they had top sails, and we realized that it was Willem Barents with his yacht joining us again, which we celebrated with great roar and cheering" [15 August 1594, in L'Honoré Naber 1914, p.113-114]. They fired several of their guns to greet their colleagues. "Skipper and pilot Willem Barentsz of der Schelling, citizen of Amsterdam, a very experienced and skilled man in the Art of Navigation, bringing a Schellinger fishing vessel." This small reference is in fact the only historically verifiable piece of biography of Willem Barents (note that Jan Huyghen uses the patronym, omitting Barents' last name).[5] "Willem Barentsz invited us on board, where we received each other with great happiness and many stories of how we had fared. He disclosed to us some details of his journey, reaching 78°N. For details I refer to Barentsz' own report."

The rapid sailing to 78°N – and back – was spectacular. The sheer magnitude of this achievement and the rapid decline, its melting away you might say, under our modern lights is strikingly illustrated by Charles Beke. In 1853, Novaya Zemlya was still remote and frozen as it had been in centuries prior. Beke, after careful plotting by August Petermann, outlines the zig-zag course followed by Barents over 25 days, moving north following the Novaya Zemlya coast. "[Between 10 July and 3 August], Barents put his ship about eighty-one times, and sailed [...] not much (if anything) short of 1700 miles. This is equal to the distance from the Thames to the northern extremity of Spitsbergen, or from Cape Nassau [northern Novaya Zemlya] to Cape Yakan, not far from the Bering Strait. And all this was performed in a vessel of one hundred tons' burthen, accompanied by a fishing smack!" [Beke 1853, p. cix]. Furthermore, Mr. Beke subtly notes, Barents on the northern route had approached Cape Tabin nearer than his collegues at Yamal Peninsula.

"Now, having ended our first journey, we reported to the council of the states, and thus I have been summoned to The Hague and have in person presented our faring to his Excellency, the State Attorney Jan van Oldenbarnevelt Esq.," wrote Jan Huyghen. "I handed him a report with summary and figures, word for word and identical as I have done here [...]: although those of Plancius in their Treatise have made it understood that I presented matters more favorable than they in effect were [...]"

View of the northern coast of Novaya Zemlya.

Second expedition 1595: To the east

Jan Huyghen kept a detailed daily journal of his voyage ('While I am writing this the weather is clearing up") which he did not publish until six years later. His 1601 book "Journeys to Vaygats in 1594 and 1595" demonstrates the reconnaissance nature of the first two expeditions, sounding depths, gathering intelligence from locals, trying to figure out the geography and not run aground. The second expedition consisted of no less than seven ships, freighters, and well-armed yachts. Yugor Strait to everybody's best knowledge was the gate to the Northern Seaway. A relatively protected channel, "as between England and France," according to Jan Huyghen [15 September 1595]. "Bring two hundred men for a fortification", wrote Balthasar de Moucheron [April 6, 1595, in l'Honoré Naber 1914 p. 231-240]. "It is of the utmost importance that you [the States] are assured of possession of the Strait [Yugor], otherwise you are playing a dangerous game that would be to the disadvantage of our nation. [...] I admit that [building] a fortress [on Vaygach Island] could cause a problem with the Muscovites, to whom the land belongs, and also the Danes, who still pretend control of the region, and the English who do not want to see the passage closed. Further difficulties can be expected with the inhabitants of the country. Facilius est excludere quam expellere: it is easier to exclude them than to expel them by force." But this 'advice' was quickly brushed aside. No one wanted to start troubles in waters that were friendly and safe. The State issued explicit instructions to their commercial agent Jan Huyghen van Linschoten, "to show friendly intentions wherever they called, and to make it clear that their country maintained contacts with nations and regions over the entire world."

The explorers were to explain what advantages trading contacts entailed and, whenever interest was noted, to offer to send a more appropriate delegation at the first opportunity [July 1995, in L'Honoré Naber 1914, p. 140]. Indeed, many of the goods recovered from the Saved House were meant for bartering or as gifts. The clock that was retrieved from the Saved House was probably carried into the Arctic two times, because Jan Huyghen's correspondence from the bishopric palace in Goa had shown a particular interest in clock mechanisms at the Chinese imperial court [Grimbergen and Wijnberg, in Braat et al. 1998].

The fleet returned in October all wet and shivering, with insufficient, dirty clothes, suffering from scurvy, and shocked by what they had witnessed. The frustration of the expedition in August 1595 running into sea ice, in the Yugor Strait, is on every page. Problems started barely a month into the voyage, when on 6 August Barents collided with *Hoop* in a storm, breaking masts and Jan Huyghen thinking this would be the end of them. Five men went overboard, of which only some could be rescued [Hulsius plate 21]. They continued in rough seas, with an unfavorable and cold wind from the north-northeast. The first ice floes and ice fields where already spotted when the flotilla had just passed the White Sea. When they arrived at the Yugor Strait, ice was spilling out. The ships sought shelter in Train Bay, under Idols Cape, where "we were lying as trapped" ["ligghende aldus in een Vuyck;" L'Honoré Naber 1914, p. 155].

The cold weather held on for days, "sometimes with snow flurries and hail" and the land was barren and uninhabited. It was an unfortunate year: there was much sea ice and the summer season would be short. On 20 August a yacht was sent out, but only came as far as the next bay, Cross Cape. At last, on 24 August they make contact with a Russian lodya, anchored on Vaygach's west coast. The Russians visited the Dutch vessel and were treated herring. Meanwhile, Willem Barents' yacht had discovered a group of about 25 people on the mainland across the strait. "They told us that the strait would be freezing over in about three or four weeks which seems more credible that what the Russians had said and agrees with what the other Samoyeds said last year," wrote Van Linschoten. These communications were also recorded by Willem Barents according to his only surviving note, salvaged between Henry Hudson's papers [below, *stilo novo* refers to the 'new' Gregorian calendar]. They are at the origin of the dispute with admiral Nay and the other skippers, to push on and spend a winter if necessary.

The 24th August, stilo novo, 1595, we spoke with the Samoyeds, and asked them how the land and sea did lie to the east of Vaygach. They said, after five days' journey going northeast, we should come to a great sea, going southeast. The sea to the east of Vaygach they said was called Marmoria, that is to say a calme sea. And they of Wardhouse have told us the same. I asked them if at any time of the year the sea was frozen over? They said it was. And that sometimes they passed it with sleds. And the first of September 1595, *stilo novo*, the Russians of a *lodya* or bark affirmed that the sea is sometimes so frozen, that the lodyas going sometimes from Gielhsidi to Pechora are forced to winter, which Gielhsidi was won by the Tartars three years ago [from Beke 1876, p. 273].

The Arctic climate and the threat of the Arctic night put men and boats to the test. On 2 September, Willem Barents, after words with Nay on the 30th and 31th, lifted anchor, fought through the strait and reached Staten Island (now Ostrov Mestnny) with great effort the next evening. "What would yóu do then?" Nay had asked, and when Barents suggested to push through, spend the winter if necessary, stroke out: "Willem Barents, mind what you say!" But the fleet followed, which resulted in them all getting stuck between the small island and the mainland, under a leaden sky, barely protected from extensive, moving fields of sea ice. The crew of the fleet, "murmured," upon seeing the fearful white masses stretch in the mists; fearing that the expedition would get stuck they insisted that staying longer equaled to suicide [Van Linschoten 1601, in L'Honoré Naber 1914, p. 176-177]. And then, in front of all the others two men were killed by a bear, causing a panic. "As soon as the bear had its fill of the first man, he turned towards the group, that fled upon seeing the furious beast come running towards them, in short the one who couldn't run paid for it." This horrifying accident scared and angered the crews – shocked by Mother Nature showing teeth. When the panic threatened to turn into a mutiny, Nay and his skippers again were unforgiving, and five men were hanged on Staten Island for insubordination. (As vividly as the bear attack was described in both journals, the death sentences are not mentioned in either, but shown in Hulsius Plate 27).

The option of wintering was again brought to table by Willem Barents and Jacob van Heemkerck on 8 September, before the captains drafted their apology of aborting their mission. Barents was reminded by admiral Nay that he was free to continue his journey by himself, on his own authority, "and see what they would run into from here." The fleet managed to maneuver back to Vaygach Island, then retreated to Cross

Point in the relative protection of the Yugor Strait. There, after several desperate attempts to get back into the ice by Barents, the "Amsterdammers somewhat let go of their obstinacy." Realizing that their chances were low, both Amsterdam vessels conceded and returned with the group – persistent to return in the following year with every preparation for a wintering. Willem Barents wrote:

> For the ebb and flood here: I can find none; but with the wind so runs the stream. The third of September, *stilo novo*, the wind was southwest, and then I found the water higher than with the wind northeast. My opinion is grounded on experience: that if there is a passage, it is small, or else the sea could not rise with a southerly wind. And for the better proof to establish whether there is flood and ebb, 9 September, *stilo novo* I went ashore on the south end of Staten Island, where the cross stands, and laid a stone on the brink of the water. I went around the island to shoot a hare; returning I found the stone as I left it, the water neither higher or lower: which proved as said that there is no flood or ebb [from Beke 1876, p. 273].

"I do not doubt," concluded a disappointed Jan Huyghen when the fleet was preparing to return to the Netherlands, "that we will learn by additional investigation of the Vaygach area the right time to avoid the ice and conquer the obstacles that now, for lack of experience, appear insurmountable." The next expedition of course, was Barents famed journey that resulted in the wintering – not far from the position that had been reached two years before. They barely managed to get through. As practiced in 1594 and 1595, Barents maneuvered through ice that would have stopped any other. Jan Cornelisz Rijp, skipper of the second Amsterdam vessel in 1596, attempted to follow

Barents three weeks later. "We found the island with three crosses standing on it. The Russians had said this is the farthest point ever reached by Man. Twenty miles later we encountered sea ice that we were not able to pass and turned around. We did not go ashore because those Russians had told us how those had fared that tried. There lives an evil spirit such a sound they heard coming from the hills. Whatever it is, we don't know, but we hurried back because the ice threatened to enclose us"[19].

Aftermath

Every day, daylight still falls through the stained-glass windows of the Old Church on the weathered marble skull ornamental to Jacob van Heemskerck's tomb. The Old Church is a quiet monument in the bustle and grime of Amsterdam's Red Light District, still a meeting place and underneath its stone floor, the last resting place of thousands of Amsterdammers. On the tomb (the actual grave lies a bit further in the shadows), one can still make out the words written by poet P.C. Hooft in 1610:

> *Heemskerck, who through ice and iron dared to strive, left Honor to his country, his body here, and off Gibraltar, his Life*

Van Heemskerck, forty years old, was personally invited by Johan van Oldenbarnevelt in January 1607 to lead the attack on the Spanish fleet in her home port. Van Heemskerck accepted with honor and even refused to be compensated. An anonymous etching depicting his funeral on 8 June 1607 shows the coffin being carried through the streets by fourteen naval captains. The closest relatives, among them the De Veers, walked next to the bier. Two companies of soldiers, their drums muffled, dragging the enemy's colors, led the procession from the house on the Oudezijds Achterburgwal.

"But Van Heemskerk fell in that battle in the Straits of Gibraltar. Van Heemskerck was anxious to acquire the honor of finding a passage through the Arctic Regions, like Magellan, who had discovered the passage to the South Sea," wrote envoy Pierre Jeannin to the French King in January 1609. Mr. Jeannin mediated in the peace negotiation with Spain. In a letter informing his King he pointed out that the Dutch were preparing for a fourth journey round by the north, to search for the Northeastern Passage. "Of this latter passage the States have reserved to themselves the right in case should it be discovered. [...] Having been informed that Plancius had come to The Hague [...], I invited him to call upon me, to speak with him. [...] I have spoken to Plancius only in the way of a scientific discussion, on the northern passage, as if I were desirous to instruct myself, and to learn what he knows about it, or what he concludes on scientific grounds. He has confirmed to me all the above facts, and he also told me that the late Jacob van Heemskerk, the admiral of the fleet which defeated the Spaniards in the Straits of Gibraltar, to undertake the above enterprise. Van Heemskerk had consented to do so, and Plancius had expected great achievements from him, because Van Heemskerk was greatly experienced in navigation, and was anxious to acquire the honour of finding a passage through the Arctic Regions, like Magellan, who had discovered the passage to the South Sea. The truth is, that one cannot guarantee the success of this enterprise with certainty. [...]"

The great overseas expeditions had been taken over by the Dutch East India Company. It had been the downfall of Balthasar de Moucheron in 1603. His investment in Joris van Spilbergen's journey around the world turned out to be a fatal one when creditors forced his trading empire into bankruptcy at the request of the VOC. De Moucheron left his home and possessions and fled the country. Business had been taken over by the VOC [Verenigde Oost-Indische Compagnie or VOC]. Hearing of the various initiatives being deployed to find the un-monopolized route across the Pole, the VOC hurried to contract Henry Hudson. And beat the French to it.

Henry Hudson's famous journey to the east coast of America marks the founding of the colony of New Netherlands, which later grew to New York City. Hudson's preparation for the voyage, and especially his doubts about the feasibility of the adventure, sheds light on the then vivid Arctic ambitions, more than ten years after wintering. During his stay in the Netherlands, Hudson spoke at length with Petrus Plancius and Jodocus Hondius, who had taken over Mercator's business. One week before Hudson's departure, Plancius handed him the note by Willem Barents. "This was written by William Barentson in a loose paper, which was lent me by the reverent Peter Plancius in Amsterdam, 27 March 1609," wrote Hudson. Hudson to Plancius, Hondius, and probably everyone who would here it expressed serious doubts on the voyage. Gerrit de Veer erroneously depicted and described "Costin Sarch" as a possible passage between the Barents and Kara seas, confusing 'Costinsarch' and 'Matochkin Shar.' "This place upon Nova Zembla is another than that which the Hollanders call Costing Sarch, discovered by Oliver Brownell [Brunel], and William Barentson's observation doth witness the same." Apparently, the broad inlet close to the Meelhaven settlement was recorded to yield passage to the east and used by the Pomors as such. "[...] It is as broad and like to yield passage as Vaygach [the Yugor Straits], and my hope was, that by the strong current it would have cleared itself; but it did not. It is so full of ice that you will hardly thinke it" [H. Hudson, 6 July 1608; in: Asher 1860, p. 40].

His doubts on the feasibility of the journey went around Amsterdam but the VOC felt cornered by the French. The

Company did not want to spend much money and made available only a small, dilapidated vessel: "*Yacht Halve Maen,* 40 last, bound for the North." Less than one month before Hudson's departure, the Zeeland Chamber composed a note to Amsterdam: "We duly received Your Honours' letter of the 11th [of March] and learned therefrom that the Englishman, Mr. Hudson, had great dispute with Dirck Gerritsz, the chief boatswain, concerning the wages of the Englishmen who were to sail with him, and such other matters as YY.HH. write of." This unsent note was later rephrased in fiercer language and then sent: "We are much surprised at Mr. Hudson's strange behavior and consider it inadvisable to let him undertake the voyage, for if he begins to rebel here, under our eyes, what will he do if he is away from us?" [Letter Book B, Archives of the Zeeland Chamber; in: Murphy 1859, p. 140]. The writers added that, if prospects were as good as they were led to believe, the English would not have let Hudson go. A last-minute addendum to the contract ordered Hudson explicitly "to think of discovering no other ways or passages, except as the above mentioned one around by the North and Northeast of Novaya Zemlya" [M. van Dam, Description of the status and condition of the East Indies Company; in Murphy 1859, p. 110]. On 8 April 1609, Hondius wrote to Plancius: "I have heard that Hudson began his adventure two days ago."

Jan Huyghen van Linschoten appears one more time. He was called to testify, on 2 February 1611, before a committee that was to assess the chances of another journey past the north of Novaya Zemlya [Mollema 1947]. But Van Linschoten, long retired from the business of discovering worlds, had little to add. He had been living quietly on Enkhuizen's Breestraat as treasurer for that city and its hospital. He was ill and died six days later. The Netherlands' search for the northeast passage to Asia had ended. In the years thereafter, the Arctic, under a centuries-long cold spell, would close shut, became the Kingdom of Night.

Mad about Barents

During my involvement with these Amsterdam characters, alive and dead, I was 'backstage' at the Rijksmuseum, visited its offices and storage rooms, where the 'Novaya Zemlya collection' lay well protected in broad drawers, or lay around in workshops, being cleaned and prepared for their journey through the ages. Dozens of cast iron nails, black and shiny from linseed oil. The tangible connection between the past and the present, of course, are the many objects retrieved from the ruins of the Saved House, collected by Elling Carlsen and Charles Gardiner almost 150 years ago. Their unsystematic gathering, but careful transport back to the Netherlands is a miracle. Imagine Gardiner, prying the "carefully folded and crumbled letter", Willem Barents' apology, out of its container, noticing that it was falling apart and securing the parts and pieces in a blue paper-linen folder. In our ability to hear their voices, we connect with Charles T. Beke in 1853 and Samuel L'Honoré Naber in 1914. Naber at the start of the 20th century was part of a group of archivists and librarians, one leg in the colonial past, that set themselves to the task of republishing the 'Golden Age' expedition journals with full and complete archive research. When the Nazi war machine cast its shadow, and eventually crushed over Europe, Jarig Mollema steadily kept to the task of advertising the deeds and spirit of our honorable seamen. Northern Novaya Zemlya, remote and forbidding as ever, remained an abstract fantasy land for walrus hunters and submarine captains. It was inaccessible once again during the Cold War, veritably until 1991, when we were drawn in by post-perestroika openness. There was a brief chasm in history, when the Russian Arctic opened and these two bright-orange life boats, piloted by Frans Heeres and Maurits Groen made their way through the Kara Gates. Kravchenko could barely have exaggerated the historical weight of that moment. Suddenly, we found ourselves out there in the High Arctic, unexpectedly following Barents traces and completing this journey with our own physical stay on the island. Through good fate it was exactly 400 years later.

We'll close with the poem by Joost van den Vondel, in 1613 adding Willem Barents to the ranks of maritime heroes. The *Hymnus, or laudatory on the famous navigations of the United Netherlands* (lines 231–246) had been inspired by the etching "s Lans Welvaren,' commissioned by publisher and fellow poet Abraham de Koninck. The print shows Amsterdam's cityscape and a young woman, a yacht in her lap, with the shield of Amsterdam at her feet, flanked by Willem Barents and Jacob van Heemskerck, angels and cherubs.

De hope van gewin zoo wijd de saeke brocht,
The hope for lavish profit set expectations wide
Dat tot twee malen toe dees streke werd bezocht,
So twice in just two years they northern route tryed
Wijd onder t' Beersche licht: maar laas! met weinig bate,
Ways under Ursal glare: but alas! The bleak fate
Niet wijders opgedaan als der Nassouwen strate.
Had gained them nothing wider than the Nassau Strait

Maar Willem Barentszoon, als voogd en principaal,
But Willem Barentszoon, as guardian and leader
Den Noordpool, met nog een, gaat voor de derde maal
The Northpole plus one, for the third time either
Bestoken, op vier min als vier-maal twintig trappen,
Will assault, at 4 minus 4 times twenty steps
En daalt ter Hellen waart, daar nergends menschen stappen,
And descends into Hell, where no humans tread

Daar hem Corneliszoon, in nood en lijfsgevaar,
For [Jan] Corneliszoon [Rijp], in distress and mortal danger
Om al des werelds schat geenszins wil volgen naar;
For all the world's treasures did not want to follow him
Dan Barentszoon (die niet vindt raadzaam zich te wenden)
Then Barentszoon (who did not find it advisable to bend)
Tot Nova-Zembla toe, verzeilt aan 's Weerelds ended.
At until Novaya Zemlya, reached at last the World's end

Natuere word beroert, sal ick dan gantsch verkracht
Nature is touched, will I indeed be totally raped
(Seght sy) ten lesten zijn van 't menschelijck geslacht?
(She says) at last by Humankind
Zal dan een sterflijck dier de palen overspringen,
Will then a mortal animal jump the poles,

Die eenmael heeft ghestelt de Moeder aller dingen?
That were once set by the Mother of all things?
Zal dan geen plaetse zijn op 's Werelds aengezicht
Will there be no place on the face of the Planet
Daer desen woesten hoop zijn zoolen niet en licht
Where this savage bunch does not place its feet
Natuere sal vele eer, vele eer als dit ghedoogen
Nature will sooner, much sooner than tolerate
Geheel ontwapent zijn van alle haer vermogen
Be stripped entirely and subjugate

Detail of *'s Lans Welvaren*, 'the Country's Prosperity' (1613) commissioned by publisher Abraham de Koninck, showing Amsterdam's cityscape and the only confirmed portrait of Willem Barents (3 cm-tall).

Chapter Twelve

Summer on Vaygach Y2K

Moscow

It is a fine summer evening and there is quite a bit of wind, so I open the double windows, obviously designed to keep the cold out, for a breeze, and hear the bustle outside: barking dogs, accelerating trucks, claxoning, multi-toned car alarms, chants. Between all that buzz, there are shreds of popmusic and a Russian house beat. We are back at the Heritage Institute, our host of three expeditions to Novaya Zemlya: in 1993, 1995, and 1998. This year, we are set to return to the southern end of the archipelago, to Vaygach Island. The institute is in a guesthouse opposite of the 'All-Russia Exhibition Center' or the Park of the People; opposite also of the towering Cosmos Hotel, which has bright, pulsating strips of white light running up and down on it. On the square in front are kiosks and pavilions with improvised terraces. Young people stroll around and buy bottles of beer. A gigantic overpass is being constructed straight through the neigbourhood, obstructing the park's gold-gilded gates. Sparks from welding are flying. The sleek obelisk 'for the Conquerers of Space', a beautiful 107-m tall titanium monument representing the stylished plume of a spacerocket, is right around the corner. In the exhibition center, however, the dusty spacecraft, *Sojuz*, *Salyut*, and landers for Venus and Mars, have been shoved aside to make room for an imposing German car display. Mercedes, Porsche, BMW. Black and shiny, each more than the other: a glimpse into Russia's desired future. It is August 2, year 2000. Y2K.

Tonight, I am in the King's Room (4-40), two floors above the dark corridor where still lies the 4-m-long part of Willem Barents' vessel. Occasionaly, we see someone in the wide, red carpeted hallways on slippers heading for an electric samovar. These are permanent residents; we seem to be the only guests. A lady signals to us that we can eat if we want to. In a small kitchen she opens a refrigerator and takes out three white plastic buckets, from which she pulls off the lids to show us its contents. I ask for two half liter bottles of *Baltica Three* beer. "Not for me...," David says, regarding the beer, while peering into the bucket. I'll take both bottles, anyways. Pyotr Boyarsky and his team are already up north in Vorkuta, we will meet them there. Dmitri Badyukov was waiting for us at the airport. He had aged considerably since 1998 and I didn't recognize him at first, walked right past him, his black beard shot with gray hair. "From worrying," he said. He was phoned after two years of quiet and asked to pick us up. He hugged me several times, even in the van on the way to the hostel. I am proof that some things have not changed. I returned to Russia, with twenty thousand dollars in rolls in my luggage and taped to my body. The Americans are sponsoring this journey and because bank transfers didn't work, not since the ruble crash of August 1998, expedition funds were collected in cash from a local bank office, like in a movie (not the robbing kind). My boss had to put an extra mortgage on his house to get me all this money.

After the 1995 expedition, we cleaned up and finished everything. I left Amsterdam and continued on my way, which led me to Chicagoland. Russia was now drawing in cash and initiatives at an unprecedented scale. The country had never been this inviting. With some old and some new sponsors, we returned in 1998 to the north of Novaya Zemlya, to search Cape Vilkitsky for the grave with the bear skull and to investigate

Ice Harbor with a remote-controlled underwater vehicle. But we found the bay filled with sea ice, moving and piling up and piling on the beaches. On Cape Vilkitsky, there was nothing even resembling a grave. Kravchenko, for everything he wanted to see, made it more beautiful than it was.

Then, while we were all on board in the middle of the Ice Sea, the house of cards collapsed. Flu was raging through our vessel, R/V *Ivan Petrov*, which Dave and I evaded by staying on shore as much as we possibly could, when the ruble crashed, an event aptly named the ruble crisis or the Russian flu, on 17 August 1998. Our Russian teammates over hours lost every possible saving. They would not be able to afford their tickets home. Next to the usual and familiair anger, merriment, stoic humor, there was a new and earnest emotion: panic. On return to Archangelsk, the ship was moored at a gated, closed part of the harbor from which we were unable to leave – kept hostage, you could say (in hindsight). Our teammates went in and out through a hole in the fence to fetch bottles of beer and dried fish which lay shriveled and dead next to my yellow notebooks. All life had been sucked out of them.

It proved to be very difficult to return to Novaya Zemlya. Russia was going through a major financial crisis and after a winter and spring nursing faxes and unintelligable phone calls we had to skip the 1999 field season. Then suddenly, came the invitation to join the group on Vaygach Island, the southern end of the archipelago. And we embraced the possibility of going to Vaygach to see what we could find there. Vaygach – "Has in places descending beaches, of gray and black sand with many pebble stones, and all these beaches are full of driftwood tossed one over the other with roots and all," wrote Jan Huyghen van Linschoten [July 1594, in L'Honoré Naber 1914, p. 64]. "... Mostly flat expanse, except for some elongated low ridges, hills, and lows. Here and there still and enclosed waters or swamps, which I think must originate from snow melt. Has everywhere many kinds of field flowers of every color, some excellently smelling; here and there also clear grass but mostly a saturated green vegetation [...], peat-like or as mosses, indeed like moving over feather beds or cushions, very hard to go..."

Over dinner, David and I look over an elongated photo of Vaygach Island, shiny black and white with hard contrasts, laminated in clear plastic. This photo will guide us over the next month and will be our main instrument to chose field sites. It is an espionage photograph taken by the first generation of spy satellites in the 1960s, called *Corona*, simply on 70 mm film strips that were shot to Earth in capsules. Special planes flew around with trawls that were able to intercept the photo rolls descending on parachutes. Just imagine. Russian topographic maps and air photos are still classified, not in the last place because Novaya Zemlya and Vaygach remain under military authority. But through the ending of a 30-year Cold War embargo, the old US spy satellite imagery was recently released by the Geological Survey. I got my hands on it and went with a roll of film to the university photo lab in a warehouse across the tracks. With a crayon I marked out the portions that interested me. The man at the photo lab printed all these glaciers and coastlines on large sheets of photographic paper, possibly acknowledging some of their esthetic quality. The result of this unlikely process – satellite, parachute, finding this film on the USGS's brand new internet – is on the table here in Moscow.

The Arctic

From Moscow we travel to Amderma, a small coastal town, or rather a settlement if you consider its small size. Amderma like most places in the Russian Arctic has lost 80% of its inhabitants over the past decade. First, we spend two days on the now familiair long-distance train, then the last stretch from Vorkuta to Amderma we fly with an An-24 passenger plane. Next, we continue by helicopter, an Mi-8 of the Russian border guards, in camouflage colors and including small wings with rocket pods for ground targets. While I am seated on a small bench along the side of the aircraft, five men lift a large, rusty fuel barrel on board and leave it in the door. The helicopter is being fueled by an Army truck and the air in the cabin soon becomes saturated with kerosene vapors. The whole process is observed by three soldiers in their typical slack boots and a single weary-eyed Nenets. The carelessness and neglect of the potentially catastrophic risk – a major explosion – reflects a fatalism that seems to have become quite normal in Russia. I pretend not to see the actions of the flight engineer, who removes a panel and will use the half hour of our crossing the Yugor Strait to complete his soldering work.

I feel rather ill, I got something from the two-day train journey. We were placed next to the disgusting and sour smelling toilet. Steel door slamming for two days. Thank God Dave has peptobismol, norit-like active carbon stuff, which I swallow with a splash of water from the canteen. At last the helicopter's turbines are started and begin their deep wail. The temperature in the cabin immediately rises. Adrenaline rushes through my body. The entire machine rattles and vibrates like it may fall apart anytime. When the moment arrives that the blades are up to speed and the helicopter is bouncing on its wheels, the turbines drop away and the engine takes over. Frightening: it sounds like it's failing. But we are going: the flight engineer closes the hatch. My heart jumps: this is probably the most dangerous part of the journey. After a flight of about half an hour over the blue polar water, rather spectacularly by Staten Island and 'Bear Beach,' we jump out of the helicopter in mud and driving rain. We're next to the Idols Cape and erect camp by the elongated lake that provided the 1595 expedition with drinking water. First, we pull the tents out of their expedition boxes and create some shelter. Nothing too soon: when the tents are up, it starts to rain harder. Everything is already damp in the first hour.

The Russians are even more jovial and amical than on the previous trips and seem genuinely happy with this expedition. Lots of winks and pats on the shoulder. We are with a large group that will have their basecamp here for a week or two. We will make our preparations and then continue north in a couple of days. Hard discussion in Vorkuta, over the money and our schedule, because the program had already been confirmed by the FSB security service. There is a huge naval exercise going on in the southern Barents Sea, the largest in a decade, and we really shouldn't be here. The requested rifle has not been brought for that reason, which I suspected, because the subject was constantly avoided during our preparations over fax and the occasional email. "We brought three types of cartridges," they smile amicably: "yellow, red, and green." For a flare gun, mind you. "The Nenets always travel without a gun," the Russians claim. I find that hard to believe. We did not get a radio either, because this is a military controlled expedition and they do not want to arm foreigners or leave them with a radio.

So this year no 'license to kill'. David does not like it at all, after keeping polar bears away for five years on Franz Josef Land. He is thinking aloud to call it off. Dave insists that we have a rifle at the ready in the field, in addition to the flares and mace, because, as he says, it is not worth dying for research, even if the chances are small. I now have a holster on the left with a flare gun, on the right a dagger and a can with pepper spray, one that covers about fifteen meters. There is just a small chance of us crossing a bear, unlike our journey two years ago on Novaya Zemlya. I accept it and it saves us five kilos. Dave is sulking, which is not appreciated by the Russians. Sergei is already well aware of it. "It's on your list, it's in your notebook, and you want to cross it off, right?" he says, teasing Dave with his records.

Sergei is a new face, (and a remarkable face: shaved skull, with deep-set eyes, a small nose and tight-fitting skin), sensible, calm, humourous, and observant. Sergei is one year older than Dave at 35, and two years older than me. He speaks rudimentary but constant English and has earned enough doing web page designs that he was able to bring a sleek, lightweight, two-person tent and a digital photo camera. He will take photos and film our trip as long as his batteries last.

Kitchen master, cook and stock manager is Valera. Quiet, a very tough marine captain. We travelled together on R/V *Ivan Petrov* two years ago, and he spent a week on Cape Vilkitsky with George Maat and his assistant Jorrit-Jan, putting to use the dissecting skills of both doctors after shooting a reindeer. There is a lot of food, including sacks of rice, beans, pasta, whole potatoes, raw ingredients for porridge, whole tomatoes, onions, carrots, cabbages, tins of meat and tins of condensed milk, chocolate, and jute sacks with candies and biscuits. We make a wide selection and pack everything we can carry in our boxes.

I am back at Cape Diakonov, which was known centuries ago as the Afgodenhoeck or Cape Idols.[12] A rock bridge encloses the gate to the underworld – still a place where our world and whatever is behind it meet. Now it is a quarter to ten in the evening and a continuous rain comes down, sometimes so that speaking is drowned out by the drumming of it on our tent. Except for some parts with frost shattered rock, the entire landscape is overgrown by peat bog. Thick layers of peat curl over the rocks into the sea. We are south of the only settlement on the island, Varnek. The helicopter mistakenly left a Varnekker's shopping bag here, and tonight a Nenetsman appeared with two shy girls of maybe 5 and 8 years old, shivering in the hard cold wind, looking very serious. Father cautiously tied their hood and Boyarsky brought out three sandwiches with very thick bacon and a steaming cup of tea. Then the father knelt down by them and pointed across the strait. "There is Khabarova," I heard him say, "and behind it, Amderma." They briefly caught their breath and then started the ten kilometer walk back. I watched them climb against the twenty-meter-high ridge (the actual cape) next to our camp. The youngest kept up with difficulty, until the other two stopped and waited for her to arrive. She caught up and soon let go again because she found something and stopped to pick it up up from the ground, then ran after her sibblings. She will be a tough one.

The rain stops for ten minutes and I quickly get out. Through the mists I can see the barracks and barbed wire fences or what's left of it of the former prison camp Khabarova on the other side of the Yugor Strait. Flattened rock islands everywhere spread across the sea. We help the Russians stretch plastic over their heavy cotton tents. Apparently, these tents were known to leak quite a bit, as they brought in large rolls of plastic to cover them up. We fixate it with duct-tape introducing a handy American invention used by Moon astronauts but it meets with sarcasm on Vaygach. We marvel that we are suddenly in that black and white *Corona* photo, alive and well.

Polar Station Fedorov

Vaygach is the southern end of the nearly 1000 km-long Novaya Zemlya Archipelago. The guards of the Kara Gates, the broad strait that connects the Barents Sea and the Kara Sea, are young boys in camouflage uniforms. They interrogate us on August 3 in the living room of polar station Fedorov. The station from the outside looks like a countryside school building. It has a central corridor and rooms on either side. At the end of the corridor, to the right are the engine room and airlock. Why an airlock? Because it is dark here half of the year with two meters of snow and -40°C. To the left are the kitchen and cosy living room.

It must have been like this in better times at Cape Zhelaniya, or any of the other polar stations closed down in the past decade: without the mold, well lit and warm and dry, and occupied by two friendly souls who seem to have forgotten how to speak. The last entry in their guest book was made by Dmitri Kravchenko and his two apprentices (22 July 1991). "With deep respect and gratitude for the help to the polar explorers [provided by] the Evgeny Fedorov meteorological station – on behalf of the members of the 'Arctic Circle' expedition." Who would have believed we'd be hosted here on Vaygach Island, by the 'KGB' according to Frans Heeres on his pass here, nine years ago. How times have changed now that we shelter with a former enemy. With a mighty jump we went across the 100-km-long island and will spend a comfortable week in Polar Station Fjedorova, on Cape Bolvansky Nos, connected with Vaygach by a narrow isthmus of shingles.

Silhouetted on the bare peninsula across the bay stands the compound of the border guards, and shortly after our delivery by helicopter (with mail for the station and its crew), we saw a tracked personel carrier detach and creep towards us. It took a while for it to arrive, because it needed to drive around the laguna and over the isthmus to get to its neighbors, who were not at ease about the upcoming passport checks. Did we even have permits?, they asked nervously. Sergei will do all the talking. The farewell of the group today was moving. Pyotr Boyarsky escorted me and hugged me twice, next year I can go for free, he said, "at Putin's expense." Vladimir Putin this year has taken office as new and promising president and all hope is on him to drag Russia out of the mess it is in. "I'll be honored," I answered, "I hope we'll go through Matochkin Shar next time." Also solid embraces with Dima (visibly hung over, "Very bad mood today") and Valera ('My friend'). Goodbye everybody.

Questions asked during the interrogation: do you have children; what kind of car do you have? Do you have many girlfriends? Over the *Corona* image we explain our goals and are seriously questioned. One of the men introduces himself as major, the other other one is lieutenant. We selected three areas that could be useful (meaning not covered by peat bog) and need to get clearance for that. "Problem, problem," they shake their heads. They need to radio to headquarters, tomorrow, and find out whether we may get permission. They go through our passports back and forth.

After an hour of tight formalities, festivities break out quite unexpected. The crew of the station are Ukrainian technician Gennadi, a good-natured bear of a guy, about forty years old, and Vladimir, a timid, skinny meteorologist, with gray-blond stubble. Age unclear, probably not much older than Gennadi. Both with thick-rimmed glasses; Gennadi black rim with small glasses and Vladimir a dirty yellow rim and round glasses like a lighthouse. From the look of their worn-out outfits they've been isolated from civilization for a couple of years already. They receive us shyly, but warmly. Vladimir above his table books has lost the art of speaking. He tries all evening and one moment sits next to me, but he just can't get a word out. The words get stuck on the tip of his tongue.

The guards tell us of their days in their isolated post at the Arctic frontier. They get up at six and work until ten at night. Three hours on, three hours off, forty-five vacation days a year. They miss their wives and infants and spend three, four, some five years in sweltering, roach-infested barracks. December, January, February are the worst months: then there are only four walls. When I am outside with the smokers, the lieutenant has presented his kalashnikov and Lord Jesus! There is a shot! Everyone laughs and I'm more excited than shocked. My turn! A minute later I get my hands on the weapon. It weighs little, I put on, the shot slips smoothly and sparks fly from a sea container parked a hundred meters away. From across the barrel of the gun ("How to swith to automatic?", I ask) I see one of the dogs walking by and then when I aim at a row of fuel barrels, Gennadi intervenes firmly and removes the cartridge holder with a decisive smile. "Typically Russian," says Sergei, "something has to be done after drinking." "After shooting, you feel completely happy," says the lieutenant, and it's true. The men tell us that a polar bear was spotted a few days ago along the coast.

Waiting for permission

The next day, we deliver Sergei to the compound across the bay to complete the paperwork and await our orders following from radio contact of the border guards with their superiors. Large holes pierce the container that came under fire yesterday. Those small, pointed bullets cut straight through two layers of steel. We used a boat and have rowed across the 500 m-wide bay to get to the other side. It is a sinister complex with a watchtower in the center of the completely barren peninsula. David and I are not allowed to enter and prepare to explore the coast.

Waves crash on that rocky coast and wind from across the Kara Sea carries in a cold dirty mist, which splatters around us and later turns into hard rain. When we knock on the door a few hours later to pick Sergei up and hear the news, a startled soldier appears behind the window and sends us away with an uneasy laugh. In the middle of the mud flat is a cannibalized crawler tractor in which we take refuge and have an hour of lunch, until we are cold. Sergei's lunch we give to the two dogs that walked with us from the meteorological station this morning (and swam), and who are now shivering under the tractor in the wind. They run around us as we walk, providing a perimeter to the polar bear seen in this area four days ago. In the pouring rain we scramble between other waste, mostly mechanical, and oil barrels, but find nothing of interest. It is an absolutely miserable afternoon.

At half past four we again return to the compound by appointment to collect our comrades. Water is in the fingers of my leather gloves. Sergei and Gennadi get along well and come out in a very good mood. May have already enjoyed a 'little drink'. For another hour we toil through the mud and then through the heavy beach gravel before we reach the place where we crossed the bay this morning. Dave and Sergei laughingly hold up a stranded blue rope for me as a finish line when we get to the sloop. "Where's the boat? Is that our boat?" I ask and we see the battered steel dinghy filled to the brim with sea water in the heavy surf. Dave and I are used to dragging our boat out of reach of the waves against the beach, but it wasn't necessary, according to Gennadi who walked away with a careless 'normal' and said to return in half an hour. Gennadi jumps into the waves and wants to tilt the boat. He is strong as a bear, but the gig filled with water is like a block of concrete. I run along the tide line and find an empty 5-liter oil container, where I cut off the top with my dagger so that we have a container with which we can bail. Half an hour Gennadi stands chest-deep in the ice-cold water, but the colossus cannot be moved. We are on a lower shore, and every time we have the bow half a meter out of the water, the sea drags the boat back. Eventually we get it perpendicular to the beach and dig the gravel ridge with the field shovel. All the while Gennadi is still in the water, bailing. His wool sweater is wet around his upper body. He can hardly stand, sinks into the steep gravel beach. Dave and I are full in the bow line, to get the boat ten centimeters further on dry land everytime a wave rolls up. But the sea drags the unruly object back time and again. When we finally get the upper hand, my arms shake with exertion and my body feels as if I weigh three hundred kilos. We are on a lower shore but will lift the steel sloop over the shingles barrier using driftwood trunks as rollers.

There is a strong tide current through the estuary, but Gennadi is rowing ferociously, and we reach the opposite coast. Back in the polar station, I am exhausted. Gennadi fires up the sauna and we wait for it to heat. The dogs that have swum back with us immediately went to sleep on plastic crates in the portal. Very wet. The little one was rather cold at first and ran up and down the tide line as we drove away, but finally jumped into the sea to swim with the dinghy. On the other side the animal quickly ran after the terns and buntings. In the laundry room, with a cast iron roll top bath, we warm up in an electric sauna improvised with bricks and a blanket. It is a fully tiled sauna by the way, with glowing hot tiles and therefore not without risk, and washed.

It is a quarter past eight in the evening and a tube radio plays an instrumental version of 'The girl from Ipanema' with a lot of static noise. Today's physical strain on my untrained body makes me so tired that I tremble, and my arms and legs are hurting. But I am warm and dry, my stuff is drying out in the 'engine room'. In the kitchen we drink tea and eat pancakes and the lightly salted fish, which is simply cut into slices that we chew on. There are also strips of goose, brand unknown, maybe a Branta bernicla. These geese are stripped of their feathers and hung naked in the wind for several days, causing the flesh to turn purple. The drying gives the same effect as in the preparation of smoked meat, and does justice to the animal's sweet, slightly trainy taste. We drink vodka, an alcohol concentrate diluted in a glass carafe

Drop off at Cape Diakonov with Yugor Strait in background.

with Arctic water to the desired strength. Whoever thinks that we are here being cold and miserable is wrong.

Days of quiet

Here is the kind of quiet that prompts you to start talking to yourself: a quiet barely broken by the rattling of a telegraph or a lonely radio call echoing through the station's hallway. It is so quiet here that you can hear a single pump and, in the distance, the steady drone of the power generator in a small building thirty meters away. We stepped into the 1950s: there are no computers; the instruments have solid steel casings, large dials, and big buttons. Next to a desk stands an old-fashioned tube radio with a lacquered wooden casing and stations like Moscow, Kiev, and Leningrad printed on its dial. Guy wires from the radio and weather masts sing in the wind. Eventually you will talk to yourself, or you will forget to speak, like both residents of this station. After some calculations I arrive at the conclusion that it is Saturday. Clothes hanging out to dry lend the air inside the room the well-known smell of poverty. It must be exciting, especially during the polar night, to keep a spaceship like this going. They do a good job: the building is very clean and well-maintained; in the engine room all the lights are 'green'. You'd say it is a lost battle. The windows, frames, plaster, wallpaper, piping is old and needs to be replaced eventually. Like most other stations in the archipelago, things are kept running with minimal resources and patchwork; closed when improvisation also falls short. The meteorological observations will be taken over by satellites and automatic weather stations and outside, nature awaits to repossess this structure, like we have seen on Cape Zhelaniya.

Polar station Cape Zhelaniya was abandoned in 1995 after a fire crippled its power plant sometime around Christmas, in the middle of the Arctic night. We passed by three years later and found miniature plastic Christmas trees and Christmas lights throughout the station. All was left instantly and as we found it, with personal items still on desks. Photographs, cigarettes, coffee mugs next to open notebooks, one with a pencil still on it. Bedding was open as if someone had jumped out yesterday, and in several buildings, tables had been set with plates, pans half-full, now spilling over with fungi. Curtains, carpets, books, linen, wallpaper, and clothing: everything had been overgrown with a veil of mold. On shelves and desks, we saw great quantities of pharmaceuticals: pills and ampoules containing powders. People had made sure they had everything they could possibly need during their stay in one of Earth's most isolated spots. On a wall in one of the buildings was a map of the world on which Novaya Zemlya rises high above the Eurasian continent. They had painted the walls with images of flowers and trees and everything beautiful that lies beyond the barren horizon. Anything feminine showing the least bit of nudity or sensuality had been ripped out of newspapers and periodicals to adorn the rooms. Outside, planks and discarded radiators were laid next to one another to make improvised walkways across the soggy soil. Five graves were lying just steps away from the buildings, with stones stacked over the bodies. Everywhere there was litter: dog skulls, boots, jackets (quilted and jeans); books and binders with tables full of measurements, containing years' worth of observations, ten thousand glass canning jars and green bottles, so many that they spilled over the large carts in which they were piled; boxes full of unopened, rusted cans of condensed milk, peaches, or corn. A bear-claw resembling a huge hand, all knuckles still connected by tendons. Apparently fresh, water-filled tracks plowed through the dark mud, but the heavy machines that created them stood together, red-brown from corrosion. Ocean spray and snowstorms hadn't left a speck of paint on them. David and I spend a couple of days in the station, making camp in one of the buildings, stacking furniture in its entry hall to block it against polar bears and not be surprised by our white hairy friends, although I feared more being eaten by fungi. The peninsula was strewn with fuel drums, stacked in long rows by the shallow lagoon. Their steel noises would signal the cool of the night.

No news from the border guards on our permission to research the island (that we are presently on), but I am hoping that tomorrow I might be staring at the tent canvas. Check out this floor, or the poster with drawn fish, that I can touch now, perhaps for the last time. The windows have thin, flowery curtains. Terns scream outside and my heart beats and that is how this day has passed. David wants to read a few more papers and update his notes, so I decide to take an evening stroll.

Fjedorova is located on a tiny island with waves running up the steep cliffs that surround it. Waves roll in from the Kara Sea, pack together, and shatter white on the rocky coast. The uproar is great. There are walruses in the sea; they pop up in between waves as I pass. I climb over the weathered rocks to the very tip of the cape that I can reach, a narrow rock on which I let myself be sprayed with sea water. Surrounded by rolling waves and two-meter-high breakers, I watch fog entering again over the raging, white-washed water, blue as only Arctic water can be. Very nice, such a dog that runs with you, and waits patiently and looks around until we walk on together. Chases a gigantic Arctic hare, killing it for her young. We round the whole island from 9:45 to 12:45 am. On the cliff behind the station there is a small wooden toilet building on four meters high posts. During wave run-up like we enjoy today, Mother Nature clears out all the droppings. This applies to a lesser extent to the other waste, which was collected in an open steel container, probably for decades. It has been full for years, and the debris is piling up all around, blowing all over the peninsula.

August the 8th. Counting days has now officially started. There is little to do except read and gaze at the sea. At the dinner table (soup, macaroni-and-cheese soul food) we discuss our most profitable tactic for our twelve remaining days, because with all the effort we have put in to get to this island, we must make the best of it. The major showed up with the tracked vehicle unexpectedly last night and offered us a ride on his fishing trip to a lake that holds Arctic trout. Now we know we are surrounded by miles of impenetrable swamp. We have the best chance in the rocky areas in the southeast of the island and should skip all the rest.

While I'm writing this on the bed, the radio blares. It is the major who dropped us off inland last night and now inquires whether the geologists have returned properly. Very thoughtful.

Polar station Vaygach

Spend two days on the location of abandoned polar station Vaygach. One day sunny, one misty. On the 9th the major has personally driven us about 12 kilometers southwest of Fedorov. We have a new companion, Petr who was dropped off by helicopter on the day of our departure from the weather station. The sky was a clear blue, the landscape sun-drenched. The black dog ran all the way with us, twelve kilometers. Petr is carrying a gun, perhaps as a result of that bear spotted: someone is taking care of us, Boyarsky or the major. The official version is that he will count the numerous snowy owls here. These snowy owls are found in cold winters to Ukraine and central Europe, he says. From our encampment we enjoyed a spectacular view across the Kara Gates with small rock islands spread in front of us. The other side of the ~50 km-broad strait cannot be seen, because southern Novaya Zemlya has little relief. This must have been a nice post, with high windows, small rooms, and a stove in each room. Old scenes, partially decayed and long gone in the past, come back to life: the heated rooms, the bedroom with the cast iron bed frame, a quiet afternoon in this secluded post. I walk outside between grass and little tundra flowers. The year of construction is unknown, but from the history of this area, I would guess early twentieth century.[20] On top of the hill are two graves, and two more further down in the tundra, plus a small box that has frozen out of the ground and that may have been for a baby.

Skinny, tall Sergei still walks in casual clothing on sneakers. He mocks our gear and, in the evening, sits with his wrinkled pale feet by the fire, his socks and shoes next to it steaming. The Russians are much more trained in hardship than I am. The Russian on his high rubber boots, with bandaged feet, a leaky tent, his dacha-bred immunity to parasites, endures much better – they're always ready to lug more, work harder. Time becomes space in the tundra. Every step is a heartbeat. There is simply no end to it, all day long you look forward to getting someplace, but you don't seem to get any closer. With every step I squeezed water out of the peat and left footsteps behind. The tough leather boots we were using up north are useless. The weather was exceptionally fine, with the air carrying a whiff of water and rosemary. Petr took off his gun during a break, completely undressed in the cold wind, and washed in the river. We sat on top of the hill, on the large orange-lichen-stained stones, encouraging him and shouting that it was like a scene from a Soviet Union propaganda film. We collected *Hiatella arctica* shells for radiocarbon dating, from a 10-m thick section up there. Some were complete with both shells attached, in situ as we say, indicating that they are in original position. I am very curious what ages the laboratory will return on these. Very good catch.

Waiting for our ride

On August 12 we prepare to be taken to the southeastern part of the island by helicopter. "It was 12, wasn't it?" I ask David. Sergei shakes his head, isn't totally sure. "August 12, I'm almost sure," Dave says, going through his notes, yes that's what it says in his notebook: between 10:00 and 13:00. At ten o'clock we must be packed and ready to leave. Thus, we lay ready, between our bags and gear on the ground, which we cleaned of glass shards and other objects that could go airborne in the rotorwash. The unmistakable drone and silhouette of the helicopter along the eastern horizon makes us all jump up and cheer, but we have to be patient a bit longer. At 13.20 we see a dot above the horizon and know it is our 'ride'. First, we ask each other: did you hear something? What did you hear then? Listen, I hear it again [...] The distance is still about ten kilometers, because it stopped at the border guards' station first. Then it arrives, that beautiful machine, with beating blades and howling turbines. It shows us its belly and circles over the sea before landing right on top of us, with the blades well over me, a lot of wind and an unearthly noise. It bounces twice on its rubber wheels and then establishes a tight lock with the ground. While the blades continue, the pilot jumps out with a smile to shake hands and help us load our boxes. The co-pilot is filling out the log.

As long as it took us to get to this place, we get out in the blink of an eye. The airmen have fun between the 'mountains' of Vaygach: bare clusters of rock ~100 m high in rolling terrain. The unwieldy machine slowly drags itself through a few bends. It reduces forward speed to gain altitude while I see a hilltop full of large boulders approach and pass just three meters under the wheels. On top, the helicopter tilts forward and down the slope again makes speed. It is blazingly hot in the cabin under that thumping engine. The cockpit is cramped, with space for two pilots and a navigator in the doorway. The pilot has a wimpy little fan running. Dave, Sergei, Petr and I view the monotonous green-grey landscape from behind the portholes. The portholes open to allow a machine gun to be protruded and mounted on supports under each window. Dozens of braided black lines pass underneath, indicating the route followed by the major on his fishing trips.

After flying for fifteen minutes, a few patches of fog shoot by, causing some commotion in the cockpit and the navigator, a boy of about seventeen in oversized Army wear, gestures at me with the plastic-lined map. I quickly move forward. He points to the cross I have placed on the map, and I confirm that we want to be dropped there. The boy briefly consults with the pilot and the helicopter immediately slides into a sharp turn to the right, so I have to hold on to the doorway of the cockpit. The mist is rising and through it I see a shiny mixture of watery plains and green grass. There seems to be some confusion or panic because of the fog, and a small windshield wiper frantically swipes away the fine droplets that cling to the convex cockpit windows. We fly very low and I can count reindeer antlers, snowy owls and arctic foxes that shoot underneath us. Suddenly the speed drops, apparently, we are there: the pilot is already turning to find a dry spot. "Get ready to debark!" I shout to David and Sergei and shake hands with Petr.

The depths of Vaygach

A gloomy dusk has descended over the bog. I am about twenty-five minutes away from camp. Amid the lakes and puddles of Vaygach Island's interior, I watch an owl as it wings stealthily away from the low bedrock ridge it had used as a lookout, bright white in the dark atmosphere. It flies silently past me, looking me straight in the eye. Our journey has taken a bizarre turn. David and Sergei have been gone for a day now. When I got out of the helicopter, my boots sank to the ankles in a wet bog. I knelt to stay clear of the rotor blades and switched on the GPS. It takes about thirty seconds for it to calculate a position. Following our usual routine, I pulled the Xeroxed Russian topographic map out of its protective folder and plotted our position: 69°53.612 N 59°56.852 E. As I double-checked the plot of coordinates, Dave and Sergei hauled the last box from the helo and gave the engineer a thumbs-up. The hatch closed and the engine started gearing up. "Wrong place!" I shouted above the tumult, feverishly searching my pockets for the flare gun. The machine stood shaking on its wheels and then miraculously disconnected from the earth. I loaded a red flare and fired the gun: pop! But the helicopter had already dissolved in the low clouds. Too late, too late, they don't see the red glow, or they don't want to see it. "We are twenty kilometers off!" I called, as the helicopter's thunder turned into a distant drone.

"How are they ever going to find us?"

There was little else we could do but hike to the rendezvous marked on the navigator's map and await our retrieval, scheduled three days later. We had to split-up, to exclude the possibility of the helicopter returning to our recorded position and find everybody gone. Sergei dreaded the very thought of being left behind. As tough as he is, he refused to stay alone. David and I on the other hand are committed to make the most of every field day. We must get to the southern part of the island; David must get there to sample either rock or shells. It is the least we should do. We are little soldiers in a science that is almost obsolete. So I offered to stay. Should the helicopter fail to locate them, David and Sergei are to continue to Varnek, twenty kilometers through the bog, and organize my evacuation. I stayed, and solitude closed in on me as I watched their silhouettes fade into the mists.

Let me be quick to add, I find the experiment of being alone in this place exciting, yes, a certain excitement has taken hold of me. I am plain curious how I will keep myself. To start with, I am busy for an hour to turn the tent around so that the opening is more favorable on the wind. Then I stretch the blue tarp and enforce it with lines to make a roof, under which I can cook and be protected from the wind. It bulges like a sail under the steady stream of air and draps around my back with knocks and blows. A shower passes every few hours. I am in a wet sandwich: rainwater from above and below the saturated mire. The substrate consists of approximately 5 cm of moss on top of a soft silty clay, which is squeezed up under your weight. Just behind the tent are the half-a-meter-deep hoof prints of the helo, mostly filled with water. Because of the rain and our walking around, the ground is messy. The oval or rectangular lake that I stand next to, and from which I draw my drinking water, is half a meter deep at most. It is continuously churned by wave action: the water is brown, and I can't block the thought that radioactive fallout from the atomic bomb tests has bound to the sediment.

Safe and well in the tent, and the rain continues; it rained in the morning and after a few hours the rain even intensified for a while. I hope the others keep up as well. The confusion over the landing site is probably caused by the fact that the stream circling this swamp has a name very similar to the river I designated. I lie on my back with my hands folded over my stomach, leaning against a huge duffel bag. I calmly listen to the wind and the tapping of the rain on the light-yellow canvas, which is constantly rippling under gusts of wind and stroking my face moistly.

18:00 The rained stopped and in its place came a thick fog. I am surrounded by a white wall. My camp is the eye in this quiet storm. I finished afternoon tea half an hour ago. The big Russian gasoline stove sprays poorly and produces flames and a lot of soot. Dave and Sergei took my burner with them. Wood was abundant on the coast, but there is nothing to burn in this swamp and I have to rely on two lemonade bottles with petrol, taped together. That should be enough for three days, although it is going through too quickly with this apparatus. Under ideal conditions the machine already takes a long time to get up to temperature, but under the present wet conditions it sometimes refuses to start up completely. My countrymen, four hundred years ago, explored the inland of the island to several miles from Varnek but found it boring and impossible to walk.

Dense fog and rain prevent exploration of the area. First, you don't see a thing, second, I want to avoid getting my clothes soaked, because how do I ever get dry here? Third, if the GPS gives out, how will I ever find my tent? Five steps away I

View inland from polar station Cape Zhelaniya: 'And outside, the silent wilderness surrounding this cleared speck on earth struck me as something great and invincible, like evil or truth, waiting patiently for the passing away of this fantastic invasion' (Joseph Conrad, Heart of Darkness 1902).

only see the contours of my camp through the fog. So I spent the day in the tent, which luckily gives a sunny yellow light. There is a lot of food left, cans of very gross meat, consisting of waste, whole pipelines and patches of intestinal wall or skin or lung, all contained in congealed fat. We have boiled soup of it a few times and then nothing remains. Furthermore, pasta, beans, sugar, but also: rice, honey, dades, chocolate, cans of *Dutch Lady*, jam, and peanut butter. In the chest on which I sit while cooking are my daily supplies, the rest I packed in the large duffel bag that I lean into while sitting in the tent. I feel healthy, also because of the simple, but solid food, oats for breakfast made with *Dutch Lady* and raisins, beans, rice, or mashed potatoes for dinner. In between a selection of outdoor nut mix and sugars, chocolate.

Fear of the stillness of this place and whatever lurks here grows when dusk sets in around 9:00 in the evening. The footsteps are back, and I hear falling objects, weird voices; probably invisible geese or the wind in my collar. It is known that for lack of stimuli the brain itself will fill the void and I wonder if that is what's happening now. My mind starts to wring already:

I expect figures or faces when I leave the tent, and once outside there is something that keeps me from going back into the tent. I fear seeing myself sitting when I open the tent and have spent ten minutes standing and watching tonight until I managed to pull myself together and get back inside. In the tent when night falls and it becomes too dark to read, I hesitate to light my Petzl headlamp because the light will expose me. When I finally do it, the lamp gives a weak and shaky light. I'm not here. Nobody is here.

Out and about

To make peace with my surroundings, I venture into that wall of white and practice navigation with compass and GPS. The permanent mists cast a dim, bleak light on the ponds and bogs that hide my small camp. These are the depths of Vaygach: Khebidya Ya, the Sacred Island of the Dead. I hear footsteps, falling objects, and eerie voices, a fine rain tingles in my face. Through the water I step on my rubber boots and search for dense and higher places where I can make more speed. The GPS says that I get 4-5 km per hour on those parts. Hollow tracks as if a bunch of cyclists have passed testify to the presence of lemmings, which must be water-repellent. Many bird's nests, neatly braided and attached to blades of grass. Very alone in the middle of a green sea, a green circle, and I don't think much of it except dammit, I sink too deep when the water gets to the edge of my boots, that is, just above my knee. Within such a green circle, the white dot of a snowy owl can always be seen in the distance. If it's not the same guy watching over me, there must be quite a number here. I hold up a bright white feather in the wind and feel the lift it provides.

The night went well, I slept through it. I've been alone for 48 hours now. Strong wind tore the tent pegs out of the soft ground last night. At times there is rain, or an annoying spray hissing softly on the thin polyster cover that shields me. Better visibility than yesterday, sometimes kilometers, but still hazy. I cleaned the stove as well as I can and finally got it working, so I had breakfast with tea and oats. I shaved and brushed under the billowing sail. I only have one thought all the time: will the helo come tomorrow and how bad must the weather be to prevent this. It shouldn't get much worse, I think, but the way it is now would be fine, if they know exactly where I am. I decide to leave the tent up until they show. My lower back is stiff and painful from lying and sitting on the cold ground. I walk like an old man for the first minutes. On with the show.

After looking long and hard at the *Corona* image I spotted a linear feature that calls for closer inspection. Not bedrock, it is a deposit of some kind that perfectly separates a lake in two halves. Now that I have mastered navigation in my netherworld, I can undertake a hike: the feature is about six kilometers away. At half past three I headed northeast, following the narrow little river until I came at a point that I could pass through in a quick few steps. Emptiness, silence, and as in an evil dream I only make slow progress. The atmosphere suddenly clears, at last. After only two kilometers I see a bulge protruding above the horizon, which continues to grow, and I cannot keep my eyes off it. After another half an hour three shapes lie in the otherwise flat landscape. Sometimes Dave would say we do 'random geology' by the lucky or unlucky nature of our work. But it isn't random, intuition underlies it. In this case, however I cannot deny that through good chance I landed in the vicinity of this discovery.

The three features that I found are so-called eskers: the fillings of meltwater tunnels in the edge of the glacier or ice cap that one time covered this area. They are up to 20 m-high and wind like dikes over a distance of about 2 km. There are three longer ones as well in the north (we must have flown right over them). The landforms appear rather fresh, with 45° sides. This is the first solid proof of that ancient ice margin. The orientation of these lines through the landscape point to a glacier coming from the northeast: from Novaya Zemlya. Glaciers extended to about 500 km from the ice cap's center on that island, curving onto Vaygach and deepening the Yugor Strait, possibly forming it. The location of these three eskers here, in the middle of a big lake, suggests a dead-ice, melting environment. Slumping on the side exposes the filling of unsorted glacial outwash, silty clay, local calcite limestone boulders. The landform despite its steep angled sides can be climbed with ease, over compacted larger and smaller rocks and sandy sediments. Victory! When I stand on the ~2 m wide top of the structure and see it wind in front of me, the clouds part briefly: a blinding moment of sunshine in an otherwise dark world. Very dramatic.

I feel cozy again in the tent after dinner and having dried up. When the wind drops, there is a great silence and my ears rustle. I have cooked and wait until tomorrow morning before packing, because tonight, after eleven it is already quite dark with those heavy clouds. I really hope the heli comes tomorrow. In total I covered 15 km today. When returning, I saw that tiny yellow tent in which I lie flat, visible to everyone and shielded from the elements by no more than a double layer of nylon, a fraction of a millimeter thick. Except for the sleeping bag, everything is wet and damp, if not from precipitation than from condensation. I have the feathers of snowy owls that I collected today in my awning to ward off evil.

Supernatural

In one of the low rocky hills furtheron I found the castle of the Arctic fox that was passing by my tent this afternoon. On another ridge was a large snowy owl that this time allowed me to approach and I came to within five meters of that big bird before it winged away calmly. The owl sat on a low pile of crushed vomit balls and lemming bones, a dirty wet spot. Notwithstanding the presence of this predator, a lemming 'swam' before me in the swamp and those animals are indeed water-repellent. I managed to grab one by the neck and held it to my face as it squeaked loudly. On the way back, a greasy fog came up that thoroughly soaked me in the last ten minutes. I can see the tent an hour in advance, but as in a nightmare I do not seem to get any closer and even up close it is as if you sooner die or wake up before reaching that goal.

Here is a thin red plant, which, against a low hill in the fog, gives the impression of a small human figure. It freaked me out more than once. Under the circumstances, the spiritual essence of this dark world can be sensed in every bit. I am part of something bigger, I have been allotted a place in it. It is in the rocky outcrops that I see on the horizon. It is in this entire green bog that I am in. That fox certainly is spirited, and these owls are, too. The Nenets catch young animals and domesticate these, only to release them when they are mature. Thus, they know individual animals by name, their fellow creatures in this world. Foxes do very well and can be even called back. But the snowy owl cannot be tamed, we were told. 'The island of the idols,' the first visitors called this place that I have landed on, observing the indigenous life-death rituals with wonder, to say the least. For centuries, the Nenets had a tradition of human sacrifice. Openly, until outsiders penetrated their territory, my Russian colleagues argued; implying that they still carry out these practices in the secret depths of Vaygach, but they do not reveal. Life is cyclic: a person is born, dies, and is reincarnated in a new individual – newborns are given the names of the deceased. The rocky arch of Cape Diakonov, the Idols Cape, where supernatural entities enter and leave our world, is like a *torii*, the gate of that other animistic faith, Shinto. And I am in the temple. Now be careful and avoid contacting spirits other than your own, or you will open that whole box of Japanese horror movies, of wandering souls looking for someone to see them and look in their mad dead eyes.

Day Six (?)

This sleeping bag has too much dead space: when I move, the hot and cold air mix and a chill runs through me. The hood is downright clumsy and stretches far too small around my head (or my head is too big, anyway I put my wool cap on). I spread the gold insulation foil under the neoprene mat because the ground is stone cold. You can feel the water through the groundsheet, on which my breath condenses, and permafrost ground ice is sixty centimeters lower. Dreamt of a homely situation three or four years ago. Ms. Eri she was lying on the couch reading a book, while I walked on the concrete of the driveway of our house, still warm under my bare feet, checking if all the insect screens and storm windows are secure and in place. There's a warning for severe weather. I looked into the deserted yard and walked along the oak by the bedroom window; the play of the sun through its leaves makes shadows dance on the window in the afternoon. The screen door flipped once in the wind and I stepped across the porch with hollow steps. Silence descended on the land. Only the crickets would be heard in the quiet before the storm. When I woke it was a quarter to four in the night. The tent cloth softly waved in the passing wind. During the 'interval' sleep I have here, I dream a lot, dreams full of absurdities. I slept in. Now wide awake and considering getting out, but I don't know what I could do. The pointlessness of walking through that empty world out there, at this instant is overwhelming. I grab a book and start reading. From its light bristle on the tent, I hear the fog keeps coming. This is the fourth day of bad weather. You could say my expedition has become an internal journey.

August 17th it is. They were able to drop me off in this weather, but the pickup is not so good. It rained, and it was cold. At half past ten this morning it was suddenly very light, and windless; the condensation drops that have been all around me in the tent for days disappeared in a short while. Out: blue sky, sun, I have never seen that glory radiate over this landscape before. In the distance on the horizon, I can now see the low undulating irregularity of the rocky part of this island, where my partners have headed, and I would have liked to be. I pull everything out of the tent to dry. The helicopter is definitely coming! But twenty minutes later the gray veil of fog pulls over the island again. The wind turns very rapidly from east to south and that plastic tarpaulin of mine almost becomes airborne.

My afternoon program starts at 14:00 at the earliest because I have to be ready for the helicopter until then. After 14:00 they probably won't be coming. But who knows. Twelve o'clock noon: the day is still ten hours long. Two hours of that will be spent reading, as this stimulates the mind. There will be an hour of sleep, and by three o'clock I ask everyone to gather for the usual walk, four hours today. (I could go back to my discovery of yesterday and get more luminescence samples). I take an hour for dinner. This leaves two hours that are impossible to fill other than by staring.

13:45 This is the worst moment, when you know that it really won't happen again and the window closes. Dave and Sergei have food and fuel until today and are probably already in Varnek or will get there today to establish radio contact. The weather is calm, cloud ceiling >500 m.

15:45 Spent the last two hours looking along the completely blown horizon, with growing frustration. I've been hearing phantom helicopters for two days. Confusingly I am also not looking forward to resuming my regular life back in Chicago when this will all be over again.

17:15 At least two or three more days, I repeat aloud, perhaps more. You might think you could sleep through it, but no one needs that much sleep. I go back to the small stream that winds around this swamp, just west of me. In one of the bends is an exposed laminated section of medium to fine sands, alternating with silty clay. Each layer is 2-5 cm thick. I have short, black pvc tubes to sample these deposits for luminescence dating, my boss Steve's specialty. I hammer three of them into the side of the riverbed, then cap and label them. From the look of it this has been a lake, in front of the melting ice cap an estimated 10.000 years ago. This has always been a lake.

Collecting meteorites

Two years ago, we had several brilliant weeks working between glaciers and polar bear. On the morning of 27 August 1998, after our ship had delivered George's party to Cape Vilkitsky, David, Dmitri and I landed in Ivanov Bay. As our Zodiac sped to shore, I was laying on the bow to keep the nose down and quickly made out that one, square building on the beach that I had come to know intimately through the stories of friends. Since 1995, the cabin had been blown askance and damaged by the powerful Bora winds. The greater part of the roof and its front were ripped off, and the door, carved with the names of those six, swung in indestructible hinges of walrus leather, because it had not been closed properly. In the haste of departure, Nicolai even left behind a backpack with plant samples. Inside the building, there is an elevated floor on which the lads slept side by side. The Russian sleeping bags, white with a thin, blue stripe, lay beside the hut, torn by polar bear and leaking their kapok filling. Our collegues never told of Ivanov

Bay's wild beauty: a pebble-strewn desert, separated from the icecap by dark brown, debris-covered mountains. There was not a sign of life in the entire vale, not even grass or moss. In the middle of that expanse stood the shelter erected in 1995, a rectangular edifice measuring 2 x 4 x 5 meters. We worked for about five hours to repair the construction, re-attaching planks and tarpaulins and nailing cross beams along the sidewalls for stability. Behind the cabin we wedged in a driftwood trunk to support the heeling structure, sunk firmly into the beach gravels. (In 2023 it can be seen still standing on Google Maps). As I rested and squatted against the sun-warmed planks, Dima laughed and said: "A Russian polar man can tolerate the cold well and can work hard with little food. But a Russian polar man does not like cold, hard work, or little food." Before I fell asleep that night, I lay still listening to the humming of the guy wires of our five-meter radio antenna, and the croaking and squealing sounds of moving parts.

The next day again there was a massive, radiant blue sky over that broad, sun flooded landscape. The sun brought out all the fine greys and ochers, and inside the cabin bright dots of projected light crept steadily across the rough wooden floor, reflecting the Earth's spinning motion. At last came the glorious day of our hike to the ice cap. We climbed up through the valley following the Snezhnaya River until it cut deep in the spectacularly layered rock, forming a broad and steep canyon. In the past, deluges of meltwater have fought their way down the canyon towards the sea. Black moraines with white lines of snow running parallel loomed high in front of us. We managed to find a way around them and there, saw the ice, shining and glittering with smaller streams running down the concave surface of the cap. Somewhat tired from our rush up the mountain we sat down on big rocks in the icy cold glacier wind to enjoy lunch with dried bread and bars, drinking the glacier

Climb towards the ice cap through the valley of the Snezhnaya River.

water. The view from our elevated position was spectacular. Before us we could see the entire north cape of the island, with the two Orange Islands as flattened rocks in the blue expanse of the Arctic Ocean. You search for a ship or a plane in the sky until you realize that there is no one there as far as the eye can see. Just a few white icebergs from the IJshoeck glaciers floated steadily by from west to east, further out in the sea. I walked around on the first hundred flat meters of ice while Dima hung a magnet on a rope in one of the streams that ran of the ice cap. When an hour later we readied ourselves to go back, he pulled up his catch. The magnet had been covered by tiny black iron spherules: meteorites [a paper was published about it by Badyukov & Raitala 2002]. On our distant ice caps, the only dust that settles is cosmic dust.

In the evening, when the sun was low and every part of the terrain was nicely accentuated by shadows, we took the Zodiac and crossed the bay to Cape Varnek. For safety reasons, Boyarsky had explicitly forbidden us to round the cape in our boat, so we crossed it on foot, passing over patterned ground between the Gagarii Lakes. We passed the remains of the camp of surveyors, who worked here in the 1950s to validate Novaya Zemlya's new topographic map. Before us lay the remarkably wide beach of Cape Varnek, 800 m-wide with dozens of beach ridges. The cape protrudes about 2.5 km into the sea compared to Ivanov Bay, which is on the leeward side and was probably filled with ice. Therefore, the winterers on their return journey must have landed here. "Is this where it all happened?" I wondered, as we moved across the low-ridged plain. How far away were these castaways, when they buried their dead, from where I am now? Would they have been close enough to see us? Driftwood scattered across the beach and far into the land showed that storm surges had repeatedly washed the area. We found nothing resembling a grave. All we found was a large round Nazi sea mine filled with molten paraffin explosives.[21] Dmitri took some of that white stuff and lit it, and it burned bright and fierce.

Back at the cabin we created a huge bonfire with heavy bleached logs that we burned in half and then stacked them again. Sitting around the fire, with our mugs on a washed-up fish crate, we watched the northern horizon glittering with the colors of a lengthy sunset. We were the only ones on this distant, mythical North Pole Island. Dmitri distributed shots of vodka, visibly relieved that things were progressing as fortunately as they were. He told us that he was forty-four years old and has two brothers, one fifty and one sixty-five, and that his father was the commander of a Soviet submarine. Economic and personal struggles had not left him untouched. A stern expression was etched on his face. Another bad tiding, of the ruble crash, was received just days earlier, sending our shipmates into a state of panic. But that night, the peace and tranquility of our remote position evoked a solemn sense of detachment all three of us. With the murmur of waves on the beach and the crackling of burning wood, I watched in awe how smoke from our fire drifted slowly inland in a ghostly swirl, remaining static on the cold dense air in the central parts of the valley. Our voices and sounds echoed for kilometers across that silent landscape. At 11:00 p.m. I observed a bright planet, Jupiter, above the mountains in the blue-gray twilight rising from the Earth. Arctic twilight, which just doesn't progress to darkness, but instead freezes the whole peaceful scene in time.

Weekend

Just be patient now. Another opportunity missed today to get me out of here. I hope Dave and Sergei are alright. I hope they find something good. The wind has turned 180° today and is now coming from the southwest again. I have shifted the sail so that tonight I am on a less boggy stretch. Eaten potato soup while the sun peers brightly through the thin slit between the horizon and the cloud cover. From three to seven o'clock tonight I walked twelve kilometers to get rid of the frustration. I think a lot here: "It's only been a week... Better this, than...," and other internal dialogues (monologues, rather). Now at a quarter to nine, the tundra becomes very cold.

The stove has almost exploded. That horrible device leaked gasoline and a large ball of fire started less than three meters from the tent. Flames broke out under the reservoir, which was heated by this. I heard the liquid fizzing and boiling. With the shovel I managed to turn things around, to stop fuel leakage. Then I ran away twenty meters and waited for the blow. However, the fire went out and when everything had cooled, I made another attempt, preparing soup and tea. I intend to take it apart again tomorrow. Fuel has to be rationed. I lost more of it because of the bumbling than I could have imagined. Everything is covered in soot. It is a mess of water, clay, and gasoline.

Boy it's quiet here. The birds make strange noises. As I am writing this there seems to be a howling somewhere – could be that little fox that has come to see me every morning, dancing by on it's four legs and always in a hurry. Hurry, hurry, there is a big rush to finish and close things, then start something new. I would absolutely move the camp to higher ground if I only knew that it would take another week or even a month, or two months, for that matter. But the miserable certainty that I must stand ready every morning limits my every move.

17:45 Today's hike as usual started at three o'clock. I went in the direction of the coast to see how far I would get. The problem with the coast is that there may be polar bear and I am unarmed, so I got cold feet. Bears probably won't come in this swamp because it sucks. But the last thing I want to do is attract a bear to follow me here. I am relatively well hidden. Still walked more than eight kilometers and struggled hard. Emergency scenarios crystallize further on these walks: I must have an escape plan. To make the most of it, I'd follow a route to the coast and see some more of the island. This one is also the riskiest. Straight to Varnek is a possibility but then I have to go through 20 km of swamp. Dave and Sergei probably arrived in Varnek yesterday.

20:30 Cold mist hisses on the canvas. Been listening to my walkman for an entire hour to some tapes that I bought for cheap at a kiosk in Moscow. (I am glad I have been saving batteries for the GPS). To go forward or backward I swing the cassette around a BIC pen. It is hopeless. Just when the sun would reach the underside of the cloud cover, promising the fire works I enjoyed a few days ago, a very dense fog drifted in. It takes me over an hour with this cold and wind to bring a liter of water to the boil (I cleaned the stove and it finally works).

Each time I hear the pan begin to sing, the wind will pick up, the flame flares, and the sound disappears; it goes like this for half an hour, until I put the stove between my legs, between the crates; petrol has been spilled and the flames are pouring out on all sides: but the water is boiling!

This day was killed. Tonight I am a bit gloomy. At some point I have to decide to leave things behind and find a way out, get out of this swamp. Where are the other two? There comes a time, I know, however unimaginable, that I wish I could be here again, enjoy these wasted days again, but then they are behind me in the elusive past and I will be so busy with things considered important, that this island will seem impossibly far away. If only I could hold on to it. The loud flapping of the blue sail keeps me awake. The wind picks up, turns to blow from another direction. In my dreams people come to me who I haven't seen for a long time. Images of regularity and peace.

Camp Desperado

Like yesterday, completely packed, I write this leaning against Dave's big duffel bag. Writing is a simple routine that forces you to organize your thoughts. Under the current circumstances, this communication with myself is of vital importance, because it helps me prepare my decisions. Moreover, it is 'cozy'. It should be emphasized that my moments of weakness, my anger and frustration would have been less severe and more manageable had I not been deposited in this green expanse of water. In a rocky part I could have gotten around better and would have had more opportunity to establish some sort of a camp. On the other hand, the conditions in this bog contribute to the intensity of the experiment. There is more emotional adventure in being alone.

10:45 When the time comes, I think, rehearsing my evacuation in mind, I roll up the sleeping bag and mat, I collect the tent pegs, remove the tent poles and then fold my house together for shipping. I think I can complete all these actions within two minutes. I got up at a quarter to nine, after a restless night. There was dense fog, and a strong north wind producing a lot of noise. In the west, the fog cover has lifted from the landscape an hour ago and the clearance has already blown here; within two hours the weather will be good for flying.

12:30 Dirty weather is moving southeast, where our helicopter is based in Amderma. Hello, Roger! The airspace above Vaygach is clear. You have permission. Strong wind may keep them on the ground. There will always be something here, especially now that autumn is knocking on the door.

13:55 Rain beats the tent with hard taps, for about an hour, but it could be done. Yes, you fly if you try. The chances of it still happening today are decreasing rapidly. It is a desolate situation. Day Nine at Camp Desperado.

15:15 Brief showers, a lot of wind. The sky is black in the direction this weather is coming from: we'll be visited by a new cyclone of three or four days. Look at it this way: as long as we are here, at least we have something to look forward to. From here we will start all over. The thought that I may have resumed my usual office activities in a week or so, is so trivial that it makes me disgusted. The fox did his round this morning and does not seem to be very impressed by my presence. I threw a piece of rock-hard bread towards him, but he did not look up or anything.

17:10 Hour walk around the lake. There are no reeds or woody bits around this lake, it is just a hole, a puddle, one of the thousands of water-filled craters in this green bog. The wind ripples the surface of the lake with regularly spaced brown waves.

20:30 The mood is good, especially since from eight o'clock the sun finally showed under the clouds and made this black and grey land in color. The green of the tundra, black of the hills, in the distance; the pink neon glow of the underside of the cloud cover, the bright and transparent horizon, lemon and copper yellow, patches of pastel blue sky in the gray deck.

A plan to get out

August 22. Dutch weather, the clouds are low and sail on by, clear white, there is a lot of blue sky, wind, but not so much that, for example, a helicopter would not be able to fly into it. At two o'clock tonight I woke up to the bright sun, which after a couple of hours made me feel like being in an incubator. I am now writing leaning against the duffelbag outside in the sun and it is fine. The tent is open on both sides and everything dries out nicely. Breakfast with sun for the first time here. There is still petrol for a maximum of two days. Therefore, I now decide that if nothing shows today, this afternoon I will walk to Varnek along the route that David and Sergei have followed.

12:00 Our daily window of opportunity is open and we are in the middle of the action. Nervous, I keep the binoculars and flares ready. I have seven flares and have given as many to David and Sergei. Yesterday my heart jumped because I saw a dot above the horizon. It was a bird of prey hanging still, maybe a rough-legged buzzard. I also considered the scenario, in which Dave and Sergei were indeed collected on August 16 but

Helicopter crew chats with Nenets man during brief stop in Varnek.

crashed with the helicopter and disappeared into the swamp. What then? It will be assumed that I was on board. Nobody knows that we split and that I am sitting here. It would open up enormous possibilities. How long would I be able to keep such a secret? The sun has shifted south: it is exactly the middle of the day. Time is a current that takes you along. The days they flow by themselves, even though nothing seems to be moving when you are away from all the shores. The shores of hope.

Then suddenly the helicopter comes in from the south. It is a dot above the horizon much larger than the birds that before have put me on the alert. I can't hear it yet. Like lightning, I stow my binoculars and begin to take down the tent. I can't see it approach but when the machine has reached me there is a deafening roar and it blocks the sky with rocket launchers spread wide. I look up and, in the door, see David and Sergei, smiling like madmen. This time, the heavy Mi-8 doesn't put its full weight on that spongy soil and keeps the blades blasting at full speed while I shove in my goods and hop aboard. While I reorganize and pack, the beast is working, and through the open door I watch myself being lifted above the tundra.

"Two more minutes of Vaygach," David announces as we fly by the Idols Cape and look over the blue water of the Yugor Strait.

"What took you so long?" I ask. He says there has been an accident with a submarine in the Barents Sea, and all aircraft were kept on standby for the rescue.

"Besides, the past two days were Saturday and Sunday, and they don't fly on weekends. They told us they don't fly on weekends, but you didn't write it down, did you."

Closing the circle

Euphoria prevails and I shake many hands. On the landing strip, a little way from the helicopter, there is an empty Antonov-26 cargo aircraft that will take us from the coast to Vorkuta. The tailgate is lowered and through the empty tube of the plane I spot the crew in front. The pilot beckons and I walk into the plane over the green painted steel. The plane is empty except for two brand new spare wheels, one large and one small. Behind a narrow door, two men sit in the cramped cockpit and the third, a base employee, is standing with a half-liter bottle of beer. The pilot smiles and shakes my hand. The co-pilot bends backwards towards a red crate with bottles.

"Tundra njet pivo," he says and hands me a bottle of beer: there is no beer in the tundra. The helicopter and crew were kept on standby for several days in connection with the major rescue operation that is going on off the coast of Murmansk. There, on the twelfth, nuclear submarine *Kursk* had a big accident and disappeared with more than a hundred men. The rescuing is still in progress. There are no more details. Severe weather prevented the helicopter from flying just one day, I am told. Dave and Sergei started from their camp on the seventeenth and arrived in Varnek in five hours.

"We tried to get you out the next day. It was too far for the tractors, which are no longer considered reliable. Then the plan was constructed to go and get you with reindeer. A horrific accident happened that night. A party was organized to celebrate the rescue plan. One of the men who was going to save you fell of a table while drinking and broke his skull."

"We have to believe he fell," adds Sergei.

"Ivan told us, almost casually, with his hands covered in blood. Another drunk Nenets then offered to go find you that same night." Sergei explains that this man was not drunk. "Okay, good too. In any case, we have not been able to explain to him how many people were involved and where you were."

"Wait, who is Ivan and what's with his hands?" I ask.

"He's a Nenets boy just back from Chechnya. He was in the war. Because, what else can you do if you want to leave Varnek then sign up in the army," Sergei says.

"Did he say anything about the war?" I asked.

"'It was terrible,' was all he wanted to share – and that the Army had paid for his return only up to Pechora," Sergei says. "The Army provided cell phones to them to call home. But Varnek doesn't even have a phone system. He was very relieved to be back in Varnek." My companions had hidden their tent just outside the village and through the rain they heard men moving across the tundra, drunk, looking for them.

"Besides, there was too much broken glass everywhere to set up a tent," says David. By invitation, they spent the last night in a room and drunk children tapped the window until morning.

Flames burst out when the plane starts its engines, one after the other. We quickly climb to a relatively low cruising altitude, and the steady resonance of the propellors echoes through my skull with a very low robotic voice that hums or chants then when they step on the gas it goes up an octave higher; shifting to a thin buzz, to revert again later. The flight lasts an hour and we sink in clouds while approaching Vorkuta. The clouds are very dense and as we continue to descend, darkness falls, for the first time in over a month. Suddenly the plane drops obliquely into turbulence and bounces violently. On a bench along the side of the plane we shake patiently with it and hold on to its gray-painted steel construction. I have surrendered to Providence and am perfectly at peace with the situation, disguised in my heavy boots, canvas pants, and dirty woolen gloves with cut-off fingers. While the plane is banking, the engineer makes his way towards the back, struggling to hold on to pipes and handles mounted. He looks out of the rear porthole towards the rudder, then holding a torch light opens a hatch under the tail fin. After landing, it is immediately looked at.

We spend the night in Vorkuta, one of the world's few polar cities. It rains softly and it is totally dark. There is little street lighting in this tundra city, but it is 'cozily' busy on the street. Warm light pours out from the apartments, people are walking around with shopping bags, standing in line at the post office, where I try to make a phone call to tell of our safe return. I smell exhaust fumes, find the traffic noisy. In my mind the image keeps repeating of the helicopter small above the horizon.

No hot water in this city either, but while I am washing with cold water, a young Russian boy brings a glorious bucket of very hot water to make a delightful bit of a bath. The bumpy hotel bed with the broken springs and the worn-out mattress is like floating on the hands of thousands of swamp elves. The next morning, I see the tundra out-there behind concrete appartment buildings. And even further in the distance, the Ural Mountains, where my Russian adventure began eight years ago. No man's land. I was in those mountains, with Mikhail telling me of Kravchenko's cross that he had been at, and this man, Barents. Tall birches line the streets, very beautiful indeed.

The streets are deserted, and a cold wind blows through it. Hammer and sickle are still high on the buildings, rusted and without paint. A man comes out of a housing block, stumbles to a tree, leans against it with one arm. He pauses for a moment, then spits once, wipes his mouth and goes back inside. Another man asks, "Say there. Can you tell me the time?"

"It is half past three."

"Half past three in the morning or half past three in the night?" He demonstrates how to walk: with a cigarette, swaggering, a bottle, a leather jacket, looking slightly below your forehead, spitting occasionally along the path.

From Chicago

Saturday night August 26, Y2K and I'm back in Chicago, back in the summer, full of flashback memories. Someone is throwing a party and now I'm leaning against the stove in an apartment somewhere on the north side of Chicago, a block from the lake. All windows are slid open and through the back door, from the fire escape occasionally slips in a gust of warm air. It is about midnight and the appartment is still full of people. Tonight, life has returned to a state of normalcy: outside are excited voices, now soft, then they flare up again. "Five more minutes," says Greg, who drove me here, "and then we go."

"Darling, I'm so glad you're back in one piece," the host interrupts with a big smile, "how was it?" He has lost a lot of excess weight this summer. With his thumbs he pulls on the waistband of his pants and shows the amount of space that has become available. He drops to his knees and stretches out on the kitchen floor to do push ups and demonstrate an exercise he has learned from a personal trainer. I already know that if it doesn't work out with that personal trainer, the pounds will be right back on.

"So how are you?"

“I need a haircut,” I answer. My colleague Todd who came over with a new girlfriend, Chloe, says: “You should go to my hairdresser. I will go again next Saturday morning and you should come. I will make you breakfast first. He says he was the hairdresser of Eva Braun and Leni Riefenstahl. He’s very good with the razor. “

“I bet he is.”

“Exactly. He delivers very consistent haircuts. There is always an old Serbian who hails from the same village as Albert Einstein.”

“It is very important that a hairdresser is consistent.”

“Why don’t you come with me? What are you saying, two men are going to the hairdresser, eh? A nice Saturday morning outing.”

“I don’t know. Those razors...”

“You watch him do me, and if you don’t like it, you can always change your mind.”

You don’t hear conversations like that at her office, says Chloe, politely. It’s hot, everyone’s a little dewy in the face. Chicago, like Moscow, is a city of extremes, blazing hot in the summer and bitterly cold in the winter when we are exposed to the aptly named ‘Arctic Blast’. There are many complaints about it on television: it is agreed that it was too hot today.

Tuesday morning, I sat in front of my tent, Thursday afternoon in a Chicago cab on the Kennedy Expressway in the hot summer sun on my way to town. Half past one and the sun was high in the sky. It scorched my arm and shoulder. The black leatherette of the backseat sofa burned hot, but I couldn’t move because of the heavy plastic expedition box next to me. Traffic was slow and I had time to take in the tired faces of the drivers: Latinos in an old van, a middle-aged woman with dyed blonde hair in a sedan. A plane, landing, sailed noisily overhead, the subway train rattled by. My travel clothes so carefully stowed in a waterproof latex bag during my adventure, got wet where my body touched the seat. Above the door was a vacuum cleaner-hose with holes to carry cool air from the air conditioner in the front to the rear of the car, but I chose to keep the window open. Next to the taxi a sedan with four young women stopped. They stared at me for a moment and then one of them shouted at me from the back seat, but I didn't get it and tried to decide which one was the prettiest, yes she sat in the front right and smiled at me.

"He can hear you, stupid," the lady behind the wheel said to her friend in the back, and I glanced at the taxi driver who pretended not to register. Back in my appartment I showered and lay there, not knowing what to do. Wasn't all that tired. Big and yellow, that same sun was over the water on Friday morning as I cycled along the lake to the city, through the park, where elderly gentlemen were playing baseball in the sun; tennis, callenetics, tai chi and yoga – a few swimmers were crawling near the beach and the bike path along the boulevard was full of roller skates and inline skates despite the early hour. Between the skyscrapers through dusty downtown, I saw a woman turn a corner, step out of the shadows and cast a silhouette, pitch-black across the broad concrete sidewalk, and the sun exploded in her face. Crowds, danger, sirens and horns. A sign next to a small barbershop among the skyscrapers read: "Thou shall not kill".

Steve is happy with our results. We beat the Norwegians to it, so it couldn't be better. He was anxious that we wouldn't get to Vaygach first. "Why don't you take a week off. We'll look at what you've found afterwards," he says gently. "Buy a newspaper and sit in a coffee shop." But I can't, I have to move on. A man is visiting our department who I recognize from the Discovery Channel and I tell him, "Hey I saw you on the Discovery Channel. You had a beard."

"Yeah, I shaved it two days ago," he answers wearily, brushing his chin. In the laboratory I open the large plastic boxes of the expedition. Their contents are wet; of condensation moisture, of the rain and fog that went into paper and canvas in the past month. My pants and the pockets that I used to carry my things are soaked. The cotton bag with dirty clothes smells the bitter smell of homeless people that I sit next to on the subway train. The physical proceeds from our expedition are below it: a dozen black PVC pipes containing sediment samples and another dozen clear sample bags containing marine shells. It may not seem like much, but it was worth it. I put the shell samples together in a small cardboard box and contacted FedEx to ship it all to the lab.

I often recall the image of a small family of nomads I saw from the door of the helicopter during a brief stop somewhere inland, about ten kilometers north of where I had been. Their camp consisted of a large red tent and a skin tent. There were a few reindeer between rolling rock ridges, and sleds only partially unloaded; a skimpy man and a skinny woman, and two children, all standing close together and watching the screaming monster that had descended on them. They were exactly as Gerrit de Veer had described them four centuries ago: "as we used to paint wild men, but they are not wild, because they are of reasonable judgment." Two little girls with "caps of deer skin closed around their heads" were lifted in through the door. Summer was almost over and the kids were heading back to school in Narian Mar. I sat them on the bench next to me and noticed their small, pretty hands, which they had been taking good care of, as girls do. The helicopter took them to Varnek and there I shoved out the duffel bag with spaghetti, rice, tins of meat, and beans from our expedition. It was monstrously heavy, with all these tins and hard objects, and it was dragged away with difficulty by a Nenetsman. The remaining cans of *Dutch Lady*, the chocolate, and the honey; a man had spotted these treats for his own use during the short flight and gritted it all out, collecting it in a plastic shopping bag. While he was busy scavenging other pieces of luggage in the tail, I gave his precious plastic bag to the girls, who were hesitant to accept and then went off with it.

The next evening, I lay in the Heritage Institute's hostel bed and watched neon lights bounce up and down the gigantic Cosmos Hotel. On the highway to the airport, the taxi driver offered me a smoke.

"Kurit?" Alright: one more then. Within two days, I was back in Chicago, and at 6:30 in the morning, just as I imagined it while I was out there on that distant island, I heard the muffled voice of a television evangelist penetrate from the apartment below. Meanwhile, my footprints remain in that faraway bog, and that little fox probably still comes by every day, wondering where everything has gone.

Epilogue

Letter of Robert Le Canu to Willem Jansz Blaeu (1627)
Good friend Willem Jansz: you have asked me that I would reproduce from memory, the discussions I had with Jacob Heemskerck, Gerrit de Veer, Jan Cornelisz Rijp, and some other of my students, about the journey they undertook in 1596 to explore the Kingdoms of China and Cathay, returning in 1597, without completing anything of the mission they had been send on. In November 1597 they came to visit me, to tell me of their miraculous experience, amongst many other things, the most remarkable was the observation of the early return of the Sun [...]. This would keep all the scholars busy for a while. And because you told me that Mathematicians in all of Europe are still upset about this, I will briefly tell you of the discussion I had with these students of mine. My arguments were: in summer, they had more than ten weeks of continuous day and no night, and the days were not always clear, to observe the path of the sun. Then how could you know it was 4 November when you lost the sun; because the sun at that time was more than 15° below the equator. They replied that they always had their watches, clocks, and hourglasses before them so that there wasn't the slightest of a doubt. I asked them if these clocks never had failed and they not once had found the hourglass empty [these had to be turned every half hour] and wanted to know what phase the moon was in when the sun disappeared. They couldn't tell me, for which reason I believe that the day of 4 November is incorrect. But

assuming (I said) that you are correct about 4 November, and in summer didn't miss a day in counting, then how can you be so sure during the winter, when it was night for more than eleven weeks and you spend most of the time sheltering from the cold and snow drift, didn't even dare to stick out your head, and couldn't see the sun, the moon, or the stars. Gerrit de Veer answered me that they could see the northern star through the chimney, and how often the watcher stars [*Ursus Minor*] moved around it. Added to this they had every day (said Gerrit de Veer) paid close attention to their clocks and hourglass. I didn't want to dispute but I couldn't accept this because in summer they had enough to do, defending themselves (they claimed) against bears, and in winter were often occupied by the fox hunt, so that they, in my opinion could perhaps not always have found the necessary devotion to the observation of the heaven or the clocks and hourglass, which they may have often have found empty or frozen.

Then Jacob Heemskerck said to me 'Do you, Master Robert, say that we have been mistaken in the time and erred?' I don't just believe that, I answered, but I am entirely sure that the mistake is so great that you could impossibly have known whether it was the end of January or beginning of February. Although I did ask several questions to find out, where on 24 January (when they said they had seen the sun) they had seen and measured the Moon, some fixed stars, or wandering stars [planets], at six in the evening, at midnight or even at six in the morning. They couldn't answer, because they failed to make such observations and therefore, I conclude that they were mistaken by ten or eleven days (or more). The next day they eagerly returned to tell me that they did indeed know where the moon was at on 24 January, but I replied that they found it in the *Ephemeriden* [tables of Moon and Sun] and yesterday when I asked, hadn't known what to say. Gerrit de Veer, the writer of the navigation round by the north, had more unfounded words, that I meant to write down, but I didn't think it necessary and crossed it out; because he stuck by his opinion and published it in his journal, even in a different lettering on pages 34, 35 (to make it stand out). He writes that he will gladly be held accountable on his story, but I know very well the account he sent to D. Martinus Everardus Bruggensius, experienced almanac keeper from Leiden, who wrote him a letter demanding explanation. De Veer personally let me read that letter and asked me what would be best to do. I replied that the best advice would be to plead guilty, and openly admit that he and his company had perhaps overslept a couple of days during that long journey they had made. But of course, he didn't write his book to have it corrected, and continued in his misjudgment until the end of his life. [...] And this Gerrit de Veer has been able to include 56 days between 24 January and 21 March during which he mentions that the Sun was 14° above the horizon, while it should have been 19°. Therefore, it is my conclusion that Gerrit de Veer added 13 or 14 days to compensate [...] and triumph with wonderful observations and keep learned men talking about Gerrit de Veer's journal. I leave it to others to think what they want about this, but I find that Gerrit de Veer is like that verger with a watch that would never synchronize with the Sun and when asked, would answer that the Sun was possibly off, but not his watch. [...] This in short is my answer to your question: I have never believed and will never believe [these measurements], it is against my nature and reason. These navigators round by the North couldn't separate the long days in summer and the long nights in winter, or count them, understandably, and therefore can be forgiven.[22]

Acknowledgements

This has become a wonderful book thanks to the dedication and enthusiasm of many. The making and publication of the Russian edition in 2022 was initiated by Denis Khotimsky from Boston, Massachusetts. Denis, editor, engineer, map collector, helped me with a critical eye and document research to rework the entire manuscript. Denis advocated use and translation of Vondel's Ode to Barents, producing the first stanza in English himself. I thank Raisa Kolosova of Paulsen Publishing House (Moscow) for arranging and supporting this project, done and completed under challenging conditions, not to mention a Covid-19 lock-down.

For the 2023 edition, the historical chapter ('Aftermath') was newly written and researched. 'Vaygach Y2K' was written after the previously unpublished expedition journal from August 2000.

Pieter Floore and I, following a night in beer bar *De Zotte* discussing C. Ransmayr's book *The terrors of ice and darkness,* and some other favorites, composed our wild scrapbook of experiences published by Elmar in 1997 (in Dutch: 'Nova Zembla'). Thank you Pieter, for trusting your journal notes to my care. The 'Ice Sea'-chapter was composed from excerpts of the logs by Frans Heeres and Maurits Groen. Frans in 1996 provided me with Xeroxes of his notes. Maurits' story appeared in the *Alkmaarsche Courant/ Noordhollands Dagblad* (Peter Heerkens, 26 October 1991), and a series of reports in *Maritiem*

Nederland (Ron de Vos, February July 1997); courtesy of Maurits Groen and Ron de Vos. Before the expedition, Maurits was interviewed by *Dagblad Kennemerland/ Noordhollands Dagblad* (18 June 1991) from which the dialogue with Kravchenko is taken. Included in the chapter are also events from a brief report of the expedition's rescue posted by Dmitri Kravchenko (1936 - † 2020) in his 2010 internet blog. In August 2018, I visited ship-builder Gerald de Weerdt on his yard in Harlingen. While completing this manuscript, I again consulted Gerald in November 2020 on the name and size of Barents' vessel. Texts from Gerrit de Veer's *True and Perfect description* and Van Linschoten's *Voyage round by the North* I translated from the originals reproduced in L'Honoré-Naber (1914 and 1917). The *Letter by Robert Le Cannu* I translated from the original Dutch, collection Utrecht University. Thank you, René Gerritsen, for making available some of your expedition photos once again!

Our vessel 'Into the Ice Sea' was cast off by Jack Wormer, schoolbus driver from San Diego, California, who in 1998 proposed and started the translation of 'Nova Zembla.' Together we translated these texts, I mostly on Chicago's Red Line train between work and home. Help and support was received over 1999 and 2000 from Robert Headland (Cambridge). The resulting text was edited by Luisa Alexander Izzo (Calgary) and first published in 2005 by Auke van den Berg (Rozenberg Publishers, Amsterdam).

The expeditions in 1993 and 1995 were organized under supervision of Henk van Veen († 2012) and made possible through the financial support of Wegener Publishing Group (Apeldoorn) and the University of Amsterdam. The 1995 expedition was also financed by donations from the Russian Ministry of Culture. National Science Foundation award

OPP-9796024 bore the costs of the research in 1998 and 2000. Svetlana Gusarova and the Arctic & Antarctic Research Institute of St. Petersburg organized access to Novaya Zemlya in 1993. Pyotr Boyarsky and the Heritage Institute (Moscow) provided access to Novaya Zemlya in 1995 and 1998 and to Vaygach Island in 2000. Boyarsky's *Integrated Marine Arctic Expeditions* received technical and logistical support from the Russian Defense Ministry, the Federal Organization of Border Patrols, the Ministry for Nuclear Energy, and the Chief Staff of the Russian Navy, Central Nuclear Polygon, Archangelsk. Field work on north Novaya Zemlya was organized and executed in 1998 with Leonid Polyak (Ohio State University), Steven Forman (University of Illinois at Chicago), and Henk van Veen (Willem Barents Foundation). To the States General of our small nation, let this be a report of a mission completed. In August 2003, on my way to October Revolution Island (Severnaya Zemlya), the team and I made a stopover for helicopter refueling on Cape Chelyuskin, the most northerly cape of the continent and, as such – Cape Tabin. "Upon reaching that cape, you accurately establish its coordinates and chart the area," reads the instruction issued by the States in May 1594. I do warmly acknowledge family and friends, who have heard me say 'nearly done' for 25 years.

Thank you, Pieter Floore and Els Lenting, Perry Pierik and Mr. Pierik Senior, René Gerritsen, Henri Hoogewoud, Hans Bonke, Dirk van Smeerdijk, Victor Dershavin, Vadim Starkov (Russian Academy of Sciences), Yuri Vanda, Victor Galitzyn (boatsman) Alexander Ivanov (leading seaman), Stanislav Bogushevich (leading seaman); Captain Yuri Lekarev (R/V *Ivan Kiriev*, Archangelsk), Captain Valery Pustoshny (R/V *Ivan Petrov*, Archangelsk), Alexander Rogatov (first engineer), Vladimir Loukinyh (engineer and metal worker),

Gennadi Iljin (first chef); Jerzy Gawronski (University of Amsterdam), Mark Glotzbach (Haagse Courant), Bas Kist (Rijksmuseum, Amsterdam † 2003), George Maat and Jorrit-Jan Verlaan (Leiden University), Anton van Munster († 2009), Herre Wynia, Danila Badyukov († 2020), Dimitri Badyukov, Konstantin Blinov, Pyotr Boyarsky (Heritage Institute), Anatoli Kuliyev, Nicolai Labutin (doctor), Roman Labutin, Yuri Mazurov (Moscow State University), Jevgeni Salikov, Vitali Teplyakov, Nicolai Vekhov, Yuri Zakharov, Ilya Baryshev and Valera Shumilkin (Heritage Institute); Valentin Lobyntsev (Russian Navy, St. Petersburg), Petr Glazov, Sergei Pchyolkin (independent), Eri Iwata, Naomi, Sam, Chrisje, and Jimi Hendrix. I particularly thank Steve Forman (University of Illinois at Chicago), who shaped and sharpened me, and my three-time companion and field partner, David Lubinski (University of Colorado). Special thanks go out to the Army airmen of the Mi-8 'Hip' (Amderma); Gennadi and Vladimir from Polar Station Fedorov; to the officers of Border Patrol Station Vaygach, and to the Varnek community.

Notes

1 Vladimir Rusanov (1875-1913) was exiled in 1903 for Marxist activism and moved to Paris. Now inspired by Fridtjof Nansen's books, he took part in five Arctic expeditions (1907-1911), both French and Russian, the latter being organized with the support of the Arkhangelsk provincial government. He became the first geologist to survey Novaya Zemlya and to cross it on foot; charted the southeastern coast in 1908 [Barr 1974, 1984, 1987]. In 1912, following the west coast he dared to sail by the north of Novaya Zemlya and into the Kara Sea – and disappeared. The search for remains of the expedition in the 1970's was led by D.M. Shparo and promoted by newspaper Komsomol'skaya Pravda. Shparo's search produced a fireplace on Mikhailov Peninsula – (p. 15 and 33).

2 In August 1933, the remains of Barents' camp represented nothing more than a small number of beams and boards, some of which – for instance, the remains of the frame of the hut, 9 m long and 6 m wide – obviously had retained their original disposition. Large, forged iron nails (evidently ship nails) were sticking out of the boards and beams. Lying apart from the boards was found a forged iron door-hinge. Inside the frame of the hut were two piles of rather large stones, which showed traces of burning: obviously remains of a hearth. Outside, close to the northern wall of the hut, was a small pile, apparently the refuse heap of the wintering party. Scattered about near the southern side of the hut lay odd pieces of a barrel: rivets, bottom, and large forged iron hoops. About eight paces from the barrel, the soil was covered with a thin layer of well-preserved pitch. Close to it lay the bottom of a small jar with some stringy, bad-smelling yellow mass. Between the hut and the shore, pieces of some rather large octahedral cork plates were scattered about. Pieces of a small broken jug were found a short distance from the hut. These pieces were of grey clay, covered both outside and inside with yellow glazing. At the foot of the escarpment, about 100–150 m from the shore, some boards and two half-rotten timber ribs of a small boat were found, and close by, a piece of a roughly made oar [Miloradovich 1934] – (p. 49 and 241).

3 Fragments of Willem Barents' ship were identified in Moscow's Heritage Institute in May 1994 by Ab Hoving, the Rijksmuseum's expert on Dutch seventeenth-century ship building techniques, with Jerzy Gawronski and Pieter Floore. "It is hard to describe the feeling I had," writes Hoving, "when, in a dark corridor of the anonymous Moscow hostel that accommodates Boyarsky's institute, we came across a part of one of the most famous ships in Dutch history. From all the vessels of discovery that have traveled the globe, not a single piece has been recovered: not from Columbus' Santa Maria or Cook's Endeavour, let alone the brigs in which Vasco da Gama or Magellan explored the Pacific Ocean. From Barents' vessel there is a piece measuring 1x4 m in

Moscow, and it stuns me that no one at all is taking care of it, not the Dutch authorities and not a single research institute" [Hoving & Emke 2004, p. 33]. The largest part, measuring 3.85 x 0.93 m, was apparently part of the vessel's lower hull. From this it can be deduced that the vessel's hull was 18 m-long and 6 m-wide – (p. 78).

4 The Russian expedition identified at least two other possible graves, on either side of Ivanov Bay, capes Vilkitsy and Cape Petrovsky. "In the western part of the bay near Cape Petrovsky we found a 1,1 m-high and 20 cm thick pole, with a 1,5 m base of rocks. After removing the rocks we found that the pole went into the permafrost, which starts here at 35 cm depth. On the flattened side fairly clearly we found imprinted 'Bar' and, below that, barely readable '55' or 'SS' (two fives are more likely)" (Kravchenko 1979, p. 110, Dutch translation [1983], prepared by the Institute of Prehistoric and Protohistoric Archeology of the University of Amsterdam) – (p. 87).

5 The only verifiable biography of Willem Barents is the short reference by J.H. van Linschoten on 15 August 1594 [in L'Honoré Naber 1914, p. 113-114]. "Skipper and pilot Willem Barentsz van der Schelling, citizen of Amsterdam." Van der Schelling was an influential Amsterdam family in the 15th and 16th centuries. The oldest known member of this family, Tymen van der Scellinc, was alderman between 1408 and 1412. The geographic occurrence of the family name has a focus on Rotterdam. However there exists no record connecting Willem Barents with the family, nor with the island of Terschelling. Association with the island is made by the mention of a Schellinger fishing yacht, which may also refer to the small village opposite Amsterdam. The spelling of 'Barents' as a surname was adopted by Beke (1853) and was used around the same time for the naming of the Barents Sea – (p. 101 and 289). The 1595 Caertboeck is authored by 'Willem Barentzoen' and signed 'Your humble servant, Willem Barentszoon.'

6 "Am 13. August [1886] sah ich bei völlig klarem Wetter von der Mündung des Flüsschens Mogur (nördlichste an der NW-Spitze der Insel Kotelny), unter 76°NB und ca. 139°OL die scharfen Konturen von vier stumpfkegeligen Tafelbergen, an welche sich im Osten ein niedriges Vorland anlehnte" [Von Toll 1898, PGM-1898-VI-P.125].

"Bei einem Gespräch über das auch von mir im Jahr 1886 gesehene Land gab mir mein Begleiter Djergeli, der siebenmal auf den Inseln übersommert hat und mehrere Jahre nach einander das sagenhafte Land gesehen hatte, auf mein Frage: 'Willst Du dieses ferne Ziel erreichen?' die Antwort: 'Einmal meinen Fuss dorthin setzen und dann sterben.'" [Von Toll 1894, PGM VI, p. 159] – (p. 126).

7 Albanov with a party of 10 people in April 1914 left their drifting ship to try to reach land on sledges and kayaks. Only two of them survived. The search for the schooner itself and the 13 people remaining on board was unsuccessful. In 2010, human remains and objects belonging to members of Albanov's party were discovered on Georg Land in the Franz Josef Land Archipelago. Leaving the drifting *Fram* on March 14, 1895, Fridtjof Nansen and Hjalmar Johansen attempted to reach the Pole by sleigh, and failing, returned to Franz Josef Land and spent the winter there. On May 21, 1896, they continued their journey, reaching Cape Flora, Northbrook Island where they ran into F. Jackson's party in June 1896 and with them returned to Norway – (p. 139).

8 The hut had a portal or porch about 1.4 m (2 ells) wide. During the construction phase, the south wall was left open until all the barrels and bales had been transferred inside and piled up

against the west wall. The scarcity of finds in a strip 1.5 m wide on the east side of the hut suggests that the bunks were constructed along the eastern wall, which faced the frozen sea. Carlsen, at the request of August Petermann, drew a sketch of the building remains about a year after his return from Novaya Zemlya. His drawing shows a row of five bunks along one wall and a sixth bunk against the short (south) wall. One engraving in de Veer's journal [in Hulsius 1598] shows six bunks along one wall. The archaeological survey indicates a row of five bunks along the eastern wall and another bunk on the south side, next to the door, where De Veer was lying [7 December 1596]. In a living space with a total length of 8.90 m (10.3 m-1.4 m), each bunk would be 1.70 m long. Kravchenko found remains of smaller beams and planking that might have belonged to these bunks. The four beams that remain of the building structure were part of a foundation about 80 cm high formed of driftwood trees, which Carlsen could still see in 1871. Carlsen did not sketch a porch because it had been used for firewood on 22 May 1597 – (p. 229).

9 Barents' ship was a 'yacht,' a relatively small vessel that could make some speed as well as manoeuvre between the ice floes. The large piece kept in Moscow was enforced with double planking, two layers of oak wood each 4 cm (1.5 thumbs) thick [Hoving & Emke 2004]. Because ships were built with strict width-length ratio's, Barents' vessel measured 64 feet (19 m) by 20 feet (6 m), excluding the 12 m-long bowsprit. It weighed as much as it could carry: 30 last or 60 metric tons [G. de Weerdt 2004, p. 83]. Between 2010 and 2019 a group of volunteers reconstructed Barents' vessel from oak wood, with hand tools and materials that would have been contemporary.

The ship sizes are expressed by De Veer and Van Linschoten in carrying capacity. A last (nid. scheepslast), literally, cargo, is approximately 2 metric tons. The armament of 40-last *Swaen* from Veere during the 1595 expedition is documented in Veere's city archives (Zeeland) [l'Honoré-Naber 1917; Kist 1998]. Van Linschoten [1601] furthermore recorded that *Swaen* was equipped with double planking to make it more durable among ice floes. Can this *Swaen* be the double-planked vessel that Barents used in 1596? Ship-builder Gerald De Weerdt searched the archives of the most common Amsterdam shipping notaries who made the cargo contracts. He discovered that over the '90s of the 16th century the smaller vessels were disappearing from the registers in favour of the larger ships, consistent with the rapidly expanding trade. However, he did find a matching record. Notary J.F. Bruyingh on 14 April 1595 registered de *Witte Swaen* [Inv. No. 70, fol. 41-43], shortly in fact after De Moucheron's plea for another expedition [6 April 1595]. As it does not return in the registers of 1596, the *Witte Swaen* may for a small sum have been sold to the city [G. de Weerdt, personal communication 2 November 2020] – (p. 232).

10 Alexander Mikhailovich Sibiryakov (1849-1933) – Russian entrepreneur, explorer of Siberia and philanthropist who sponsored many Arctic expeditions, including the voyage of A.E. Nordenskjold with *Vega* 1878-1879. He spent the last years of his life in Nice, receiving a pension awarded by the Swedish government – (p. 257).

11 The indigenous people were called Samoyeds, a combination of saam-yedno, meaning 'land of the bog people', the Saami. The Samoyeds, an Ugrian [in Russian: Yugorski] tribe, call themselves Nenets [Nentsi], meaning 'people' – (p. 257).

12 De Veer calls this Cape Beeldthoeck, Jan Huyghen uses the name Eylandt de van Afgoden to refer to the small peninsula on which it is located. Both words are a direct reference to the Ten

Commandments, book of Leviticus (26: 1): "Do not make for yourself idols and statues, and do not put pillars in your place, and do not put stones with images in your land to bow before them." [Gij zult ulieden geen afgoden maken; noch gesneden beeld, noch opgericht beeld zult gij u stellen, noch gebeelden steen in uw land zetten, om u daarvoor te buigen] – (p. 261).

13 Editor's note: Adriaan Daniël de Vries (1851-1884) – Dutch art critic, historian of engraving. The only know print of the ''s Lans Eer' engravin (52x161 cm) in 1907 was acquired by the Royal Library in Brussels, where it is kept to this day. The 30mm miniature portrait of Barents on it most likely is nothing more than a symbolic detail. De Vries published his own enlargement of it, enlarging it many times over and artfully refining it. It is this image (in fact, created in 1883) that can be found everywhere today as a supposedly reliable portrait of Willem Barents [DK] – (p. 274).

14 Six months after his return from Novaya Zemlya, Van Heemskerck left with the second Dutch fleet to the 'spice islands' and between April 1601 and July 1604 captained Gelderland [Gelria]. Proceeds from a gigantic load of porcelain captured with a Portuguese freighter made him a wealthy man. His wife, Ms. G. Colterman died during childbirth in 1605. Preparing for the raid against Gibraltar, Van Heemskerck made his will in the presence of three other captains in the Red Lion hostel ('De Roode Leeuw') in Den Helder (27 February 1607). Albert de Veer kept custody of the will and, according to a record by notary Joannes Pylorius in Amsterdam's city archives, opened it on 23 August 1607. He left all his possessions to his brother Cornelis (b. 1561), imprisoned in Buenos Aires since 1599, and to his cousin Simontgen Jansdochter Schaeck, Albert de Veer's wife [Dutch Biographic Dictionary] – (p. 276).

15 Editor's note: As far as I know, there are no other sources that would confirm Oliver Brunel's stay in Astrakhan and Kazan. None of the historical characters in this book has caused so much trouble for historians and did not give them so many reasons to point out to each other errors and inaccuracies, as Oliver Brunel. The first mention of Brunel's visit to the Costin Schar in 1584 or 1585 is contained in the navigation book Thresoor der Zee-Vaert by Lucas Janszon Wagenaer (Leiden, 1592). It is believed that having returned to the White Sea, Oliver Brunel made one or two more unsuccessful attempts to reach the Ob by water. On the way back in 1585, his boat capsized at the mouth of the Pechora River, and Oliver Brunel drowned. "But his ship, together with the crew, was able to return to Enkhuizen," continues Wagenaer (1592). Veniamin Aleksandrovich Kordt (1902) described the same events in a different way: "His ship with cargo went to the bottom, but he himself survived." At the same time, Kordt cited evidence of the subsequent service of Oliver Brunel to the King of Denmark and his participation in Danish voyages to Greenland, and also noted with reference to S. Mueller that Brunel died "probably at the end of the 16th century." See V.A. Kordt 'Essay on the dealings of the Moscow state with the Republic of the United Netherlands up to 1631', Sbornik IIS Volume 116. S. Petersburg, 1902. S. xlv – xlvii [DK] – (p. 281).

16 Johan van Oldenbarnevelt (1547-1619) – statesman and diplomat of the Republic of the United Provinces, associate of William of Orange in the proclamation of independence, since 1586 the de facto head of government of the United Netherlands. Due to political and religious disagreements with Prince Maurits related to the Armenian disputes, he was arrested on charges of treason, sentenced to death, and beheaded with a sword in The Hague – (p. 284).

17 Gerard Mercator showed Tabin promontorium Plinio on his world map of 1569, that he later reworked into a new folio plate for his famous 1595 atlas. (Gerard died in 1594 and the Atlas was published by his son Rumold, who died not much later.) Tabin was a legendary mountain protruding into the ocean, mentioned by Roman authors Pliny the Elder and Pomponius Mela in the first century AD. The maps by Petrus Plancius [1590, 1592, and 1594] and Willem Barents [published posthumously, in 1598] also prominently show Cape Tabin. After discovery of the Severnaya Zemlya Archipelago (1913), one could make a point that the Vilkitsky Strait is on Mercator's map as narrow passage between Cape Tabin and the hypothetical Arctic Continent [DK] - (p. 284).

18 Editor's note: the original used 150 vadem, a measure of length (6 feet) or depth. While the English foot is 304.8 mm (1 fathom 1,828 m), the Amsterdam voet is 283.1 mm (1 fathom 1,698 m). Thus, 150 fathoms are between 255 and 275 meters. In Russian translations of 1936 and 2011, the Russian word 'sazhen' was used. In this case, the fathom, as a measure of length, is usually equated to seven English feet [DK] - (p. 286).

19 Declaration by shipmate Anthoine Claeszen (Theunis Claesz) Hermans, Leiden, 1613. Rijksarchief, published in the *Nieuwe Rotterdamsche Courant* on Saturday 6 August 1910 [L'Honoré-Naber 1917, IV-VII] - (p. 295).

20 Vaigach polar station was one of the first in the Novaya Zemlya region (1912); only Malye Karmakuly station on the western coast of Yuzhny Island (1896) is older than it - (p. 320).

21 'Operation Wunderland' entailed a ten-day sweep of the Kara Sea by Admiral Scheer in August-September 1942. 'Wunderland' was laid out with air photos of Novaya Zemlya taken by the airship Graf Zeppelin in July 1931, en route to Franz Josef Land via Cape Zhelaniya (Samoylovich 1933; Barr 1975). A minefield was laid before northwest Novaya Zemlya during Operation Zarin in September 1942 (Woodman 1994). In 1943 research vessel Academician Shokal'ski was sunk off Cape Spory Navolok. On 30 August 1943, Soviet submarine S-101 sank U-639 off Cape Zhelaniya, with the loss of all (47) hands (Boyarsky et al.1996) - (p. 336).

22 Translated from the explanatory text to the map of Novaya Zemlya in the Atlas Maior (Dutch edition 1662), written by Johan Blaeu, quoting the letter that his father had received 35 years earlier. In 1627, when this letter was written, Robert le Canu was 64 years old, and Willem Blaeu was 56 years old. "J. Blaeus grooten atlas, oft, Werelt-beschryving, in welcke 't aertryck, de zee, en de hemel wordt vertoond en beschreven," Folio 5, c. pages 76-78 (Universiteitsbibliotheek Utrecht) - (p. 353).

References

Albanov, V. 2000. In the land of the White Death. Modern Library, New York, 205 pp.

Allen, J.P. & R. Martin 1985. Entering Space. New York: Stewart, Tabori & Chang, 2nd Edition.

Arctic Pilot 1959, 1990. Volume 1 (USSR). London: Hydrographic Department of the Admirality.

Asher, G.M. 1860. Henry Hudson the Navigator. New York.

Badyukov, D.D. & J. Raitala 2002. Micrometeorites from the northern ice cap of the Novaya.

Zemlya archipelago, Russia: first occurrence. *Meteoritics and Planetary Science* 38, 3, 329-340.

Badyukov, D.D. 1997. Geology of Cape Spory Navolok and the archaeological site. *In*: Gawronski, J.H. and Boyarsky, P.V. (Eds.): *Northbound with Barents*. Amsterdam: Jan Mets, 58-62.

Barr, W. 1974. Rusanov, Gerkules, and the Northern Sea Route. Canadian Slavonic Papers. 569-609.

Barr, W. 1975. South to Zemlya Frantsa Iosifa! The cruise of Sv. Anna and Albanov's sledge journey, 1912-1914. *Canadian Slavonic Papers* 17, 567-595.

Barr, W. 1984. The fate of Rusanov's Gerkules expedition in the Kara Sea, 1913; some further details and recent developments. *Polar Record* 22, 287-304.

Barr, W. 1985. Imperial Russia's pioneers in Arctic aviation. *Arctic* 38, 219-230.

Barr, W. 1987. Charles Bénard's first expedition to Novaya Zemlya, 1908. *Polar Record* 23 (146): 511-529.

Barr, W. & Wilson, E.A. 1985. The shipping crisis in the Soviet Eastern Arctic at the close of the 1983 navigation season. *Arctic* 38, 1, 117.

Beattie, O. & Geiger, J. 1987. Frozen In Time: The fate of the Franklin expedition. London: Bloomsbury.

Beke, C.T., ed. 1853. The three voyages of William Barents to the Arctic Regions (1594, 1595, and 1596), by Gerrit de Veer [1598]. Reprint of the 1609 edition (translation by A. Philip 1607). Second edition (1876) with an introduction by L.R. Koolemans Beynen. Hakluyt Society, London.

Bonke, H. 1998. Onderdak in de poolnacht. [A shelter in the polar night. Aspects of the building and life in the Saved House]. In: Braat, J. *et al* (Eds.) *Behouden uit het Behouden Huys*. Amsterdam: Bataafsche Leeuw, 124-130.

Boyarsky, P.V. (Ed.) 1994. Novaya Zemlya. Part 2. Moscow (in Russian).

BOYARSKY, P.V., Liouty, A.A., Bronnikova, V.K., El'chaninov, A.I., Mazurov, Yu.L., & Stolyarov, V.P. (Eds.) 1996. Novaya Zemlya. Natural and cultural heritage. History of discoveries. Moscow, 210 pp. (in Russian).

BRAAT, J., Gawronski, J.H.G., Kist, J.B., Put, A. van de, & Sigmond, J.P. (Eds.) 1998. *Behouden uit het Behouden Huys* [Saved from the Saved House]. Catalog of objects from the Saved House. The Rijksmuseum collection, supplemented with Russian and Norwegian finds. Bataafsche Leeuw, Amsterdam, 343 pp. (in Dutch).

BRADLEY, R.S. & JONES, P.D. 1993. 'Little Ice Age' summer temperature variations: their nature and relevance to recent global warming trends. *The Holocene* 3, 4, 367-376.

BRIGHAM, L.W. (Ed.) 1991. *The Soviet maritime Arctic*. Annapolis: Naval Institute Press, 336 pp.

BUISMAN, J. 2000. Duizend jaar weer, wind en water in de Lage Landen (Deel 4, 1575-1675). Van Wijnen, 767 pp.

BURGER, C.P. 1930. De deurvaert bij Noorden om naar Cathay ende China. Het Boek XIX, 273-288.

CALVERT, J. (1996) [1960]. Surface at the Pole. Annapolis, Maryland: Bluejacket Books (p. 81).

CARR, J.R., BELL, H., KILLICK, R., AND T. Holt 2017. Exceptional retreat of Novaya Zemlya's marine-terminating outlet glaciers between 2000 and 2013. The Cryosphere, 11, 2149-2174.

CARPENTER, K.J. 1986. The history of scurvy and vitamin C. Cambridge, 288 pp.

CONRAD, J. 1926. Geography and some explorers. In: Richard Curle (Ed.) *Last Essays*. London: Dent & Sons, 10-17.

CREDLAND, A.G. 1980. Benjamin Leigh Smith: a forgotten pioneer. *Polar record* 20, 127-145.

FILEDT KOK, J.P. 1998. Engravings. In: Braat *et al.* (Eds.) *Behouden uit het Behouden Huys*, 169-171 (in Dutch).

FLOORE, P.M. 1996. Barents en Van Heemskerck in Amsterdam. *Ons Amsterdam* 11, 284-287.

FLOORE 1997. Dutch exploration of the Northeastern Passage and Western contacts with the indigenous population of the Arctic. Northbound with Barents. Amsterdam: Jan Mets, 18-37 (in English and Russian).

GAWRONSKI, J.H. & BOYARSKY, P.V. (Eds.) 1997. Northbound with Barents. Amsterdam: Jan Mets, 255 pp. (in English and Russian).

GAWRONSKI, J.H.G. & J.J. ZEEBERG 1997. The wrecking of Barents' ship. In: Gawronski, J.H.G. & Boyarsky, P.V. (Eds.) *Northbound with Barents*. Amsterdam: Jan Mets, 89-92.

GAWRONSKI, J.H.G. 1997. Trapped in wood and ice. A preliminary reconstruction of the *Behouden Huys*. In: Gawronski, J.H.G. & Boyarsky, P.V. (Eds.) *Northbound with Barents*. Amsterdam: Jan Mets, 77-86.

GROSSWALD, M.G. 1980. Late Weichselian ice sheet of northern Eurasia. *Quaternary Research* 13, 1-31.

GUTTRIDGE, L.F. 1986. ICEBOUND. The Jeanette Expedition's Quest for the North Pole. Naval Institute Press, 355 pp.

L'HONORÉ NABER, S.P. (Ed.) 1914. Reizen van J. Huyghen van Linschoten naar het Noorden 1594-1595. Werken uitgegeven door de Linschoten Vereeniging VIII. The Hague (in Dutch).

L'HONORÉ NABER, S.P. (Ed.) 1917. Reizen van Willem Barents, Jacob van Heemskerck, Jan Cornelisz. Rijp en anderen naar het Noorden (1594-1597), verhaald door Gerrit de Veer. Werken van de Linschoten Vereeniging XIV & XV. The Hague (in Dutch).

HOVING, A. & EMKE, C. (Eds.) 2004. Het schip van Willem Barents. Een hypothetische reconstructie van een laat-zestiende-eeuws jacht. [Barents' ship. A hypothetical reconstruction of a late-sixteenth century yacht]. Amsterdam: Verloren, 128 pp.

HOVING, A. 1998. Het schip. In: J. Braat *et al.* (Eds.) *Behouden uit het Behouden Huys*, 143-147.

ISRAEL, J. 1995. *The Dutch Republic*. Oxford: Clarendon Press, 1000 pp.

JOHANSEN, S. 1999. The origin and age of driftwood on Jan Mayen. *Polar Research* 17, 125-146.

JONGE, J.K.J. DE, 1872. Nova Zembla. De voorwerpen door de Nederlandsche zeevaarders na hunne overwintering aldaar in 1597 achtergelaten en in 1875 door Kapitein Carlsen teruggevonden. 's-Gravenhage, 23 pp., 1 map.

JONGE, J.K.J. DE, 1877. Barents relics, recovered in the summer of 1876 by Charles L.W. Gardiner, Esq. and presented to the Dutch government. London: Royal Geographical Society.

KIST, J.B. 1981. Het begin van het Smeerenburg-project. In: *Spitsbergen 79'NB*. Amsterdam: Elsevier, 44-71.

KIST, J.B. 1998. Armament. In: J. Braat *et al.* (Eds.) *Behouden uit het Behouden Huys*. Amsterdam: Bataafsche Leeuw, 193-194.

KOLCHAK, A.V. 1904. The expedition to Bennett Island mounted by the Academy of Sciences, in search of Baron Toll, 1903. From: *Izvestiya Imperatorskoy Akademii Nauk*, Vol. 20, No. 5, 1904, p. 149-157; and *Izvestiya Imperatorskogo Russkogo Geograficheskogo Obshchestva* Vol. 42, No. 2, 1906, p. 487-519. Reprint in: *Polar Geography and Geology* 16 (1992), 179-206.

KOOLEMANS BEYNEN, L.R. 1876. Introduction to the second edition. In: Beke, C.T., ed. 1876. The three voyages of William Barents to the Arctic Regions (1594, 1595, and 1596), by Gerrit de Veer [1598]. Hakluyt Society, London.

KRAVCHENKO, D. 1981. Mysterie van de 16de eeuw wordt ontraadseld! [Mystery of the 16th century revealed!] *Netherlands-USSR Bulletin* 34, June, p. 16-20 (in Dutch, translated from Russian).

KRAVCHENKO, D. 1983. Report of the Arctic Komplex Exploration-Historical Expedition (AKIE 1979 and 1982). Cultural service and regional museum of the Archangelsk Oblast. Fund III, List 3, Nr. 234. Original report by I. Michailova, N. Belyakova, A. Kazakov, S. Kovalevskaya, with drawings by S. Voronin and collegues of the Moscow Architectural Institute (original in Russian, translated into Dutch by L.W. Prins, Rijksmuseum, 207 pp. and 180 pp.).

LINSCHOTEN, J.H. VAN, 1596. Itinerario, voyage ofte schipvaert, naer Oost ofte Portugaels Indien inhoudende een corte beschryvinghe der selver landen ende zee-custen. [Itinerario, voyage to East or Portugese India including a short description of these countries and coasts]. Amsterdam: Cornelis Claesz.

LINSCHOTEN, J.H. VAN, 1601. Voyage van bijnoorden om door de engte van Nassau (Straat Jugor) tot voorbij de rivier Oby, etc. [Voyage round by the north through the Nassau (Yugor) Strait and past the Ob River]. Enkhuyzen.

MAAT, G.J.R. & FLOORE, P.M.F. 1997. A search for Willem Barents in the Ivanov Bay area. In: Gawronski, J.H.G. & Boyarski, P.V. (Eds.) *Northbound with Barents*. Amsterdam: Jan Mets, p. 97-99.

MAAT, G.J.R. 1981. Human remains at the Dutch whaling stations on Spitsbergen. In: A.G. F. van Holk (Ed.) *Early European Exploitation of the northern Atlantic 800-1700*. Groningen: Arctisch Centrum, p. 213-217.

MILORADOVICH, B.V. 1934. Poseshchenie zimovki V. Barentsa v Ledyanoy Gavani na Novoy Zemle [Visit to W. Barents' winter quarters at Ledyanya Gavan, Novaya Zemlya]. *Arktika* 2, p. 187-190.

MOLLEMA, J.C. 1943, ed. revised by A.H.J.Th. Koning, 1963. *De Nederlandse vlag op de Wereldzeeën* [The Dutch flag on the high seas] Part 1: *Op gegist bestek*. Scheltens & Giltay, Amsterdam, 232 pp.

MOLLEMA, J.C. 1947. *De Nederlandse vlag op de wereldzeeën* [The Dutch flag on the high seas] Part 4: *Driemaal is scheepsrecht*. Amsterdam: Scheltens & Giltay, Amsterdam, 360 pp.

MURPHY, H. 1859. Henry Hudson in Holland. Brothers Giunta d'Alboni. (Reprinted by Martinus Nijhoff 1909, and Lennox Hill, 1972).

NANSEN, FRIDTJOF [1897] 1999. Farthest North [Fram over Polarhavet]. New York: Random House.

NANSEN, FRIDTJOF 1911. In Northern Mists. Frederick Stokes Company.

OTA (Office of Technology Assessment) 1995. Nuclear wastes in the Arctic: an analysis of Arctic and other regional impacts from Soviet nuclear contamination. Congress of the United States, OTA-ENV-623, Washington, 239 pp.

PAYER, J. 1876. New lands within the Arctic circle. Narrative of the discoveries of the Austrian ship 'Tegetthoff' in the years 1872-1874. London: Macmillan; 2 vols., 335 pp.; 303 pp.

PETERMANN, A. 1872a. Die neuen Norwegischen Aufnahmen des nord-ostlichen Theiles von Nowaja Semlja durch Mack, Dörma, Carlsen u. A. 1871. *Petermanns Geographische Mitteilungen* 10, 395-396.

PETERMANN, A. 1872b. Die fünfmonatliche Schiffbarkeit des Sibirischen meeres um Novaja Semlja erwiesen durch die norwegischen Seefahrer in 1869 und 1870, ganz besonders aber in 1871. *Petermanns Geographische Mitteilungen* XVIII, 381-395, 2 maps.

RANSMAYER, C. 1984. Die Schrecken des Eises und der Finsternis [The terrors of ice and darkness]. Wien, 256 pp.

SALIKOV, J.A. 1997. Following the signs of Pomors and Dutch seamen. In: Gawronski, J.H.G. & Boyarsky, P.V. (Eds.): Northbound with Barents. Amsterdam: Jan Mets, p. 92-97.

SCHAMA, S. 1987. The Embarrassment of riches. Knopf, New York, 698 pp.

SELM, B. VAN, 1980. Amsterdam stock catalogues with printed prices from the first half of the seventeenth century. *Quaerendo* 10, 3-46.

SIDES, H. 2014. In the Kingdom of Ice. The Grand and Terrible Polar Voyage of the USS *Jeanette*. Oneworld Publications, 454 pp.

SPIES, M. 1994. Bij Noorden Om. Olivier Brunel en de doorvaart naar China en Cathay in de zestiende eeuw. Amsterdam.

Spörer, J. 1867. *Nowaja Semlä in geographischer, naturhistorischer und volkswirthschaftlicher Beziehung. Petermanns Geographische Mitteilungen. Ergänzungsheft* 21. Gotha: Justus Perthes, 112 pp., 2 maps.

Starokadomsky, L.M. 1946. Charting the Northern Sea Route. Translated and edited by W. Barr, 1976. Montreal: McGill-Queen's University Press, 332 pp.

Toll, E. von, 1894. Mitteilung über eine Reise nach den Neusibirischen Inseln und längs der Eismeerküste, ausgeführt im Jahre 1893. *Petermanns Geographische Mitteilungen*, Heft V, p. 131.

Toll, E. von, 1898. Plan einer Expedition nach Sannikow-Land. *Petermanns Geographische Mitteilungen*, Heft VI, 125-131.

Van der Werff, S.Y., Können, G.P., Lehn, W.H., and F. Steenhuisen 2000. Waerachtighe Beschrijvinghe van het Nova Zembla-Effect. *Nederlands tijdschrift voor Natuurkunde* (April), p. 120-126.

Vaughan, R. 1994. The Arctic. A history. Sutton, 340 pp.

Veer, G. de, 1598. Waerachtighe beschrijvinghe van drie seijlagien ter werelt nooit zo vreemd ghehoort, drie jaren achter malcanderen door de Hollandse en Zeelandsche schepen bij noorden etc. Cornelis Claesz, Amsterdam. See Beke (1853); l'Honoré Naber (1917); Nimwegen (1978).

Verhoeff, J.M. 1983. De oude Nederlandse maten en gewichten [The old Dutch measures and weights]. Amsterdam: Meertens Instituut.

Vize, V. Yu. 1936. Barents Navigation (Diarum Nauticum) 1594-1597 [Translation of De Veer 1598]. Leningrad 308 pp. (in Russian).

Vries, A.D. de 1883. Het portret van Willem Barentsen. November 1882. Oud Holland Vol. 001, p. 112-118.

Weerd, G. de 2004. Een interessante variant. In. Hoving & Emke 2004, Chapter 4, 81-97. Amsterdam: Verloren.

Werner, A. 1990. Lichen growth rates for the northwest coast of Spitsbergen, Svalbard. *Arctic and Alpine Research* 22, 129-140.

Witsen, N. 1671. Aeloude en hedendaagse scheepsbouw en bestier [Classic and contemporary shipbuilding]. Amsterdam.

Woodman, R. 1994. The Arctic Convoys, 1941-1945. London: John Murray, 532 pp.

Zeeberg, J.J. 2001. Climate and glacial history of the Novaya Zemlya Archipelago, Russian Arctic, with notes on the region's history of exploration. Rozenberg Publishers, 176 pp.